CHINESE CLASSICAL PROSE
The Eight Masters of the T'ang-Sung Period

唐
宋
八
大
家
文
選

A *RENDITIONS* Book

General Editors

Stephen C. Soong
George Kao

RENDITIONS BOOKS

are issued by the Comparative Literature and Translation Centre,
The Chinese University of Hong Kong,
publisher of *Renditions*, a Chinese-English Translation Magazine

This book is published
with the aid of
a grant from
THE ASIA FOUNDATION

CHINESE CLASSICAL PROSE
The Eight Masters of the T'ang-Sung Period

Selected and Translated

by

Shih Shun Liu

with Notes and Chinese Texts

A *RENDITIONS* Book

The Chinese University Press
Hong Kong

International Standard Book Number: 962-201-179-9

Distributed by
The University of Washington Press
Seattle and London

Printed by South China Printing Co., Limited, Hong Kong

TO MY CHILDREN AND GRANDCHILDREN

with the hope that they may help keep alive the noble thoughts
expressed in these essays which form a part of
the heritage of our people

By the same Author

In English

Extraterritoriality: Its Rise and Its Decline. New York, 1925.

A Syllabus on Extraterritoriality. Nanking, 1930.

One Hundred and One Chinese Poems. Hong Kong, 1967.

The Confucian Way: A New and Systematic Study of the "Four Books". (Translated from the Chinese original by Chen Li-fu 陳立夫：四書道貫.) Taipei, 1972.

Vignettes from the Late Ch'ing: Bizarre Happenings Eyewitnessed over Two Decades. (Translated from the Chinese original by Wu Wo-yao 吳沃堯：二十年目睹之怪現狀.) Hong Kong, 1975.

In Chinese

The Undying Fire. 不滅之火 (A translation of the novel by H. G. Wells.) Peking, 1926.

The Question of Extraterritoriality. 領事裁判權問題. Nanking, 1930.

Mission to Canada. 出使加拿大回憶. Taipei, 1972.

Sohrab and Rustum. 沙場尋父行 (A translation of the poem by Matthew Arnold.) Taipei, 1976.

Introductory Note

The literature of China, like the people of that most populous country, presents an extraordinary singularity when seen beside the products of other lands. Merely in view of its extent it is unique. Thus Kenneth Scott Latourette speculates that "as late as the close of the eighteenth century the Empire possibly contained more printed books than all the rest of the world put together." Of course the majority of these books, like the majority of men, are inevitably forgotten. Even the most devoted scholar need not regret their demise. But the sheer quantity of important works in Chinese is indeed phenomenal. Because of the recent political upheavals, much of value is now shrouded in obscurity. Translations into the Western languages inevitably present only a minimum of substantial and potentially lasting worth. Certain fields have in particular been neglected. The classical essay is a conspicuous case in point. The English reader and even the Chinese reader have been denied a favorable opportunity to familiarize themselves with this highly representative type of writing.

Few Chinese literary types were more eagerly cultivated than the brief essay. The great majority of such compositions typify Chinese culture in being studies in human relationships viewed in the light of moral generalization. Of all literary forms stimulated by Confucian thought this proved, perhaps, the most popular, revealing values central to the Chinese view of life. One of the most influential groups of essayists is represented in Dr. Liu's collection. His contribution is timely and important, happily supplying material not readily available to either the English or the Chinese scholar. Few persons have in recent years made an equally important contribution to our view of Chinese civilization. On the one hand, a major literary form is admirably illustrated. On the other hand, the scope of material within what might at first be thought a delimiting form is truly impressive. The essays range from general speculation on moral values to such virtually lyrical and poetic personal expression as Han Yü's "Funerary Message to Nephew No. 12," surely one of the most moving and beautiful memorial tributes in any language. Of course no single type of art or literature expresses more than a fraction of the genius in a civilization. But these essays reveal much in Chinese thought that is scarcely so well presented elsewhere. Dr. Liu's judicious selections and eloquent translations make the book a truly valuable aid to Asian studies in the humanities. Whoever values this heritage must welcome this book.

Henry W. Wells

Preface

In my school days, the study of *ku-wen* or classical prose in China was like that of the Three R's in this country. In this fundamental pursuit, the writings of the eight great masters of the T'ang and Sung dynasties stood out so prominently that each of their names had become a veritable household word. Even now that the school curriculum has been greatly affected by the vernacular movement, there are few Chinese who have not read a good sampling of the works of the eight men. I was especially fortunate in receiving in my early teens a great favor from my grandfather, who, being apprehensive that my Chinese education at school might not be sufficient, selected one hundred essays, dating back to the Chou and Han times, for me to copy and read, after explaining each piece of writing to me in minute detail. To this day, I regret very much the loss of this hand-copied volume in the terrible turmoil we have had to live through.

Not that excellent anthologies were not extant even then, but each man had his point or points of emphasis in making his selection. The most outstanding of these anthologies are of course *Ku-wen tz'u-lei-tsuan* 古文辭類纂 by Yao Nai and *Ching-shih pai-chia tsa-ch'ao* 經史百家雜鈔 by Tseng Kuo-fan. Through the ages there have been attempts to add to the names of the T'ang and Sung masters, and in fact at least one anthology, which contains the writings of ten masters, has been handed down. But these attempts have all failed, and, to this day, when we speak of the classical style of prose writing, the reference is indubitably to the works of the eight men dealt with in this volume.

It is amazing how many subjects are treated by the authors in their essays. They range widely over philosophical and historical disquisitions, biographies, memorials to the throne,

ix

private correspondence, records of interesting events and buildings, funerary messages, tomb inscriptions and other material. There is even one sketch, which I have been lucky enough to dig up, which incidentally takes up the question of sex, a subject generally taboo for most Chinese writers, especially those of earlier times. This essay by Liu Tsung-yüan, like many of his other writings, had a special moral to point, which in this instance was particularly unexpected and interesting. It is highly regrettable for posterity that a man of the genius and brilliance of Liu should have been the shortest-lived of the eight.

Except for Su Hsün, all the eight masters passed their imperial examination and won their *chin-shih* degree. This fact alone testifies to the excellence of their scholarship. However, it is not for this reason that only two essays by Su have been included in this collection. The truth of the matter is that outside of these extremely forceful and lucid compositions, old Su's writings present certain difficulties to the translator which are well-nigh insuperable.

As in the case of my poetic renderings,[1] I have to a certain extent employed the test of translatability in making my selections here. For this reason, one or two of the leading works of the masters—fortunately in the minority of cases—have been left out, because they interpose such difficulties that I have not ventured to tackle them, but have chosen to leave them to be studied in the original by those who have a reading knowledge of classical Chinese. Examples are such famous essays by Han Yü as those on the "Origin of the Way" 原道 and "An Explanation of Learning"進學解. Though there is at least one translation of the former in English, by no less an authority than Herbert Allen Giles,[2] I can scarcely recommend it, and it is his hardly successful attempt that has convinced

---

[1] *One Hundred and One Chinese Poems*, Hong Kong, Hong Kong University Press, 1967.
[2] *Gems of Chinese Literature*, pp. 113-118.

me of the futility of any further effort.

How important the study of the writings of the eight masters is can be gauged by the very large number of stock phrases and expressions in our literary as well as popular parlance that have unwittingly been derived from them. This alone justifies the method of learning by rote, which was followed exclusively in the old days and quite extensively even nowadays in Chinese schools. I still recall how hard I and other children had to work to commit to memory the essays handed down by the eight great masters (as well as other famed writers), most of which are reproduced in this volume. For that matter, even today, can any country in the world be entirely immune to the process of learning by rote in its educational system?

The emphasis on this part of a Chinese child's schooling was and is so strong that it is most surprising that, while numerous translations exist of Chinese classics and poetry, the great essays and writings of the eight masters have somehow been consistently neglected, and that even their names, especially as a group so prominent in the development of Chinese literature, are so little known to Western sinologues.

Although sporadic attempts have been made by scholars of earlier generations to render some of these *ku-wen* essays into English or French, the results are too scanty and scattered to provide a representative view of this important genre in Chinese literary history. Not infrequently, individual translations are abbreviated from the original or marked by imperfect understanding of the extremely concise and sometimes rather obscure texts. There is thus abundant room for a current and more systematic attempt at the translation of masterly Chinese prose writings. In my humble effort to fill the gap as best I can, I have not contented myself with the existing anthologies of a general nature. I have gone through the complete works of all the eight masters individually and unearthed much new material which has thus far not been incorporated in any of the existing anthologies referred to above.

To facilitate understanding, I have included brief biographical sketches of all the writers translated. Though of all the eight men there was only one, Wang An-shih, who attained the high distinction of twice serving as Prime Minister, others played an equally important part either in government or in society. Their contributions and their personalities are a fitting background to the study of their writings.

The authenticity of this material can be guaranteed since it has been garnered from the biographies in the formal dynastic histories, supplemented by relevant information from other reliable sources. It will be noted that in some instances the judgments of contemporary authors of note have been incorporated virtually verbatim in the dynastic histories. For example, the comments of Han Yü on Liu Tsung-yüan and those of Su Shih on Ou-yang Hsiu form part of their respective biographies in the history books.

The present work was produced under a fellowship granted by Ford Foundation's National Translation Center at Austin, Texas, whose generous financial subvention is deeply appreciated. In this venture, my good friend, John Cairncross, has collaborated with me to a considerable extent, and I am glad to express my appreciation of his invaluable assistance. The late Dr. Henry W. Wells, Curator Emeritus of the Brander Matthews Dramatic Museum, Columbia University, and himself author of many volumes on Chinese art and culture, was good enough to look over the manuscript and make a number of helpful suggestions.

Mr. Keith Botsford, the National Translation Center's director, was gracious enough to make it possible for me to spend over two months in Taiwan to further my project. While there, I had the opportunity of consulting many rare and precious editions of the anthologies of the eight masters and other material. For the facilities afforded me by the Central

Library in Taipei, I am indebted to the late Mr. Pao Tsun-p'eng, its curator, and his staff. My thanks are also due to Mr. K. T. Wu, then Head, Chinese and Korean Section, Orientalia Division, Library of Congress, Washington, D. C., for letting me use the wonderful collections found in that library and for bibliographical and other aid extended to me.

Three of the essays collected here first appeared in the magazine *Renditions*, a publication of the Comparative Literature and Translation Centre of The Chinese University of Hong Kong. I am grateful to the Centre for seeing fit to bring out an entire volume of such pieces, printed side by side with their Chinese texts. I sincerely hope that this sampling in English of what the Chinese people for centuries have truly regarded as "deathless prose" will serve to reflect, however inadequately, the original and fill a small gap in the reading materials available to Western students of Chinese literature.

My thanks are due to Mr. Stephen C. Soong and Mr. George Kao who, as General Editors of "Renditions Books", have given their unstinted effort in making this book possible in its present form. I also appreciate the painstaking editorial work performed by Mr. Frederick C. Tsai and Dr. Chou Ying-hsiung of the Comparative Literature and Translation Centre and wish to acknowledge the assistance of Mr. C. C. Ho and Mrs. Pansy Wong of the Chinese University Press in production and jacket design, respectively.

Only a small portion of the large number of anthologies and other books used in connection with the project are listed in the Bibliography appended at the end of the volume. With one exception, all these books are in the Chinese and English languages. This is to be expected, since the purpose of the project has been to translate Chinese works into English.

Princeton, N. J.   Shih Shun Liu
October 1978

Contents

Contents

xvii

Contents

Introduction

The *ku-wen* 古文 style of Chinese prose is traceable to the pre-Han times. Then writing was divided into two styles: the rhymed and the unrhymed. The former characterized poetry and the latter, prose. After the Han dynasty was established, the *fu* 賦 style arose, which resembled both poetry and prose. As time went on, however, this genre of literature took another form, that of *p'ien-wen* or parallel prose. This ultimately became so florid, frivolous and devoid of substance that it began to be frowned upon by a certain school of writers. That is how the movement for the revival of *ku-wen* or ancient prose arose.

THE *FU*

Here are the characteristics of the Han *fu*: (1) As stated above, the Han *fu* had both the features of poetry and prose. As prose, its sentences were irregular both in structure and in length. Nevertheless, with its stress on tonal euphony, rhyming and poetic expression, it was not unlike poetry in some respects. (2) The Han *fu* was rich in its diction. It had a tendency of padding by way of piling up the best phraseology that could be found in the language. (3) The *fu* writers were in many instances pedantic in their presentation. To display their knowledge and erudition, they would frequently make use of obscure material hitherto inaccessible to the less initiated.

The Han *fu* was evidently an offshoot from both the *Book of Songs* 詩經 and the *Ch'u tz'u* 楚辭. The development of the former into the latter was already one step toward the evolution of poetry into prose. The Han *fu* was another step in the same direction. Furthermore, in the development of the Han *fu*, the influence, not only of the *Book of Songs* and

1

Ch'u tz'u, but of the philosophical writings of the "hundred schools," was clearly discernible. Naturally, the Han *fu* could not have come out of the blue; it must have been the result of an evolutionary process which responded to the requirements of the times. On the one hand, purely rhymed versification had been found lacking as a genre to express the increasingly complicated subject matter that had to be dealt with. On the other hand, unrhymed prose had become inadequate for depicting the emotions of the writer. As a consequence, a new genre, the *fu*, combining the features of both poetry and prose, made its appearance.

The stress of elegant and pleasing diction by the Han *fu* was an indication of the reign of peace under the benevolent rule of Emperors Wen 文帝 (r. 179-158 B.C.) and Ching 景帝 (r. 156-143 B.C.), which rendered possible a period of tranquil repose, not only in politics, but also in literature. It was in such an age that good literature, with fanciful diction, appealed to the Emperor. Perhaps the same thing could be said of *Ch'u tz'u*, preeminently exemplified by Ch'ü Yüan's (*circa* 343-278 B.C.) *Li sao* 離騷 , which, with its similar flights of imagination that found expression in its fantastic wording and phraseology, had a tremendous influence on the Han *fu*. The only difference is that, while resort to embellished language was employed in the *Li sao* to show disaffection with the Emperor, the same course was adopted in the Han *fu* as a distinct attempt to please him.

Thirdly, the emergence of the Han *fu* was attributable to the competition that had arisen between the philosophical and literary scholars in the North and those in the South. The former were writers on Confucianist themes, while the latter specialized in *fu* writing. It was a coincidence that, while one group came from the North, the other hailed from the South. It is also interesting to observe that, while the northerners adhered to Confucianism more or less tenaciously, the southerners were influenced tremendously by Taoism.

During the reigns of Emperors Wen and Ching the Han *fu* was in its embryonic stage. The outstanding *fu* writers of this period were Chia I 賈誼 (201-169 B.C.) and Mei Sheng 枚乘 (2nd century B.C.). Their works of note were respectively the "Dirge on Ch'ü Yüan" (*Tiao Ch'ü Yüan fu* 吊屈原賦) and the "Seven Stimuli" (*Ch'i fa* 七發).

It was in the reign of the great Emperor Wu 武帝 (140-87 B.C.) that *fu* writing reached its climax. The most outstanding of the representative writers of this age was of course Ssu-ma Hsiang-ju 司馬相如 (179-117 B.C.), whose works are among the best known and have been most widely read of all the Han *fu*, serving as models for many imitations, in particular, those of one of his followers and admirers, Yang Hsiung 揚雄 (53 B.C.-A.D. 18). For example, the latter's compositions on "Ch'ang-yang" 長楊賦 and "Yü-lieh" 羽獵賦 were close imitations of Ssu-ma Hsiang-ju's "Shang-lin" 上林賦 and "Tzu-hsü" 子虛賦.

Later *fu* composers included such well-known men of letters as Pan Ku 班固 (32-92), who wrote "The Two Capitals" 兩都賦, and Chang Heng 張衡 (78-139), who also produced a *fu* on the same subject.

To show how enduring the *fu* was even after the end of the Han dynasty, we may cite the name of Yü Hsin 庾信 (513-581), whose famous work, "Lament for the South" (*Ai Chiang-nan* 哀江南賦), has served as an example of the highest development of the *fu*. It was due to his influence that a new form of the *fu*, the *lü-fu* 律賦 or regulation *fu* was evolved. This form extended to later times. In the T'ang dynasty it consituted part of the requirements for candidates in the state examinations. Even in the Sung dynasty, when the *ku-wen* movement had made considerable headway, many scholars who were active promoters of the movement, devoted themselves to the writing of *fu*, though in a very much modified form. Outstanding among these scholars were Ou-yang Hsiu 歐陽修 (1007-1072), who is best known for his *fu* composition, "Sounds of Autumn" (*Ch'iu sheng fu* 秋聲賦), and Su Shih 蘇軾 , better known as Su Tung-p'o (1036–1101), whose "Red Cliff" (*Ch'ih-pi fu* 赤壁賦) and its sequel are widely read.

THE *P'IEN-WEN*

The Tsin dynasty (265–420) and the Southern and Northern Dynasties (420–589) are described as the dark ages. Fortunately this appelation was applicable only to the politics, not to the literature, of the time. In the latter field, it must be said, not inconsiderable progress was made, and one of the great achievements identified with this period was the development of the *p'ien-wen* 駢文 or parallel prose. This genre of literature has often been criticized as downgrading the level of classical writing; but, to speak the truth, the high quality of the *p'ien-wen* style can hardly be denied. Even the stalwart standard-bearers of the *ku-wen* movement, including Ou-yang Hsiu, started as outstanding *p'ien-wen* writers, and it was only later that they diverted their attention to the revival of the classical prose. To this day, the *p'ien-wen* genre has not completely died out, this being explained by the intrinsic beauty of the style. Very often the balanced and concise nature of this form of writing makes it so attractive and so succinctly yet aptly phrased that it has a useful purpose of its own to serve and cannot be entirely replaced by the classical prose.

Here again the influence of the age in which the *p'ien-wen* style was introduced cannot be ignored. Many of the ingredients of the style were clearly attributable to the *fu* form. Such, for example, were the use of the long line of six or seven words, rhyme, tonal euphony, balance or parallelism in sentence construction, refined diction, and historical allusions. However, the *p'ien-wen* was all in all different enough from the *fu* to stand out as a new form of writing. Especially distinctive was the much greater restriction in the balance or

4

parallelism of wording. In fact, this special feature has given the style another name: the "four-six" prose. This is because a *p'ien-wen* composition was generally made up of four-word and six-word couplets preceding or following each other, or of one four-word sentence following another six-word sentence or vice versa.

The Chinese language, being monosyllabic, is especially adaptable to parallelism or balanced writing, although a certain amount of the latter is characteristic of almost all languages. In ancient Chinese classics it is most easy to find many expressions placed in antithetical positions, such as heaven/earth, ruler/subject, superior/inferior, wise/foolish, high/low, noble/ignoble, *yin/yang*, etc. These tended to give rise to parallelisms which form the most significant part of the *p'ien-wen* style.

Another factor which contributed to the development of the *p'ien-wen* was the distinction made by a well-known literary critic, Liu Hsieh 劉勰 (6th century), in his work *Wen-hsin tiao-lung* 文心雕龍, between *wen* (belles lettres) and *pi* 筆 (utilitarian prose). All rhymed literature fell in the former category, and all unrhymed literature in the latter. The criterion for the division was style, and content had nothing to do with it. This gave writers an impetus to vie in the florid fashion of composition in order to achieve distinction in the literary field.

The name of Yü Hsin has already been mentioned above in connection with the development of the *fu* in its highest stage. Together with Hsü Ling 徐陵 (507-583), he also perfected the *p'ien-wen* prose style. Their literary style had so much in common and was held in such high regard that it was known at the time as the "Hsü-Yü style."

The *p'ien-wen* prose flourished even after the end of the Southern and Northern Dynasties. Early in the T'ang dynasty, for instance, there were still a number of famous *p'ien-wen* writers, such as Wang Po 王勃 (648-675) and Lo Pin-wang

5

駱賓王 (who died in 684), whose *"T'eng-wang ko hsü"* 滕王閣序 and *"T'ao Wu Chao hsi"* 討武墨檄, respectively, were masterpieces handed down from generation to generation to be read and admired by all students of literature.

In addition, there were Chang Yüeh 張說 (667-730) and Su T'ing 蘇頲 (670-727)—known as "Masterful Hands of Yen and Hsü" 燕許大手筆 after the respective dukedoms awarded them—whose writings were still in the *p'ien-wen* style. The former was responsible for the drafting of most important state papers, while the latter's works, being of the same high quality as those of Chang Yüeh, were greatly relished by the Emperor. Other well-known *p'ien-wen* composers were Chang Chiu-ling 張九齡 (673-740), who was praised by the T'ang Emperor, Hsüan-tsung 玄宗 (r. 712-755) as the "general in the literary field," and Li Yung 李邕 (678-747), whose specialty was the composition of laudatory and memorial salutations, for which the *p'ien-wen* style was particularly suited.

PRECURSORS OF THE *KU-WEN* MOVEMENT

As time went on, there was gradually some realization on the part of scholars that the *p'ien-wen* had served its useful purpose and that there was the necessity for raising the level of literary composition. Even during the Southern and Northern Dynasties a difference was already discernible in the development of the literary style, and there was a definite tendency to move against the *p'ien-wen*. For example, the decrees and state papers drafted by Su Ch'o 蘇綽 of the Northern Chou dynasty (557-581) imitated the style of the ancient *Book of History*. In the Sui dynasty (589-618), during the reign of Emperor Wen 文帝, who ruled until 604, Li O 李諤 memorialized the throne to present his views on the decadence of the literary style and plead for reform. In response, the Emperor issued an edict ordering the adoption of a form of writing that would conform to the earlier

6

standards of free and untrammeled expression. However, this turned out to be a futile attempt.

One of the earliest advocates of classical prose in the T'ang dynasty was Ch'en Tzu-ang 陳子昂 (656–695), whose letters and memorials to the throne, though still couched in the phraseology of *p'ien-wen*, tended to usher in a new trend — that of inclining toward the classical style. For this reason, many scholars, including Han Yü and Sung Ch'i 宋祁 (998–1061), the latter of whom lived in the Sung dynasty, praised the special effort made by Ch'en. However, even he and some of his contemporaries could not shake off the traditional leanings toward the florid and artificial *p'ien-wen* style.

It was left to other lesser writers to become the precursors of the *ku-wen* movement later. This group consisted of such men as Hsiao Ying-shih 蕭穎士, Li Hua 李華, Chia Chih 賈至 (718-772), Tu-ku Chi 獨孤及 (744-796), Yüan Chieh 元結 (723-772), Liang Su 梁肅 (753-793), Lu Chih 陸贄 (754-805) and Liu Mien 柳冕. Of these Yüan was doubtless the best known.

Like Ch'en Tzu-ang, Hsiao Ying-shih wrote in an unadorned classical style. He was nicknamed "Master Hsiao," and his writings spread as far as Japan. Li Hua was the author of the famous essay dedicated to old battlefields. Chia, also a poet, had a reputation that ranked him as a prose-writer between Hsiao and Li, and he was the greatest admirer of Tu-ku Chi. The influence of the latter over Han Yü was considerable. One of his pupils, Liang Su, was responsible for recommending eight scholars as candidates for the *chin-shih* degree forming part of the famous "Dragon and Tiger Roll" 龍虎榜. Of these recommendations the first happened to be Han Yü. Liang was also instrumental in helping Lu Chih achieve prominence in the literary world. The latter's subsequent memorials to the throne were so well written that they have been handed down and immortalized. Though they were still cast in the *p'ien-wen* fashion, they have deeply touched many a reader,

7

thus proving the equally appealing nature of this style. It may be noted that the *p'ien-wen* compositions of Ou-yang Hsiu and Su Shih of the Sung dynasty were generally modeled on those of Lu Chih. At the time, Yüan Chieh ranked below Hsiao and Li, but because of the unique quality of his compositions, he became, over and above his position in the field of poetry, a prominent precursor of the *ku-wen* movement.

As an illustration of the mounting momentum of this movement, we may quote what Liu Mien had to say on the subject: "Literary works should be based on the teachings of olden times, for they are manifested in the order or disorder of society and interwined with the customs of the people. . . . Although literary works might possess the descriptive power of the writing of Yang Hsiung and Ssu-ma Hsiang-ju, the vigor of that of Ts'ao Chih 曹植 (192-232) and Liu Cheng 劉楨 (who died in 217) and the beauty of that of P'an Yüeh 潘岳 (who died in 300) and Lu Chi 陸機 (261-303), they serve no useful purpose and acquire the character of a mere art, which is avoided by the gentleman." He also said: "After the death of Kings Ch'eng 成王 and K'ang 康王 of the Chou dynasty, *sung* (praise) poems were no longer composed, and poets wrote of their emotions in exaggerated terms. The functions of literature and education became divorced. Those not equipped with sufficient scholarship would not know how to express the moral principles in their writing, while others who understood the meaning of moral principles disdained expressing them. It was seldom that people who were blessed with the understanding of moral principles had also the ability to express themselves."[1]

In short, Liu Mien maintained that literary works had no intrinsic value, but that Confucian principles of morality should form the basis of all writing. This was exactly the same attitude taken by Han Yü and his school. To this great scholar it was of the utmost importance to confine one's

[1] *Ch'üan T'ang wen* 全唐文 (Complete T'ang Prose), *chüan* 527, pp. 8-9.

reading to the works produced in Han and pre-Han times, as he said: "I do not dare to read anything but the books of the Three Dynasties and the Two Hans." In another connection, he made it clear that writing is a vehicle for conveying the Way, i.e. principle. "When I write in the ancient style," he queried, "do I merely pay attention to what is dissimilar to modern sentence construction? No, I think of the ancients and regret that I cannot see them. When I learn the ancient Way, I desire also to familiarize myself with the phraseology which is based on the ancient Way."[2] In other words, he felt that the purpose of reforming the prose style was the better to propound the ancient Way as embodied in Confucianism.

In this sense, what Han Yü and his school succeeded in promoting was not merely the adoption of a new style or the revival of the ancient prose style as such, but the return to the didactic form of writing which had characterized classical literature. In addition to tracing the origin of all writing to the traditional Confucian classics, Han and his followers accepted the teachings of the Confucianist school as the foundation of personal and social conduct.

HAN YÜ AND THE *KU-WEN* MOVEMENT

Han Yü himself was a faithful practitioner of the virtues of Confucianism, and there were numerous facts to bear this out. For one thing, his memorial to the throne protesting against the welcome Emperor Hsien-tsung 憲宗 (r. 806-820) extended to a piece of Buddha's bone was an extreme example of the orthodoxy of the great scholar. Another example was his insistence on carrying out the edict of Emperor Mu-tsung 穆宗 (r. 821-824) regarding the pacification of Wang T'ing-ts'ou 王庭湊, a rebellious military governor. When this edict was

---

[2] "Postscript to the Dirge on Scholar Ou-yang (Chan)," *Ch'ang-li hsien-sheng chi* (Complete Works of Han Yü), *Ssu-pu pei-yao*, undated, Chung-hua Book Company, Shanghai, *chüan* XXII, p. 4.

issued, there were not a few in high positions who felt anxious about the heavy responsibility devolving on Han, which it was feared involved grave danger. Among those who spoke in his behalf was Prime Minister Yüan Chen 元稹 (779-831), one of the most famous T'ang poets. "It's a pity for Han Yü," said Yüan. At this, the Emperor showed his remorse and rescinded the order, admonishing Han to stop at the border and observe the situation carefully before prceeding to the area concerned. "To stop me," Han wrote back to the Emperor, "from pro-ceeding further shows Your Majesty's benevolence, but my duty is to die if necessary. How can I loiter for my own safety after receiving Your Majesty's orders?" He hastened to enter the rebel area and succeeded in persuading Wang to surrender. For this achievement Han was rewarded with the position of Vice Minister of Personnel Affairs.

In his letter to Li I 李翊, Han said: "The spirit is like water; words are like floating matter. When water rises in volume, all matter, big or small, floats on its surface. When the spirit is full, all words, short or long, with high or low sounds, will fit."[3] What he meant by "the spirit" is the motivating power which is derived from principle.

The man who could thoroughly understand the real spirit of Han's writings was one of his Sung followers, the great Su Shih, who wrote the inscription on the tablet dedicated to the temple erected in Ch'aochow, Kwangtung, to the memory of Han. In this monumental essay, Su said: "When a mere commoner can become the teacher of a hundred generations and when one word from him can be the guidance of the whole world, such a man can participate in the transforming powers of heaven and earth, and have a decided influence on human destiny, involving both progress and decline. . . . Since the Eastern Han dynasty, the Way has been lost and literature become decadent, and heterodoxy arisen. The reigns of Cheng-kuan 貞觀 (627-649) and K'ai-yüan 開元 (713-741) of

[3] *Ibid., chüan* XVI, p. 11.

the T'ang dynasty could not come to their rescue. Only the great master (i.e. Han Yü), with his high wits, could give the proper direction. For three centuries the whole empire has followed in his footsteps and restored the balance. His writing has saved Chinese literature from eight dynasties of decadence, and his Way has helped all the people from drowning."[4]

There have been innumerable subsequent commentaries on Han Yü's contribution to Chinese writing. They have all joined in the same tribute that has been paid by Su Shih. All the important essays emanating from Han's pen, except one or two which have defied satisfactory translation, have been reproduced in the following pages. Of these the most widely read is the "Funerary Message to Nephew No. 12." Incidentally, to show the abiding influence of the *p'ien-wen* style, we can detect even in this essay the use of rhyme and parallelism here and there.

Despite the praise showered upon him by Su Shih and other scholars, it was a vastly difficult task that Han Yü undertook in endeavoring to reform the style of writing. In his preface to the collection of Han's works, Li Han 李漢, one of his pupils, said: "People were at first surprised (by his new style) and then ridiculed and attacked him. But he only became more confident. In the end people changed their minds and followed his example."[5]

Fortunately his character was such that he could assure himself of success even at the very outset. In a letter he addressed to Feng Su 馮宿, he said that, although he knew that his writings did not appeal to the general public and although "I don't know what value writing in the classical style can have at present, I am willing to wait for those who understand. When Yang Hsiung wrote his *T'ai hsüan* 太玄, almost everybody laughed at him. But his words were, 'It

[4] See p. 23, below.
[5] *Ch'ang-li hsien-sheng chi, chüan* XVII, p. 11.

11

doesn't matter if the whole world doesn't know me. But if there is going to be another Yang Hsiung in future generations, he will love it.' "

While he was so self-confident that he did not care what other scholars thought of his writings, the success of his movement was perhaps due more to his ability to win over friends and followers than to his own great talent. In the *Old History of the T'ang Dynasty* 舊唐書, it is said: "Han Yü regarded those in power as mere servants and would not even look at them. But he was disposed to guide and encourage the younger generation, as many as six or seven out of ten of whom stayed with him. There were times when even breakfast proved to be a problem, but he did not mind. In general he took upon himself the elevation of moral principle and the reward of benevolence and righteousness."[6]

Several stories have been told of Han Yü's persuasive power on the one hand and extraordinary humility on the other. To illustrate the first of these two qualities, we may cite the anecdote in which Han Yü was instrumental in bringing into prominence a great T'ang poet, Chia Tao 賈島 (779-843). After their first encounter by accident, Han was so impressed with Chia's talent that he persuaded him to renounce his Buddhist faith and return to laity. This Han succeeded in doing, and later Chia Tao took the imperial examination, obtained the *chin-shih* degree and embarked upon a brilliant career. The other quality, modesty and humility, was demonstrated in Han's high praise of the talents of other scholars, and this despite his self-conceited nature. One of such instances is related in a subsequent paragraph having to do with Liu Tsung-yüan.

The most distinguished contemporaries of Han Yü were Liu Tsung-yüan, Liu Yü-hsi 劉禹錫 (772-842), Li Kuan 李觀 (who died around 800), Ou-yang Chan 歐陽詹, Fan Tsung-shih

[6]*T'ang shu ho-ch'ao* (Combined Edition of the Histories of T'ang), edited by Shen Ping-chen, 1803, *chüan* CCXI, p. 10.

12

樊宗石, Lü Wen 呂溫 (772-811) and Ch'üan Teh-yü 權德輿 (759-818). While Liu Tsung-yüan was the closest associate of Han's, his thinking was altogether different from that of Han. On the one hand, Liu had a clear understanding of both Buddhism and Taoism, and there was a free flow of this sentiment in all his writings. On the other, because of his obstinate opposition to the alien religion, Han was everywhere restrained by his steadfast adherence to orthodoxy. As a result, his writings often could not compare with those of Liu in their depth and beauty.

This was even admitted by Han Yü himself. Once when he was asked by one Wei Heng 韋珩 about the method of writing, he replied by saying that it would be more appropriate to put the question to Liu, whose prose was the best among Han's followers. Wei sent Han's letter to Liu, whose advice he sought, but who said in reply: "Han Yü's talent is several times mine. . . . He likes to commend the merits of others. He even thinks that he must downgrade himself before he can adequately praise others. That is why he is so modest. I hope that you will not believe him." While the humility of Han was a great asset, the equal modesty of Liu was something to be admired.

Liu Yü-hsi was the bosom friend of Liu Tsung-yüan. Their attachment to each other was well depicted in Han Yü's "Inscription on Liu Tzu-hou's Tomb Tablet"[7] and is referred to in my biographical sketch of Liu.[8] From one of Han's poems—"All my colleagues are great talents/Liu and Liu alone are my good friends"—we learn that he had cultivated the friendship of Liu Yü-hsi as well as Liu Tsung-yüan. The representative prose work of the former was his essay "On Heaven" in three parts.

Both Li Kuan and Ou-yang Chan took their *chin-shih* degree from the same examination as Han Yü. But in essence

[7] See pp. 90-97, below.
[8] See pp. 99-101, below.

13

Li's prose works offered no comparison to those of Han. According to the latter, Ou-yang's "writings had great depth. He was fond of pursuing his subjects back and forth and skilled in self-portrayal. He was one of my most intimate friends."[9]

Fan Tsung-shih took pride in originality, and he would never take a single word or sentence from the writings of his predecessors. This fact was also appreciated by Han Yü in his inscription on Fan's tomb tablet.

Lu Wen's writings were patterned after those of Liang Su, with great stress on elegant diction and refined logic.

As a high official, Ch'üan Teh-yü was a favorite of Emperor Teh-tsung. His writings were elegant, orthodox and all-rounded.

In addition, there were a number of Han Yü's pupils, who played a significant part in the promotion of the *ku-wen.* Among these were Li Ao 李翱, Li Han 李漢, Chang Chi 張籍 and Huang-fu Shih 皇甫湜. Both Lis were Han's relatives, and both, like their master, had strong character. Likewise, both had their *chin-shih* degree. Li Ao prduced several learned biographies and three essays on "The Restoration of Nature." Li Han's collection of Han Yü's works has been referred to above, and his preface to the collection has been lauded as offering a close resemblance to the writings of Eastern Han authors.

Chang Chi was a poet as well as a prose-writer. He was also a straightforward man. He was particularly critical of his master in that the latter never wrote a monograph against Buddhism and Taoism.

Huang-fu Shih was one of the worst-tempered scholars in the T'ang dynasty. He rated his own writings so highly that on one occasion he did not hesitate to ask an exorbitant price for one of his productions. His works were in many instances

[9] "Postscript to the Dirge on Scholar Ou-yang (Chan)," *Ch'ang-li hsien-sheng chi, chüan* XXII, p. 4.

14

moderate and unbiased, offering a direct contrast to his personality.

Curiously enough, all these pupils of Han Yü were temperamentally his exact counterparts, and their literary works were equally reminiscent of the influence he had wielded over them.

After Han Yü's time there were several outstanding *ku-wen* writers. The first name to be mentioned is that of Sun Ch'iao 孫樵, who wrote with deep thought and an unusually refined diction. Then there was Liu Shui 劉蛻, who was as highly regarded as Sun Ch'iao. Together they were referred to as the Sun-Liu school.

In addition, others whose writings were confined to the style of Han Yü and Liu Tsung-yüan and who devoted themselves to the *ku-wen* movement included Ling-hu Ch'u 令狐楚 (766-837) and Li Teh-yü 李德裕 (787-849). The former was a specialist in the writings of memorials and edicts. The latter also left a large number of memorials, but they do not possess the same value as some of his other writings.

Other famous contributions were the dirge, by Li Shang-yin 李商隱 (812-858), one of the well-known Late-T'ang poets, on Prime Minister Ling-hu and the *fu*, by Tu Mu 杜牧 (803-852), on the O-fang Palace 阿房宮賦.

The Late-T'ang period was one of decadence for both poetry and prose. Practically the only writers who could barely hold their own in the literary field were P'i Jih-hsiu 皮日休, Lo Yin 羅隱 (833-909) and Lu Kwei-meng 陸龜蒙. In their depth the prose works of these men could, of course, offer no comparison to those of Han Yü and Liu Tsung-yüan.

Although great success had crowned the efforts of Han Yü and his associates and followers, the remnant influence of the *p'ien-wen* style was still considerable. For example, the *History of the Tsin Dynasty*, compiled by such T'ang historians as Fang Ch'iao 房喬, was cast entirely in parallel prose. The renowned memorials of Lu Chih (754-805) adopted the same style. From this it is evident that the *ku-wen* movement had not yet won its definitive victory in the T'ang dynasty and that this achievement had to wait till after the advent of the Sung dynasty.

THE SECOND PHASE OF THE *KU-WEN* MOVEMENT

The influence of the florid and frivolous style of the Late-T'ang and Five Dynasties (907-959) was so strong that the beginning of the Sung dynasty was characterized by the high development of *p'ien-wen* literature. Among prominent *p'ien-wen* composers of this early Sung period were Yang I 楊億 (974-1020) and Liu Yün 劉筠. Their writings consisted principally of state papers and official pronouncements. While they were devoid of substance, they were widely copied by students who were bent on seeking fame in the literary and political realm. For a time all imperial edicts, official proclamations and memorials to the throne were written in the artificial style.

Nevertheless, as time went on, there was mounting criticism of this genre of writing. Out of this rising opposition emerged the continued vigor of the *ku-wen* movement started in the T'ang dynasty. The earlier standard-bearers of this second phase of the movement were, to name the most important, Liu K'ai 柳開 (947-1000), Shih Chieh 石介 (1005-1045), Mu Hsiu 穆修 (979-1032), Yin Shih-lu 尹師魯 (1001-1046), Su Shun-ch'in 蘇舜欽 (1008-1048) and Wang Yü-ch'eng 王禹偁.

Liu K'ai was such an admirer of Han Yü and Liu Tsung-yüan that he even changed his names to bear witness to this admiration. He was a forerunner of the *ku-wen* style in the Sung dynasty, but his prose writings did not measure up to the highest standards.

The strongest opponent to the Hsi-k'un School 西崑體, to which Yang I belonged, was Shih Chieh. The very essay he composed on the *"Kuai-shuo"* (Strange Theories) in accusation of Yang was a fine piece of classical prose.

Mu Hsiu was a staunch advocate of the *ku-wen* style. He reiterated the ideas of Han Yü, especially the view that literature should serve as the vehicle for the teaching of Confucian principles. However, even Mu had to admit that at the time "one who dares to talk about classical prose is treated as though he were talking about the weird. All the others attack him, scandalize him and deal with him as if he were either a bigot or a man not free from doubt, who would go against the time and avoid fame, and who would stand aloof from wealth and rank. None of his seniors would praise him, nor would any of his peers support him. If he did not possess a clear knowledge of himself and had no strong will-power or great confidence in what he was doing, he would lose hope and doubt himself. He would also repent and change his mind. And then he would surely change his prose style to follow that of others."[10]

Yin Shih-lu, a *chin-shih*, was a writer of classical prose. Su Shun-ch'in, though younger than Ou-yang Hsiu, had gone into the study of the classical style even before him. Together with his brother, Shun-yüan 舜元 (1006-1054), he devoted himself to the style with faithful application.

Wang Yü-ch'eng was a practitioner of *ku-wen* composition, and a number of his works have been handed down to be read by subsequent generations. But he was at the same time a skilled *p'ien-wen* writer.

The responsibility for pushing ahead the *ku-wen* movement fell on the shoulders of Ou-yang Hsiu more than anyone else. Although he had excelled in the writing of *p'ien-wen*, as many of his contemporaries did, he soon realized from experience that the *ku-wen* style had comparative merits. Here are his own words:

[10]"Reply to Ch'iao Ch'ien 喬遷," *Ho-nan Mu-kung chi* (Collection of Works of Hon. Mu of Honan), *chüan* II, p. 1.

When I was young, I lived in Hantung. . . . In the south of the prefecture there was the prominent Li family, one of whose sons, Yao-fu, was fond of studying. As a child, I often visited that family, where I saw ancient books stored in outworn sacks stacked in the walls. When I opened them, I found six *chüan* of *Ch'ang-li hsien-sheng wen-chi* (Collected Works of Han Yü) of the T'ang dynasty. The book showed some omissions and was disorderly in its arrangement. I asked for the Li family's permission to take it home and read it. . . . At that time, scholars of the empire . . . never made any mention of Han's writings. As I was trying for my *chin-shih* degree, I was engaged in the writing of poetry and *fu* prescribed by the Ministry of Rites. . . . Seven years later, I won my *chin-shih* degree and became an official in Loyang, where I joined Yin Shih-lu and others. We began to devote ourselves to the *ku-wen*, and I offered my copy of *Ch'ang-li's Works* for amplification. An effort was made to secure old copies of the book kept by others for verification. From that time on, scholars of the empire gradually tended toward the ancient style, and Han's writings came to be accepted by the whole country. More than thirty years have now elapsed. . . .[11]

Ou-yang appeared to be the most orthodox of all the Sung masters. To carry on the traditions of Han Yü, he wrote an essay entitled *"Pen lun"* (On the Fundamental Truth), which contained a severe attack on Buddhism. Thus he identified himself with the Han School, not only in continuing to promote the classical prose style, but also in defending Confucian orthodoxy. The latter practice, however, was not consistently followed by his students and followers in all cases. It was a time when what had once been vehement objection to the Buddhist faith had somehow quieted down. This accounts for the fact that scholars like Su Shih, while brought up in the Confucian tradition, were able to derive great pleasure and benefit from their association with Buddhist monks. At the same time, with the emergence of the neo-Confucianist school, it became practically superfluous

[11] *Liu-i t'i pa* (Inscriptions and Postscripts by Scholar Liu-i), *chüan* XI, pp. 513-515.

for the prose writers to share with the philosophers of that school the burden of defending Confucianism against incursions of any unwelcome heresy.

Not sharing the strong character of Han Yü, Ou-yang had a style which was soft or mellow, altogether different from that of his T'ang predecessor. It was especially one of his characteristic traits to make as many revisions as he could before he decided on the final draft of any of his writings. The classic example of his essay on the "Old Drunkard's Pavilion" is often cited to show that the version which had been handed down to us is radically different from the first draft. It is noted that, while he had made a lengthy description of the mountains surrounding Ch'uchow, he saw fit finally to be satisfied with the few words now appear at the beginning of the essay. This reveals what thought the old master gave to all his work before it took its final shape, hence the maturity and beauty of all his compositions.

Of the five remaining stalwarts of the *ku-wen* movement in the Sung dynasty, three came from the Su family of Szechwan Province. The two sons, Su Shih and Su Ch'e, were both successful candidates for the *chin-shih* degree in an imperial examination presided over by Ou-yang Hsiu. The father of the pair, Su Hsün, won high praise from Ou-yang by virtue of his learned writings. It is said that he had owed his effective style to his study of Mencius' works. Among his great contributions was his essay "On Kuan Chung" 管仲論. The younger son, Ch'e, was a great prose-writer, but he did not have the forcefulness of his father nor the penetrating thought of his brother. His outstanding works include the essay "On the Six States" 六國論.

The giant of the trio was of course Su Shih. It was no mere accident that he became one of the most distinguished talents in the whole of the Sung dynasty. For one thing, he was one of the most brilliant and diligent men that ever lived, as attested by the anecdote told in his biographical sketch which

19

follows.[12] For another, he had the highest appreciation of the lofty character and literary attainments of his seniors, and he lost no opportunity to record this sentiment, which naturally stood him in good stead. His masterpieces are too numerous to recount, but the most outstanding of them have been presented in the renderings included in this volume.

Another important follower of Ou-yang Hsiu was Tseng Kung, who was, with Su Shih and Su Ch'e, one of those who came out successfully in the imperial examination mentioned above, and who was not just a pupil of the old master, but indeed a favorite one. Tseng's style of writing was closely akin to that of Ou-yang, both of them being inclined to the soft or mellow type of composition and both showing great grace and emotion. Being a versatile composer, Tseng produced many essays of wide variety and distinctive beauty.

The last of the sextet in the second phase of the *ku-wen* movement was the well-known Wang An-shih, who achieved great distinction, not only in literature, but also in government. He gave ample evidence of being a greater genius than even Ou-yang Hsiu himself. While Ou-yang had to exercise extreme care in all his compositions, Wang's speed in literary production was unequaled, as he was never seen to alter even a single word after he got through with his first draft. He was so cock-sure of himself that he was nicknamed "the obstinate prime minister." This unfortunate disposition was the cause of his ultimate failure in politics, but chanced to help tremendously in his literary pursuits.

The part he played in his extensive reform program is well remembered. The basis of this program was outlined in a lengthy memorial to the throne, known as the "Ten-Thousand-Word Memorial,"[13] which is noted for its exhaustive discussion and eloquent appeal. Other masterpieces, selections of which have been reproduced in translation below, provide

[12]See pp. 225-231, below.
[13]See John Meskill (ed.), *Wang An-shih—Practical Reformer*, pp. 1-16.

delightful reading and rich food for thought.

In addition to the six prose masters of the Sung dynasty, there were other writers who achieved great distinction. Among these were six pupils of Su Shih—Huang T'ing-chien 黃庭堅 (1045-1105), Ch'in Kuan 秦觀 (1049-1100), Ch'ao Pu-chih 晁補之 (1053-1110), Chang Lei 張耒 (1054-1114), Ch'en Shih-tao 陳師道 (1053-1101), and Li Chih 李廌 —and three of his sons—Su Mai 蘇邁, Su Tai 蘇迨 and Su Kuo 蘇過 (1072-1123). Other highly revered names were those of Fan Chung-yen 范仲淹 (989-1052) and Ssu-ma Kuang 司馬光 (1019-1086). The former was the famous statesman and writer who established his claim as the first to worry about the world's problems and last to enjoy its pleasures. The latter was another statesman of sterling character, who found time to compile the first general history of China, entitled *Tzu-chih t'ung-chien* 資治通鑑 (The Mirror of Good Government), a masterpiece, the study of which few scholars can afford to pass by.

For a long time, even in the Sung dynasty, the *p'ien-wen* and *ku-wen* styles of writing existed side by side. However, while the former stressed mere form and was restrained by a number of rules, the latter emphasized substance and was comparatively simple and untrammeled. The battle between the two proceeded in close line with the requirements of the time and resulted in the victory of the classical prose. Thus, this style has stood its ground and reigned supreme for five dynasties—the T'ang, Sung, Yüan, Ming and Ch'ing. Even with the success of the movement of Literary Reform, which came about shortly after the turn of the century and the establishment of the Republic, and which was in favor of the extensive use of the vernacular, the *ku-wen* style has still an important place to fill and is in all probability here to stay.

韓文公

公嘗官潮州刺史。潮人廟祀公。東坡作碑中云。文起八代之衰。而道濟天下之溺。忠犯人主之怒。而勇奪三軍之帥。此豈非參天地關盛衰浩然而獨存者乎。又曰公之精誠。能開衡嶽之雲而不能回憲宗之惑。能馴鱷魚之暴。而不能弭皇甫鎛李逢吉之謗。能信於南海之民廟食百世而不能使其身一日安於朝廷之上。蓋公之所能者天地。其所不能者人也。

Han Yü (768-824)

Han Yü was the leader of the great literary movement in the T'ang dynasty for the revival of the classical style. In the view of this distinguished scholar, only the *ku-wen* (ancient prose), which had prevailed during the Three Dynasties[1] and the Two Han Dynasties,[2] could qualify as the best prose style. However, this form of writing had been corrupted by the so-called *p'ien-wen,* or rhymed prose, in vogue for several centuries up to his time. It was due to the effort of Han and his colleagues, including another great scholar, Liu Tsung-yüan,[3] that the more dignified ancient style was revived.

The devotion with which these writers promoted the movement is nowhere better demonstrated than in the confession made by Han himself that he never dared to read anything but what had been handed down from the early period. That is why he was eulogized by one of his successors in the Sung dynasty, the renowned Su Shih[4] (who was also one of the eight great masters of Chinese prose), as one whose writing had saved Chinese literature from eight dynasties of decadence (文起八代之衰), a conclusion which has been quoted and requoted by Chinese students of literature down through the ages.

Han Yü, whose courtesy name was T'ui-chih 退之 , was from Nanyang 南陽 , Tengchow 鄧州 .[5] His direct ancestor of the seventh generation, named Mao 茂 , had been granted a princely title under the Northern Wei dynasty (421-534). His father, Chung-ch'ing 仲卿 , had been magistrate of Wuchang

---

[1] Hsia 夏 (2183-1752 B.C.), Shang 商 (1751-1112 B.C.) and Chou 周 (1112-256 B.C.).

[2] The Former Han (206 B.C.-A.D. 24) and Later Han (25-219).

[3] See pp. 99-101 below.

[4] See pp. 225-231 below.

[5] Teng *Hsien* 鄧縣 , Honan Province.

武昌 ,[6] and his good government won him the gratitude of the people, who recorded his achievements on a stone tablet after he left. His father died when he was only three years of age. When his elder brother, Hui 會 , was demoted to what is now Kwangtung Province, the young T'ui-chih went along. Upon Hui's death shortly afterward, he was brought up by his sister-in-law, née Cheng 鄭 .

From his early childhood T'ui-chih was a remarkable student. He could commit to memory hundreds of words each day. When he grew up, he became well versed in the six classics[7] and the hundred schools of philosophy. He won his highest degree, *chin-shih* 進士 , in the imperial examination, when he was twenty-five years of age.

His first official position was with Tung Chin 董晉 , Military Governor of Hsüanwu 宣武 .[8] Later, he served with another military governor, stationed in Wuning 武寧 ,[9] on whose recommendation he was transferred to the Imperial University as one of its Doctors and then promoted to the Supervisory Censorship. While holding this office, he distinguished himself by outspoken criticisms. On one occasion, he offended Emperor Teh-tsung 德宗 (r. 780-805) and was demoted to Magistrate of Yangshan 陽山 ,[10] where his devotion to the people was reflected in the local custom of adopting his surname as the name of male children. Then he was re-appointed Doctor at the Imperial University and served successively in the Ministry of Justice, as Editor of the Board of History, Member of the Public Works Board, Draftsman of Imperial Decrees, ranking official at the Prime Minister's Office and Vice-Minister of Justice.

[6] A *hsien* or district in Hupeh Province.

[7] The *Books of Songs* 詩, *History* 書, *Rites* 禮, *Music* 樂 and *Changes* 易, and the *Spring and Autumn Annals* 春秋 .

[8] The jurisdiction of the military governor extended through parts of modern Honan Province.

[9] A *hsien* in Kiangsi Province.

[10] A *hsien* in Kwangtung Province.

In the latter post, he presented a memorial to the throne
remonstrating about the order of Emperor Hsien-tsung 憲宗
(806-820) on the reception of Buddha's bone at Fenghsiang
鳳翔.[11] His Majesty was enraged and showed the memorial to
his prime ministers, exhorting them to punish such audacity
by death. Prime Ministers P'ei Tu 裴度 and Ts'ui Ch'ün 崔羣,
however, protested, "Though he deserves severe punishment
for his obtrusive remarks, if he were not utterly loyal, how
could he have gone so far? May it please Your Majesty to show
lenience and thus open the door to similar remonstrances."

"While I can tolerate Han Yü's assertion that I have been
excessive in my worship of Buddha," the emperor replied, "is
it not absurd to assert that, since the Eastern Han dynasty,
those rulers who have worshipped Buddha have been short-
lived? As a government official who has displayed such
arrogance, he is unpardonable." Thereupon the whole country
was aroused, and even members and relatives of the imperial
household interceded for Han. As a result, he was demoted to
be Prefect at Ch'aochow 潮州.[12] On arriving there and
assuming his new office, he presented another memorial to
the throne, expressing in moving words his profound appreciation of the magnanimity of the emperor in sparing his life.
Deeply touched by this burst of emotion, His Majesty again
showed the document remorsefully to his prime ministers,
saying, "The advice tendered by Han Yü before was evidently
prompted by profound love for me, but he should not have
said that there can be no long life for the Sons of Heaven who
believe in Buddhism."

At the time, one man who was jealous of Han Yü happened
to be in power. He spoke to the emperor about transferring
Han to service near the Court on the ground that he could
never overcome his conceit. So he was appointed to Yüanchow

[11] See pp. 44-49 below.
[12] Prefecture in modern Kwangtung Province.

25

袁州 [13] as Prefect. In that prefecture, it had been the custom to allow men and women to become bonded slaves, or to pledge their persons for debts and to make slaves of them in the event of default. When T'ui-chih became Prefect, he instituted the system of wages for service in such cases and ordered these payments to count towards redemption of debts. As a result, more than seven hundred were released from their bondage and returned to their parents.

As a sequel to his meritorious service in Yüanchow, he was appointed to the elevated position of President of the Imperial University. Later, he was transferred to the Ministry of War as Vice-Minister, which was the last office he held before he died at the age of fifty-seven. The title of Minister of Rites was posthumously conferred on him, and he was canonized as Wen 文 .

Han Yü was a man of a perspicacious and determined nature. Never pretending to compromise, he was a staunch friend. After he became prominent in literary circles, well-known scholars, who had been successful in the imperial examination and attained their *chin-shih* degree, flocked to him for tutoring and were referred to as Pupils of the Han School 韓門弟子. He was attentive and generous to his relatives and friends. Those who had no male descendants depended on him for the support of their families after their death, and, if they had left any orphaned daughters, he married them off at his own expense. In recognition of the services rendered to him during his youth by his sister-in-law, he mourned her death for as long as he did his brother, which was longer than was customary.

When he discussed the origins of his literary style, he invariably harked back to the scholars of the Han dynasty, including Ssu-ma Hsiang-ju 司馬相如 ,[14] Ssu-ma Ch'ien 司馬

[13] Prefecture in modern Kiangsi Province.
[14] Famous writer of *fu* 賦 (rhymed or partly rhymed prose) in the Han dynasty.

26

遷,[15] Liu Hsiang 劉向 [16] and Yang Hsiung 揚雄 .[17] This shows how fundamental were his studies and explains how he succeeded in establishing a school of his own. His numerous essays, regarded ever since as masterpieces of Chinese prose literature, have made his name immortal. They represent a continuation of the works of men such as Mencius and Yang Hsiung and a monumental prolongation of the great Confucian classics.

[15] Grand Historian of the Han dynasty.
[16] Another famous historian of the Han dynasty.
[17] Another famous writer of *fu* in the Han dynasty, who also produced some philosophical works.

雜　說　四

　　世有伯樂，然後有千里馬。千里馬常有，而伯樂不常有。故雖有名馬，祇辱於奴隸人之手，駢死於槽櫪之間，不以千里稱也。

　　馬之千里者，一食或盡粟一石。食馬者不知其能千里而食也。是馬也，雖有千里之能，食不飽，力不足，才美不外見，且欲與常馬等不可得，安求其能千里也？

　　策之不以其道，食之不能盡其材，鳴之而不能通其意，執策而臨之曰：「天下無馬。」嗚呼，其眞無馬邪？其眞不知馬也！

---

[1] A horse that can run one thousand *li* a day. A *li* is equivalent to one-third of a mile.

[2] Another name of Sun Yang 係陽 , who was a connoisseur of horses in ancient times.

[3] A picul, a unit of weight equivalent to 133.33 pounds.

The Thousand-*li* Horse[1]

Only when there is a Po-lo[2] can there be a thousand-*li* horse. While thousand-*li* horses are not uncommon, men like Po-lo are rare to find. It follows that, though you have horses of a renowned breed, they will only be misused in the hands of stableboys and die side by side in their stalls without ever being known as thousand-*li* horses.

A thousand-*li* horse may consume a *shih*[3] of grain at one feed, but the men who feed it are often ignorant of its needs. Such a horse, though capable of running a thousand *li* a day, may not get enough to eat and, as a result, will not have sufficient strength. Its great talent does not come to light. It cannot be expected to be the equal of an ordinary horse, let alone a thousand-*li* horse.

A horse may not be exercised properly or fed enough to fully develop its capacity; even its neighing is likely not to be understood. Here is a man holding a whip over his horse and declaring: "There are no fine horses in the world." Alas, are there truly no fine horses? The truth is that he does not know what fine horses are.

原　毀

　　古之君子，其責己也重以周，其待人也輕以約。重以周，故不怠；輕以約，故人樂爲善。

　　聞古之人有舜者，其爲人也，仁義人也。求其所以爲舜者，責於己曰：「彼人也，予人也。彼能是，而我乃不能是。」早夜以思，去其不如舜者，就其如舜者。聞古之人有周公者，其爲人也，多才與藝人也。求其所以爲周公者，責於己曰：「彼人也，予人也。彼能是，而我乃不能是。」早夜以思，去其不如周公者，就其如周公者。

　　舜大聖人也，後世無及焉。周公大聖人也，後世無及焉。是人也，乃曰：「不如舜，不如周公，吾之病也。」是不亦責於身者重以周乎？其於人也，曰：「彼人也，能有是，是足爲良人矣。能善是，是足爲藝人矣。」取其一，不責其二；即其新，不究其舊；恐恐然惟懼其人之不得爲善之利。一善易修也，一藝易能也。其於人也，乃曰：「能有是，是亦足矣。」曰：「能善是，是亦足矣。」不亦待於人者，輕以約乎？

　　今之君子則不然。其責人也詳，其待己也廉。詳，故

---

[1] Emperor of the ancient Yü 虞 dynasty, who reigned *circa* 2233-2184 B.C.
[2] Son of King Wen of the Chou dynasty 周文王 and brother of King Wu 武王, who reigned 1111-1105 B.C.

Origin of Defamation

When an ancient gentleman censured himself, he did so ruthlessly and completely, while in his treatment of others, he showed tolerance and lenience. The former practice kept him from sloth as regards good works, and the latter made others happy to do good.

It was told that there was an ancient by the name of Shun,[1] who was a man of benevolence and righteousness. Seeking to know what had made Shun virtuous, a man censured himself and said: "He was a man and so am I. How is it that he could do this and I cannot?" He set himself to thinking morning and night, got rid of the traits in which he was unequal to Shun and retained those in which he was equal to him. It was also told that there was an ancient known as the Duke of Chou,[2] who was a man of many talents and skills. Seeking to know what had made the Duke of Chou so outstanding, the man censured himself and said: "He was a man and so am I. How is it that he could do this and I cannot?" He set himself to thinking morning and night, got rid of the traits in which he was unequal to the Duke of Chou and retained those in which he was equal to him.

Shun was a great sage, the like of whom has never been seen in later times. So was the Duke of Chou, who has never been equalled either. And yet the man referred to above said that his trouble was that he was unequal to Shun and the Duke of Chou. Was this not censuring himself ruthlessly and completely? When he came to consider others, he said: "If a man is able to do this, he is qualified to be a good man. If he is able to do it well, he is worthy of being called a man of skills." Thus, anything good was singled out for praise, while the rest was passed over; only the present was considered and the past forgotten. The fear was that the man might not reap the full benefit from doing good. One good deed is easy to accomplish and a single skill easy to acquire. And yet it was said of the man: "If he is able to do this, it is enough. If he is able to do a thing well, it is enough." Was this not treating others with tolerance and lenience?

Not so the gentleman of today. He censures others in fastidious detail, while he treats himself with lenience. Fastidiousness makes it difficult for others to do good, and lenience disposes himself to learn little.

31

人難於爲善，廉，故自取也少。己未有善，曰：「我善是，是亦足矣。」己未有能，曰：「我能是，是亦足矣。」外以欺於人，內以欺於心，未少有得而止矣。不亦待其身者已廉乎？其於人也，曰：「彼雖能是，其人不足稱也。彼雖善是，其用不足稱也。」舉其一，不計其十；究其舊，不圖其新；恐恐然惟懼其人之有聞也。是不亦責於人者已詳乎？夫是之謂不以衆人待其身，而以聖人望於人，吾未見其尊己也。

雖然，爲是者，有本有原，怠與忌之謂也。怠者不能修，而忌者畏人修。吾常試之矣。嘗試語於衆曰：「某良士，某良士。」其應者，必其人之與也。不然，則其所疏遠，不與同其利者也。不然，則其畏也。不若是，強者必怒於言，懦者必怒於色矣。又嘗語於衆曰：「某非良士，某非良士。」其不應者，必其人之與也。不然，則其所疏遠，不與同其利者也。不然，則其畏也。不若是，強者必說於言，懦者必說於色矣。

是故事修而謗興，德高而毀來。嗚呼，士之處此世，而望名譽之光，道德之行，難已！將有作於上者，得吾說而存之，其國家可幾而理歟！

Without doing any good deed, he says: "Since I have done this one good thing, it is enough." Without any real ability, he says: "Since I have this one ability, it is enough." Outwardly he deceives others, and inwardly he deceives himself. He stops short of learning by far. Is this not treating himself with lenience? When it comes to others, he says: "Though he can do this, the man is unworthy of mention. Though he has this skill, its usefulness is unworthy of mention." Anything bad about the man is singled out, while ten other things that may be good are unaccounted for. Only the past is looked into and the present is brushed aside. The fear is rather that the man may become known. Is this not censuring others in close detail? A person like this can be said to treat himself like the crowd and expect others to be sages. I do not see any self-respect in him.

However, such behavior has its origin in sloth and jealousy. The slothful cannot improve themselves, and the jealous are afraid that others may excel. I have once said as an experiment to the crowd: "So-and-so is a good man, and so-and-so is a good man." Those who agree must be partial to the men in question; or they are far removed from them and share no common interests with them, or are afraid of them. Were it not so, the strong would angrily disagree in words and the weak, in their expression. I have also said to the crowd: "So-and-so is not a good man, and so and so is not a good man." Those who do not respond must be partial to the men in question; or they are far removed from them and share no common interests with them, or are afraid of them. Were it not so, the strong would show their pleasure in words and the weak, in their expression.

Therefore, when success is achieved, slander is generated; where there is lofty virtue, defamation comes with it. Alas, living in this world, scholars can hardly hope to achieve an illustrious name and to cultivate a high moral standard! If those who would rule can take heed of what I have said, are we not justified in our hope that the country will be well governed?

師　說

　　古之學者必有師。師者，所以傳道受業解惑也。人非生而知之者，孰能無惑？惑而不從師，其爲惑也，終不解矣。

　　生乎吾前，其聞道也，固先乎吾，吾從而師之。生乎吾後，其聞道也，亦先乎吾，吾從而師之。吾師道也，夫庸知其年之先後生於吾乎？是故無貴無賤，無長無少，道之所存，師之所存也。

　　嗟乎，師道之不傳也，久矣。欲人之無惑也難矣。古之聖人，其出人也遠矣，猶且從師而問焉。今之衆人，其下聖人也亦遠矣，而恥學於師。是故聖益聖，愚益愚。聖人之所以爲聖，愚人之所以爲愚，其皆出於此乎？

　　愛其子，擇師而敎之。於其身也，則恥師焉。惑矣。彼童子之師，授之書而習其句讀者，非吾所謂傳其道解其惑者也。句讀之不知，惑之不解，或師焉，或不焉，小學而大遺，吾未見其明也。

　　巫醫樂師百工之人，不恥相師。士大夫之族，曰師曰弟子云者，則羣聚而笑之。問之，則曰：「彼與彼年相若也，道相似也。位卑則足羞，官盛則近諛。」嗚呼，師道

On the Teacher

In ancient times scholars always had teachers. It takes a teacher to transmit wisdom, impart knowledge and resolve doubts. Since man is not born with knowledge, who can be without doubt? But doubt will never be resolved without a teacher.

He who was born before me learned the teachings before me, and I take him as my teacher. But if he who was born after me received his teachings before me, I also take him as my teacher. I take the teachings as my teacher. Why should I care whether a man was born before or after me? Irrespective therefore of the distinction between the high-born and the lowly, and between age and youth, wherever the teachings are, *there* is my teacher.

Alas, it has been a long time since the tradition of taking teachers was honored! And so it is difficult to expect people to be free from doubts. Though ancient sages far surpassed the common folk, they nevertheless asked questions of their teachers. On the other hand, the masses of today, who are far inferior to the sages, are ashamed to learn from their teachers. Consequently, the sage became more sage, and the ignorant more ignorant. Indeed, is this not the reason why the sage were sage and the ignorant are ignorant?

He who loves his son selects a teacher for the child's education, but he is ashamed to learn from a teacher himself. This is indeed puzzling. The teacher of a child is one who gives instruction on books and on the punctuation of sentences. This is not what I take as one who transmits wisdom and resolves doubts. To take a teacher for instruction in correct punctuation and not to take a teacher to help resolve doubts is to learn the unimportant and leave out the important. I do not see the wisdom of it all.

Shamans, doctors, musicians and craftsmen are not ashamed to take one another as teachers. But, when the scholar-officials speak of their teachers and pupils, there are those who get together and laugh at them. When questioned, their reply is that so-and-so is of the same age as so-and-so and that their understanding of the Way is similar. If one takes another who holds a low position as his teacher, it is something to be ashamed of. If it is some high official who is taken as a teacher, it is a

之不復可知矣。巫醫樂師百工之人，君子不齒，今其智，乃反不能及，其可怪也歟？

聖人無常師。孔子師郯子，萇弘，師襄，老聃。郯子之徒，其賢不及孔子。孔子曰：「三人行，則必有我師。」是故弟子不必不如師，師不必賢於弟子。聞道有先後，術業有專攻，如是而已。

李氏子蟠，年十七，好古文，六藝經傳，皆通習之。不拘於時，學於余。余嘉其能行古道，作師說以貽之。

---

[1] A descendant of Shao-hao 少昊, an ancient emperor.

[2] A Ta-fu 大夫, government official, during the reign of King Ching of the Chou dynasty 周敬王.

[3] An official in charge of music.

[4] Founder of Taoism.

[5] A *chin-shih* during the reign of Emperor Teh-tsung 德宗.

form of flattery. Alas, the tradition of taking teachers is no longer honored! Shamans, doctors, musicians and craftsmen are not respected by a gentleman, but their wisdom is beyond that of the gentleman. Is this not strange?

Our sages had no constant teachers. Confucius took T'an-tzu,[1] Ch'ang-hung,[2] Shih-hsiang[3] and Lao-tan[4] as his teachers, all of whom were not so wise as himself. Said Confucius, "When I walk in the company of three men, there must be a teacher of mine." The pupil is therefore not necessarily inferior to the teacher, and the teacher is not necessarily superior to the pupil. What makes the difference is that one has received teachings before the other and that one is more specialized in his craft and trade than the other—that is all.

Li P'an,[5] who is seventeen, is fond of ancient literature and is deeply versed in the six arts, the classics and chronicles. Not confined by the trends of the day, he has studied under me. Pleased that he can observe the ancient tradition, I have written this essay on the teacher to present to him.

伯　夷　頌

　　士之特立獨行，適於義而已，不顧人之是非，皆豪傑之士，信道篤而自知明者也。一家非之，力行而不惑者，寡矣。至於一國一州非之，力行而不惑者，蓋天下一人而已矣。若至於舉世非之，力行而不惑者，則千百年乃一人而已耳。

　　若伯夷者，窮天地，亙萬世而不顧者也。昭乎日月，不足爲明；崒乎泰山，不足爲高；巍乎天地，不足爲容也。當殷之亡，周之興，微子，賢也，抱祭器而去之，武王周公，聖也，從天下之賢士，與天下之諸侯，而往攻之，未嘗聞有非之者也。彼伯夷叔齊者，乃獨以爲不可。

　　殷既滅矣，天下宗周。彼二子乃獨恥食其粟，餓死而不顧。繇是而言，夫豈有求而爲哉？信道篤而自知明也。

　　今世之所謂士者，一凡人譽之，則自以爲有餘，一凡人沮之，則自以爲不足。彼獨非聖人，而自是如此。夫聖人乃萬世之標準也。余故曰，若伯夷者，特立獨行，窮天

---

[1] Eldest son of the ruler of Ku-chu 孤竹君, whose domain extended through parts of modern Hopeh, Liaoning and Inner Mongolia.

[2] High mountain range extending through Shantung Province.

[3] Elder brother of Emperor Chou 紂 of the Yin dynasty, whose rule was overthrown by the Chou 周 dynasty.

[4] Younger brother of Po-i, who died of starvation with him after the fall of the Yin dynasty.

In Praise of Po-i[1]

Scholars who stand alone and act independently, with the sole purpose of complying with the principles of righteousness, without regard to the views of others, are outstanding men, who have profound faith in the Way and know themselves clearly. There are only a few who can press forward persistently and are not beset by doubts despite the objections of the family. There is only one in the whole empire who can press forward persistently and is not beset by doubts despite the objections of the whole state or prefecture. There is only one in a hundred years or a thousand years who can press forward and is not beset by doubts despite the objections of the whole world.

A man like Po-i went so far as to disregard even heaven and earth and the judgment of numberless generations after him in order to do what he thought was right. In his presence the sun and moon had no luster, the T'ai Mountains[2] lost their altitude, and heaven and earth dwindled in capacity. When the Yin dynasty came to an end and the Chou dynasty rose to replace it, a worthy man like Viscount Wei[3] had left the former with his sacrificial vessels, and sages like King Wu and the Duke of Chou attacked the Yin dynasty in conjunction with the empire's distinguished scholars and its feudal lords. No one was ever heard to disapprove of them. However, Po-i and Shu-ch'i[4] were the only ones that disagreed.

After the extinction of the Yin dynasty, the whole empire pledged allegiance to the Chou dynasty. Only these two men were ashamed of eating at the hands of the new regime, even at the risk of starving to death. Were they seeking after something that they behaved thus? No, they were merely men who held firm convictions and knew themselves well.

The so-called scholar of today feels elated even when an ordinary mortal compliments him, and imagines himself lacking when an ordinary mortal obstructs him. On the contrary, Po-i had the courage to express his disapproval of the sages and felt sure of himself, though these sages were indeed held up as examples for numberless generations to come. That is why I say that a man like Po-i stood alone and took independent action in disregard of heaven and earth and the judgment of posterity.

地，亘萬世而不顧者也。雖然，微二子，亂臣賊子接跡於
後世矣。

However, but for these two men, rebellious ministers and villainous sons would have followed in succession in later generations.

讀　荀

　　始吾讀孟軻書，然後知孔子之道尊，聖人之道易行，王易王，霸易霸也。以爲孔子之徒沒，尊聖人者孟氏而已。晚得揚雄書，益尊信孟氏。因雄書而孟氏益尊，則雄者，亦聖人之徒歟？

　　聖人之道不傳于世，周之衰，好事者各以其說干時君，紛紛藉藉相亂，六經與百家之說錯雜，然老師大儒猶在。火于秦，黃老于漢，其存而醇者，孟軻氏而止耳，揚雄氏而止耳。及得荀氏書，於是又知有荀氏者也。考其辭，時若不粹，要其歸，與孔子異者鮮矣。抑猶在軻雄之間乎？

　　孔子刪詩書，筆削春秋，合於道者著之，離於道者黜去之，故詩書春秋無疵。

　　余欲削荀氏之不合者，附于聖人之籍，亦孔子之志歟？

　　孟氏醇乎醇者也，荀與揚大醇而小疵。

---

[1] A great philosopher of the Chou dynasty.
[2] A great philosopher of the Han dynasty.
[3] More specifically by the First Emperor of the Ch'in dynasty.

On Reading *Hsün-tzu*[1]

After first reading the *Book of Mencius*, I learned how worthy of respect were the teachings of Confucius, how easily the teachings of the sages could be practiced, and how Right could prevail as easily as Might. At that time, I thought that, after the death of Confucius' disciples, the only man that respected the Way of the sages was Mencius. Lately I have obtained the books of Yang Hsiung,[2] and my respect for and belief in Mencius have since been all the greater. Since the works of Yang enhanced respect for Mencius, is this not because Yang was also a disciple of the sages?

As the teachings of the sages stopped being transmitted to the world and as the Chou dynasty declined, those who would stir up trouble sought recognition from the reigning princes by offering their theories, which were a hodgepodge of the six classics and the hundred schools. Nevertheless, old teachers and great Confucian scholars still existed. After the burning of the books in the Ch'in dynasty[3] and the introduction of the cults of the Yellow Emperor and Taoism under the Han dynasty, the works of Mencius and Yang Hsiung were the only pure studies that survived. Then I obtained the *Book of Hsün-tzu* and learned that there was such a man as Hsün. At times his words seemed unorthodox, but in the last analysis he differed little from Confucius. He was perhaps somewhere between Mencius and Yang Hsiung.

Confucius edited the *Book of Songs,* the *Book of History* and the *Spring and Autumn Annals.* He kept those parts which were consistent with his doctrines and deleted those which deviated from them. As a result, the *Book of Songs*, the *Book of History* and the *Spring and Autumn Annals* are flawless.

I intend to eliminate from the *Book of Hsün-tzu* what is inconsistent with Confucius' doctrines and then add the work to the books of the sage. Was this not also the will of Confucius?

Mencius was the purest of all, while Hsün-tzu and Yang Hsiung were largely pure, but they had some small flaws.

論 佛 骨 表

臣某言，伏以佛者，夷狄之一法耳。自後漢時流入中國，上古未嘗有也。

昔者黃帝在位百年，年百一十歲。少昊在位八十年，年百歲。顓頊在位七十九年，年九十八歲。帝嚳在位七十年，年百五歲。帝堯在位九十八年，年百一十八歲。帝舜及禹，年皆百歲。此時天下太平，百姓安樂壽考。然而中國未有佛也。

其後殷湯，亦年百歲。湯孫太戊在位七十五年，武丁在位五十九年。書史不言其年壽所極，推其年數，蓋亦俱不減百歲。周文王年九十七歲，武王年九十三歲，穆王在位百年。此時佛法亦未入中國，非因事佛而致然也。

漢明帝時始有佛法，明帝在位纔十八年耳。其後亂亡相繼，運祚不長。宋，齊，梁，陳，元魏已下，事佛漸謹，年代尤促。惟梁武帝在位四十八年，前後三度捨身施佛，宗廟之祭，不用牲牢，晝日一食，止於菜果。其後竟為侯景所逼，餓死臺城。國亦尋滅。事佛求福，乃更得禍。由

44

Memorial on the Bone of Buddha

Your Majesty's subject humbly submits that Buddhism is merely a barbarian cult, which was introduced into China in the Later Han dynasty and which never existed in ancient times.

The Yellow Emperor was on the throne for a century and lived to the age of one hundred and ten. Emperor Shao-hao was on the throne for eighty years and lived to the age of one hundred. Emperor Chuan-hsü was on the throne for seventy-nine years and lived to the age of ninety-eight. Emperor K'u was on the throne for seventy years and lived to the age of one hundred and five. Emperor Yao was on the throne for ninety-eight years and lived to the age of one hundred and eighteen. Emperors Shun and Yü both lived to the age of one hundred. During all that time, the whole country enjoyed peace and the people were happy and long-lived. But China did not have any Buddha then.

Later, Emperor T'ang of the Yin dynasty also lived to the age of one hundred. His descendants, T'ai-mou and Wu-ting, were on the throne for seventy-five and fifty-nine years respectively, and, while history does not record the ages at which they died, each is reckoned to have lived for not less than a century. In the Chou dynasty King Wen lived to the age of ninety-seven and King Wu to the age of ninety-three, while King Mu was on the throne for a century. At that time, Buddhism had not entered China either, and the longevity of these rulers was by no means due to the worship of Buddha.

It was in the reign of Emperor Ming of the Han dynasty that Buddhism was first introduced into China, and yet this emperor was on the throne for only eighteen years. Subsequently, disorder followed upon disorder, and rulers did not reign for long. From the Sung, Ch'i, Liang, Ch'en and Northern Wei dynasties on, while the worship of Buddhism became increasingly zealous, the rulers were more and more short-lived, except Emperor Wu of the Liang dynasty, who reigned for forty-eight years. Three times in his lifetime he tortured himself as a service to Buddha. In sacrifices to the Imperial Ancestral Shrine, beef, lamb and pork were avoided. He had only one meal of vegetables and fruit a day. But ultimately he was pressured by Hou Ching and starved to death in T'ai-ch'eng [the imperial palace in Nanking]. His dynasty

此觀之，佛不足事，亦可知矣。

高祖始受隋禪，則議除之。當時羣臣，材識不遠，不能深知先王之道，古今之宜，推闡聖明，以救斯弊。其事遂止，臣常恨焉。

伏惟睿聖文武皇帝陛下，神聖英武，數千百年已來，未有倫比。即位之初，即不許度人為僧尼道士，又不許創立寺觀。臣常以為高祖之志，必行於陛下之手。今縱未能即行，豈可恣之轉令盛也。今聞陛下令羣僧迎佛骨於鳳翔，御樓以觀，舁入大內，又令諸寺遞迎供養。

臣雖至愚，必知陛下不惑於佛，作此崇奉，以祈福祥也。直以年豐人樂，徇人之心，為京都士庶，設詭異之觀，戲翫之具耳。安有聖明若此，而肯信此等事哉？

然百姓愚冥，易惑難曉，苟見陛下如此，將謂真心事佛，皆云：「天子大聖，猶一心敬信，百姓何人，豈合更惜身命？」焚頂燒指，百十為羣，解衣散錢，自朝至暮，轉相倣效，惟恐後時。老少奔波，棄其業次。若不即加禁

---

[1] Prefecture in modern Shensi Province.

was brought to an end shortly afterward. Thus, the worship of Buddha, from which blessings were sought, brought disaster instead. It is plain therefore that Buddha is not worthy of fervent devotion.

Emperor Kao-tsu of the T'ang dynasty thought of doing away with Buddhism when he first succeeded the Sui regime. However, the officials of the time were not farsighted enough, and did not possess a deep enough knowledge of the rulership of ancient kings and of what was suitable for past and present circumstances, and so were unable to give effect to the wisdom of the emperor and save the country from the curse. Hence, nothing came of the emperor's good intention, to your subject's regret.

For several thousand years, no ruler has equalled Your Majesty in sagacity and courage. When you first ascended the throne, you forbade the people to become monks, nuns and Taoist clergy and prohibited the establishment of temples and monasteries. I believed that Emperor Kao-tsu's ambition would one day be carried out by Your Majesty. Though this has not yet materialized, nothing should be done to aggravate the situation. I now hear that Your Majesty has ordered monks to welcome the bone of Buddha at Fenghsiang[1] and is making preparations to watch from a tower its entry into the palace, and that the various temples have been ordered to greet and do homage to it by turns.

Though your subject is most ignorant, he is convinced that Your Majesty is not deluded to such an extent that you would worship Buddha in order to seek blessings, but that, because of this year of plenty and the happy state of the empire, Your Majesty deigns to comply with the people's wishes by letting the populace of the capital be beguiled by this bizarre and deceiving show. How could an enlightened ruler like Your Majesty really believe in this?

However, the people are simple-minded; they are easy to fool but difficult to enlighten. Once they see Your Majesty acting as you are doing, they may think that you are sincerely worshipping Buddha and exclaim, "Even a man as wise as the Son of Heaven is showing his wholehearted reverence and faith. Who are we common people to begrudge our bodies and lives?" They may burn their heads and their fingers, and groups of tens and hundreds of them may throw away their clothes and distribute their money, and emulate one another from morning till night lest they run the risk of falling behind. Old and young may in one mad

47

遏，更歷諸寺，必有斷臂臠身，以爲供養者。傷風敗俗，傳笑四方，非細事也。

夫佛本夷狄之人，與中國言語不通，衣服殊製，口不言先王之法言，身不服先王之法服，不知君臣之義，父子之情。假如其身至今尚在，奉其國命，來朝京師，陛下容而接之，不過宣政一見，禮賓一設，賜衣一襲，衞而出之於境，不令惑衆也。況其身死已久，枯朽之骨，凶穢之餘，豈宜令入宮禁。

孔子曰：「敬鬼神而遠之。」古之諸侯，行弔於其國，尚令巫祝先以桃茢祓除不祥，然後進弔。今無故取朽穢之物，親臨觀之，巫祝不先，桃茢不用，羣臣不言其非，御史不舉其失，臣實恥之。乞以此骨付之有司，投諸水火，永絕根本，斷天下之疑，絕後代之惑，使天下之人知大聖人之所作爲，出於尋常萬萬也。豈不盛哉！豈不快哉！

佛如有靈，能作禍祟，凡有殃咎，宜加臣身。上天鑒臨，臣不怨悔。無任感激懇悃之至，謹奉表以聞。臣某誠惶誠恐。

48

rush neglect their business. If they are not stopped at once, they may go from temple to temple and hack off their arms and carve flesh from their bodies as a form of sacrifice. Such unseemly behavior will make a laughing-stock of the country. This is indeed not a small matter.

Buddha was a barbarian. With his language he could not have communicated with the people of China, and his dress was different from ours. He did not speak in the manner of our ancient kings, nor was his body clad like theirs. He did not know the proper relationship between ruler and ministers and the affection between father and son. If he were still alive today and had been sent on a mission to the capital as his country's envoy, Your Majesty would probably have granted him an audience, entertained him at a banquet, awarded him a suit of clothes and seen that he left our country's borders under guard, so that he might not have deluded our people. Now that he has been dead for a long time, why should we let these decayed and rotten bones, an ill-omened and filthy relic, enter the Forbidden City of the palace?

"Reverence ghosts and gods," said Confucius, "but keep them at a distance." When a feudal lord of old presented his condolences, he generally sent a sorcerer ahead to ward off evil influences with a branch of peach-wood and a broomstick. But now Your Majesty, for no obvious reason, intends to watch this decayed and filthy object, without first sending a sorcerer and without making use of the peach-wood and the broomstick, and none of your officials points out the mistake and none of your censors offers any criticism. Deeply ashamed, your subject begs that the bone be handed to the competent authorities to be consigned to water or fire, so that it may be destroyed forever, future generations relieved of their doubt, and the people of the country may know that the deed of a sage far surpasses that of an ordinary man. "What a great gesture! And how edifying!" people would exclaim.

If Buddha should have the power to inflict disaster, your subject would be fully prepared to endure any catastrophe visited upon him. With Heaven as his witness, he would not repent or regret. It is with all sincerity and appreciation that he hereby submits this memorial.

49

御史臺上論天旱人饑狀

右臣伏以今年已來，京畿諸縣，夏逢亢旱，秋又早霜，田種所收，十不存一。陛下恩踰慈母，仁過春陽，租賦之間，例皆蠲免，所徵至少，所放至多。上恩雖弘，下困猶甚。至聞有棄子逐妻，以求口食，坼屋伐樹，以納稅錢。寒餒道塗，斃踣溝壑。有者皆已輸納，無者徒被追徵。

臣愚以爲此皆羣臣之所未言，陛下之所未知者也。臣竊見陛下憐念黎元，同於赤子。至或犯法當戮，猶且寬而宥之。況此無辜之人，豈有知而不救？

又京師者，四方之腹心，國家之根本，其百姓實宜倍加憂恤。今瑞雪頻降，來年必豐。急之，則得少而人傷。緩之，則事存而利遠。伏乞特敕京兆府應今年稅錢及草粟等，在百姓腹內，徵未得者，並且停徵，容至來年蠶麥，庶得少有存立。

臣至陋至愚，無所知識，受恩思效，有見輒言，無任懇款慚懼之至。謹錄奏聞，謹奏。

Censorial Memorial on Drought and Famine

Your subject submits that this year the districts around the capital have suffered from drought in the summer and an early frost in the autumn, and as a result, nine-tenths of the crops have failed. Kinder even than a loving mother and more gracious than the spring sun, Your Majesty has been thoughtful enough to reduce to the minimum the people's tax payments and granted maximum exemptions. But though your imperial favors have been bountiful, the distress of the people is still undiminished. It is learned that there are some who have abandoned their children and driven out their wives to obtain enough food and who have torn down their houses and felled their trees to pay their taxes. The cold and hungry are homeless and fall dead on the road and in the gutter. Those who have have paid up, and those who have not have been harried in vain.

Your humble subject has the feeling that this has not been brought to Your Majesty's attention by any of your ministers. We have seen that Your Majesty commiserates and is concerned with the people as if they were little children. Even those who have trespassed against the laws and been condemned to death have been pardoned. It is unthinkable that Your Majesty would knowingly refrain from saving those who are innocent.

Moreover, the capital is the heart of the whole realm and the center of the country. Its people are doubly entitled to compassion. Now that the coming year is bound to be good, as a result of the frequent propitious snowfalls, precipitate action to enforce tax collection would bring little advantage to the state but would instead harm the people. Deliberation would help matters and be profitable in the longer term. I humbly request that you be gracious enough to order the Metropolitan Prefecture to waive the taxes and deliveries of hay and grain not yet collected from the people this year until the silkworm and wheat harvests next year, and thus afford them a breathing spell.

Your subject is most shallow, stupid and devoid of knowledge. But he has received so many favors from Your Majesty that he seeks to be of service in return. He has therefore taken the liberty to state the position as he sees it. It is with sincerity, humility and trepidation that this memorial is submitted.

51

應所在典帖良人男女等狀

應所在典帖良人男女等

右準律，不許典帖良人男女，作奴婢驅使。臣往任袁州刺史日，檢責州界內，得七百三十一人，並是良人男女，準律計傭折直，一時放免。原其本末，或因水旱不熟，或因公私債負，遂相典帖，漸以成風。名目雖殊，奴婢不別，鞭笞役使，至死乃休。既乖律文，實虧政理。

袁州至小，尚有七百餘人，天下諸州，其數固當不少。今因大慶，伏乞令有司重舉舊章，一皆放免。仍勒長吏嚴加檢責，如有隱漏，必重科懲。則四海蒼生，孰不感荷聖德？右前件如前，謹具奏聞，伏聽敕旨。

---

[1] See p. 26, above.

Memorial against the Use of Men and Women as Surety

Topic: According to the Law It Should be Forbidden to Hold
Good Men and Women as Surety or in Slavery

When your subject was Prefect of Yüanchow[1] some time ago, he made
an inspection and rounded up within the confines of his prefecture
seven hundred and thirty-one good men and women, and effected their
release after having calculated, as the law prescribes, the amount of
wages due to them for services rendered to their masters. The reason
for their bondage had been either the failure to effect crop deliveries,
because of flood or drought, or public or private indebtedness. The
result was the gradual adoption of the custom of enslaving human
beings as surety for debts. Though it might be called otherwise, the
system of slavery was no different, with its concomitant of flogging and
harsh treatment, ending only with death. This was not only against the
law, but contrary to good government.

Even Yüanchow, with a very limited area, had more than seven
hundred cases of the kind. The number would certainly have been much
greater, if all other prefectures of the empire had been included. On the
auspicious occasion of the present celebration, it is humbly requested
that the competent authorities be ordered to follow the existing regulations and release all the men and women involved, and that the higher
officials be strongly urged to make strict searches and impose penalties
in the event of any concealment or failure to take the necessary action.
If such steps are taken, who of all the people within the four seas will
not appreciate Your Majesty's graciousness? This memorial is respectfully submitted and Your Majesty's decree humbly awaited.

圬者王承福傳

　　圬之爲技，賤且勞者也。有業之，其色若自得者。聽其言，約而盡。問之，王其姓，承福其名，世爲京兆長安農夫。天寶之亂，發人爲兵，持弓矢十三年，有官勳，棄之來歸。喪其土田，手鏝衣食，餘三十年。舍於市之主人，而歸其屋食之當焉。視時屋食之貴賤，而上下其圬之傭以償之，有餘則以與道路之廢疾餓者焉。

　　又曰：「粟，稼而生者也。若布與帛，必蠶績而後成者也。其他所以養生之具，皆待人力而後完也。吾皆賴之。然人不可徧爲，宜乎各致其能以相生也。故君者，理我所以生者也，而百官者，承君之化者也。任有小大，惟其所能，若器皿焉。食焉而怠其事，必有天殃。故吾不敢一日捨鏝以嬉。夫鏝易能，可力焉，又誠有功。取其直，雖勞無愧，吾心安焉。夫力易強而有功也，心難強而有智也。用力者使於人，用心者使人，亦其宜也。吾特擇其易爲而無愧者取焉。

　　「嘻，吾操鏝以入貴富之家有年矣。有一至者焉，又

---

[1] Ch'angan 長安 *Hsien*, Ching-chao prefecture of Shensi Province, the then capital.

[2] 742-756, reign of Emperor Hsüan-tsung 玄宗.

Biography of Wang Ch'eng-fu, the Mason

Masonry is a lowly and laborious craft. One of the men engaged in it shows by his expression that he is happy about it, and when he is heard to speak, he is concise but exhaustive. In answer to a question, he gave his surname as Wang and his first name Ch'eng-fu. For generations, his has been a family of farmers in Ch'angan.[1] During the disturbances in the reign of T'ien-pao,[2] Ch'eng-fu was conscripted, and served in the military for thirteen years. His meritorious service earned him an official appointment, but he forfeited it in order to go home. Having lost his land, he was wielded the trowel for his living for over thirty years. He lives with his employer in the city, and pays him an appropriate sum for rent and food. His wages are determined by the current rate of his room and board. If there is a surplus over this, he gives it to the disabled and the hungry on the road.

He said further, "Grain is produced by cultivation, and cloth and silk fabrics are woven with yarn provided by the cotton plant and the silkworm respectively. All other means of livelihood require human effort. While they all give me sustenance, a man cannot do everything, and each must contribute what he can to the maintenance of his own existence and that of others. This is why the ruler governs us so that we can live and the innumerable officials discharge his civilizing mission. Responsibilities may be great or small but each man does what he can, just as each object has its function to perform. If after eating, one becomes lazy and neglects one's work, catastrophe from heaven is sure to befall. So I do not for one day dare to lay down my trowel and play. The application of this tool is easy to learn. It takes little effort and it can yield results. I get paid for my work, which, though laborious, does not make me ashamed, and I have peace of mind. Physical effort can be increased to give better results, but the mind can hardly be strained to generate more wisdom. It is indeed proper that those who perform physical labor should be used by others, and those who exercise their minds should use others. I have merely chosen to do the kind of work that is easy but withal does not make me feel ashamed.

"Oh, I have wielded the trowel for years and in the process entered the homes of wealthy and distinguished men. Sometimes I revisit one of

55

往過之，則爲墟矣。有再至三至者焉，而往過之，則爲墟矣。問之其鄰，或曰：『噫，刑戮也。』或曰：『身旣死而其子孫不能有也。』或曰：『死而歸之官也。』吾以是觀之，非所謂食焉怠其事而得天殃者邪？非强心以智而不足，不擇其才之稱否而冒之者邪？非多行可愧，知其不可而强爲之者邪？將貴富難守，薄功而厚饗之者邪？抑豐悴有時，一去一來而不可常者邪？吾之心憫焉。是故擇其力之可能者行焉。樂富貴而悲貧賤，我豈異於人哉？」

又曰：「功大者，其所以自奉也博。妻與子，皆養於我者也。吾能薄而功小，不有之可也。又吾所謂勞力者，若立吾家而力不足，則心又勞也。一身而二任焉，雖聖者不可能也。」

愈始聞而惑之，又從而思之，蓋賢者也。蓋所謂獨善其身者也。然吾有譏焉。謂其自爲也過多，其爲人也過少。其學楊朱之道者邪？楊之道，不肯拔我一毛而利天下。而夫人以有家爲勞心，不肯一動其心以畜其妻子，其肯勞其心以爲人乎哉？

雖然其賢於世之患不得之，而患失之者，以濟其生之

---

[3]A philosopher of the Warring States period.

these homes after only one job, and it is found to be in ruins. At other times, I revisit one of them after two or three jobs, and it too is found to be in ruins. When asked, the neighbors say, 'Alas, the family suffered the death penalty!' On another occasion, the answer may be, 'After the owner died, his children and children's children were unable to keep up the property.' Still another version may be, 'Since the owner's death, the house has been confiscated.' As I see from all this, is it not what I would call catastrophe from heaven when one is lazy and neglects one's work after eating? Is it not straining the mind to generate wisdom where there is not enough of it and yet choosing not a task that is commensurate with one's ability? Is it not doing much that makes one feel ashamed and forcing oneself at it while knowing that it cannot be done? Is it because wealth and official distinction are difficult to maintain and their enjoyment far exceeds the contributions made? Or, is it because prosperity and adversity are mutable, coming and going as they will? There is indeed commiseration in my heart for the person concerned. It is therefore necessary to select an objective within the range of one's capability. As to being fond of wealth and official distinction and averse to poverty and lowliness, I am no different from others!"

He went on to say, "Those whose merits are great can secure for themselves greater enjoyment. Since a wife and children have to depend on me for support, I do not have to have them if my ability is limited and my merits slight. Moreover, those whom I call people that labor with their hands will have to labor with their minds too, if their effort is not enough to establish a home. To shoulder two responsibilities is impossible even for a sage."

When I first heard his story I was puzzled, but upon reflection, I see that he is after all a worthy man. He is what may be called a man who seeks his own perfection. Nevertheless, I have an adverse criticism to make of him. I say that he is too much devoted to himself and too little to others. Is he not someone who is following the way of Yang Chu?[3] The way of Yang is not willingly to dispense with even a single hair for the benefit of the world. How can a man, who refuses to support a wife and children because it involves mental labor, be willing to do for others anything that would involve the same mental exertion?

However, he is far more worthy than many other people of the world—those who are afraid of not getting anything and, again, afraid of losing it once they get it, who lose their lives after doing evil and

57

欲，貪邪而亡道，以喪其身者，其亦遠矣。又其言有可以

警余者，故余爲之傳，而自鑒焉。

deviating from the path of righteousness merely to satisfy their worldly desires. Moreover, what he has said can in some respects serve as an exhortation to me. I have therefore set down his biography in writing as a lesson to myself.

張 中 丞 傳 後 敍

元和二年四月十三日夜，愈與吳郡張籍閲家中舊書，得李翰所爲張巡傳。翰以文章自名，爲此傳，頗詳密，然尙恨有闕者，不爲許遠立傳，又不載雷萬春事首尾。遠雖材若不及巡者，開門納巡，位本在巡上，授之柄而處其下，無所疑忌。竟與巡俱守死，成功名。城陷而虜，與巡死先後異耳。

兩家子弟材智下，不能通知二父志，以爲巡死而遠就虜，疑畏死而辭服於賊。遠誠畏死，何苦守尺寸之地，食其所愛之肉，以與賊抗，而不降乎？當其圍守時，外無蚍蜉蟻子之援，所欲忠者，國與主耳。而賊語以國亡主滅。遠見救援不至，而賊來益衆，必以其言爲信。外無待而猶死守，人相食且盡，雖愚人亦能數日而知死處矣。

遠之不畏死，亦明矣。烏有城壞，其徒俱死，獨蒙愧恥求活？雖至愚者不忍爲。嗚呼，而謂遠之賢而爲之邪？

---

[1] Chang Hsün 張巡 , a learned scholar and civilian official of the T'ang dynasty, who defended the city of Suiyang 睢陽 , south of modern Shangch'iu *Hsien* 商邱縣 , Honan, with Hsü Yüan during the rebellion of An Lu-shan 安祿山 (755-757). Both Chang and Hsü lost their lives in the line of duty.

[2] 807, reign of Emperor Hsien-tsung 憲宗 .

[3] One of the great T'ang poets, who was a good friend of Han Yü.

[4] Prefecture in modern Kiangsu Province.

[5] A scholar and historian during the reign of Emperor Hsüan-tsung.

[6] Co-defender of Suiyang, who was Prefect of this area.

[7] A commanding officer under Chang Hsün, who was brave and in whom Hsün had implicit trust. He participated in every important battle and finally lost his life during the rebellion.

Postscript to the Biography of Chief Censor Chang[1]

On the night of the 13th of the 4th month of the 2nd year of Yüan-ho,[2] together with Chang Chi[3] of Wu,[4] I went over the old books in the house and found a copy of the *Biography of Chang Hsün* by Li Han,[5] who prided himself on his writing. The book is rather detailed, but it is regrettably incomplete, in that it has left out the biography of Hsü Yüan,[6] nor does it record the deeds of Lei Wan-ch'un.[7] Though Yüan did not seem to possess the same talent, he opened the city gate to Hsün and, despite his higher rank, placed himself under him without being jealous or suspicious. He even defended the same city with Hsün until death brought immortality to them both. When the city finally fell, Yüan was taken captive, and he died only slightly later than Hsün.

The children of the two families did not have the intelligence to realize their fathers' intention. They suspected that, after Hsün's death, Yüan's surrender was an indication of cowardice. But, if Yüan had really been afraid of losing his life, why did he bitterly defend the city and continue to resist the rebels without surrendering, even when he had to eat the flesh of someone he loved? When he was besieged, he did not have the slightest aid from outside, but he did not cease to be loyal to country and emperor. On the contrary, he was informed by the rebels of the loss of his country and the death of his emperor, and he could not see any relief forthcoming. As against this, what he did see was the onrush of an increasing number of rebels. In these circumstances, he was forced to believe the information of the enemy. However, knowing that no relief could be expected from outside, he still insisted on defending the city till his death, while his men were eating one another's flesh. Even a fool could have known that his days were numbered and that he could not escape death.

It is quite clear that Yüan was not afraid of dying. How could he have sought to live alone in shame and disgrace even after the collapse of the city and the death of virtually all his men? This would be something for which the most stupid would not have had the heart. Alas, could a man as worthy as Yüan have attempted it?

說者又謂遠與巡分城而守，城之陷，自遠所分始。以此詬遠，此又與兒童之見無異。人之將死，其藏腑必有先受其病者。引繩而絕之，其絕必有處，觀者見其然，從而尤之，其亦不達於理矣。小人之好議論，不樂成人之美，如是哉？如巡遠之所成就如此卓卓，猶不得免，其他則又何說？

當二公之初守也，寧能知人之卒不救，棄城而逆遁？苟此不能守，雖避之他處何益？及其無救而且窮也，將其創殘餓羸之餘，雖欲去必不達。二公之賢，其講之精矣。守一城，捍天下，以千百就盡之卒，戰百萬日滋之師，蔽遮江淮，沮遏其勢。天下之不亡，其誰之功也？

當是時，棄城而圖存者，不可一二數，擅彊兵坐而觀者，相環也。不追議此，而責二公以死守，亦見其自比於逆亂，設淫辭，而助之攻也。

愈嘗從事於汴徐二府，屢道於兩府間，親祭於其所謂雙廟者。其老人往往說巡遠時事云。

南霽雲之乞救於賀蘭也，賀蘭嫉巡遠之聲威功績出己上，不肯出師救。愛霽雲之勇且壯，不聽其語，彊留之，

---

[8]Military Governor of Honan.

There are some who say that Yüan and Hsün had defended different parts of the city and that it was the section assigned to Yüan that fell first. Such an assessment of the blame is on a par with the judgment of a child. When a man is about to die, his internal organs must have first been diseased. When a taut rope breaks, there must be a part where it severs. At the sight, one may blame it on the part. Obviously it is equally unreasonable. How prone is the mean man to criticize and how reluctant to see to it that others' merits are duly recognized! Since even Hsün and Yüan, with their lofty accomplishments, cannot be exempt from harsh judgment, what can one expect to be said of others?

When the two great men first decided on their defenses, how could they have foreseen that no relief would be ultimately forthcoming and that they should abandon the city and escape? Since this city could not be defended, what good would have been done by their withdrawing to another place? If, when no relief was received and their effort exhausted, they had taken away their wounded, disabled, starved and emaciated remnants, they could not have reached their destination. The two great men, being as wise as they were, must have gone into the matter very thoroughly. By defending one city, they safeguarded the whole country, as, when they battled with a daily growing army of as many as a million men with the remnant forces of a few hundred, they shielded the Yangtze and the Huai Rivers and stopped the advance of the enemy. In these circumstances, whose merit was it that kept the country from extinction?

At that time, there were not a few commanders who abandoned their cities for their own survival; and all around were those who retained great military strength but who chose to sit back and wait. By sparing these from reproach and blaming the two great men for their defending the city to the death, the critics concerned took the side, in fact, of the rebels and furthered their cause with absurd accusations.

I have served in Pienchow and Hsüchow and traveled frequently between the two prefectures. I have offered personal sacrifices at what was known as the Double Temple. The old people there often speak of the events that took place in the time of Hsün and Yüan.

When Nan Chi-yün asked Ho-lan[8] for help, the latter, being jealous of the prestige of Hsün and Yüan and of their superior achievements, refused to send any relief. Admiring Nan for his valor and prowess, however, Ho-lan forcibly kept him behind as a guest against his will.

具食與樂，延霽雲坐。霽雲慷慨語曰：「雲來時，睢陽之
人，不食月餘日矣。雲雖欲獨食，義不忍，雖食，且不下
咽。」因拔所佩刀，斷一指，血淋漓，以示賀蘭。一座大
驚，皆感激，爲雲泣下。

雲知賀蘭終無爲雲出師意，即馳去。將出城，抽矢射
佛寺浮圖，矢著其上甎半箭。曰：「吾歸破賊，必滅賀蘭。
此矢所以志也。」愈貞元中過泗州，船上人猶指以相語。

城陷，賊以刃脅降巡，巡不屈，即牽去。將斬之，又降霽
雲，雲未應。巡呼雲曰：「南八，男兒死耳。不可爲不義屈。」
雲笑曰：「欲將以有爲也。公有言，雲敢不死？」即不屈。

張籍曰：「有于嵩者，少依於巡。及巡起事，嵩常在
圍中。」籍大曆中於和州烏江縣見嵩，嵩時年六十餘矣。
以巡，初嘗得臨渙縣尉，好學，無所不讀。籍時尚小，粗
問巡遠事，不能細也。云巡長七尺餘，鬚髯若神。

嘗見嵩讀漢書，謂嵩曰：「何爲久讀此？」嵩曰：「未
熟也。」巡曰：「吾於書，讀不過三徧，終身不忘也。」
因誦嵩所讀書，盡卷不錯一字。嵩驚，以爲巡偶熟此卷。

---

[9] 785-804, reign of Emperor Teh-tsung 德宗．
[10] Prefecture in modern Anhwei Province.
[11] 763-779, reign of Emperor Tai-tsung 代宗．
[12] Prefecture in modern Anhwei Province.
[13] Title of a subordinate local official.
[14] The old name of a *hsien* or district in Anhwei Province.
[15] A measure of length roughly equivalent to a foot.
[16] Dynastic history of the Han dynasty.

He provided Nan with food and musical entertainment, and invited him to sit down. Nan replied feelingly: "When I left the city, the men of Suiyang had not eaten for over a month. Though I myself want to eat, I do not have the heart to do so. Even if I try to eat, I cannot force the food down." Thereupon he unsheathed his sword and cut off one of his fingers, which, dripping with blood, was handed up to Ho-lan. The entire gathering was astounded and greatly touched, and shed tears for Nan.

Since he realized that Ho-lan had no intention of sending any troops, Nan rode off. As he was on the point of leaving through the city gate, Nan took out his bow and arrow and took a shot at the pagoda of a Buddhist temple. The arrow struck one of the bricks above, penetrating half-way. Nan said, "After returning and subduing the rebels, I will annihilate Ho-lan. Let this arrow mark my determination." During the reign of Chen-yüan,[9] I went past Ssuchow[10] by boat, and someone on board was still able to point out the spot and relate to me the story.

When Suiyang collapsed, the rebels tried to force Hsün at the point of the sword to capitulate, but, as he resisted, he was led away. When Hsün was about to be executed, Nan also was told to surrender. Seeing that he did not comply, Hsün cried out, "Nan the Eighth, as a man, you can only die. You must not yield to the unrighteous!" Smiling, Nan replied, "I expected to accomplish something. But with your admonition, how dare I go on living?" So saying, he refused to surrender.

Chang Chi said that a man named Yü Sung had lived with Hsün since his youth and that, when Hsün waged his crusade and was later besieged, Sung was always with him. In the reign of Ta-li[11] Chi saw Sung at Wuchiang *Hsien*, Hochow,[12] when the latter was more than sixty years of age. Thanks to Hsün, Sung once served as Wei[13] of Linhuan *Hsien*,[14] and, being studious, he left no book unread. At that time, Chi was still very young, and, though he made certain inquiries about Hsün and Yüan, he did not know the details. He said that Hsün was more than seven *ch'ih*[15] tall and that he had a beard like that of a deity.

Once Hsün saw Sung reading the *Book of Han*[16] and asked him why he had to read it over and over again. Sung said, "I do not yet know it by heart." "I read my books," Hsün said, "not more than three times and all my life I never forget what I have read." Then he started to recite from memory what Sung was reading, without a single mistake. Sung was astonished, but he thought that Hsün had just happened to

65

因亂抽他帙以試，無不盡然。嵩又取架上諸書，試以問巡，巡應口誦無疑。嵩從巡久，亦不見巡常讀書也。爲文章，操紙筆立書，未嘗起草。

初守睢陽時，士卒僅萬人，城中居人戶亦且數萬。巡因一見，問姓名，其後無不識者。

巡怒，鬚髯輒張。

及城陷，賊縛巡等數十人坐。且將戮，巡起旋。其衆見巡起，或起或泣。巡曰：「汝勿怖。死，命也。」衆泣，不能仰視。巡就戮時，顏色不亂，陽陽如平常。

遠寬厚長者，貌如其心。與巡同年生，月日後於巡，呼巡爲兄。死時年四十九。

嵩貞元初死於亳宋間。或傳嵩有田在亳宋間，武人奪而有之。嵩將詣州訟理，爲所殺，嵩無子，張籍云。

[17] Prefecture in modern Anhwei Province.
[18] Prefecture in modern Honan Province.

66

commit the particular volume to memory. When he tried Hsün with other volumes at random, the same feat was repeated. Thereupon he picked other books from the shelf, and without hesitation Hsün instantly recited from them. Sung was with Hsün for a long time, but he rarely saw him do any reading. When it came to writing, Hsün never prepared a draft but put everything in final form as soon he had pen and paper.

When he first arrived for the defense of Suiyang, Hsün had as many as ten thousand troops, but there were several times as many residents in the city. After meeting them once and learning their names, he never failed to recognize them.

When he was angry, his beard would become taut.

After the fall of the city, the rebels tied up Hsün and scores of others, and made them sit down. Hsün stood up to make water when he was about to be executed. Seeing this, some of his companions followed his example, and others began to cry. Said Hsün, "Fear not, for death is merely a matter of fate." They all wept so bitterly that they could not even look up. But, even when Hsün was put to death, his face never changed color and he was as relaxed as ever.

Yüan was a fine gentleman who was magnanimous and kindly, and his appearance reflected his heart. He was born in the same year as Hsün, and, being a few months younger, he called Hsün his elder brother. He was forty-nine when he died.

Yü Sung died at the beginning of the reign of Chen-yüan, somewhere between Pochow[17] and Sungchow.[18] Some say that Sung owned land between the two prefectures and that the property had been seized by a military man. He went to one of the prefectures to bring suit but was killed by the usurper and died without leaving a son. The above was according to Chang Chi.

送楊少尹序

昔疏廣受二子以年老，一朝辭位而去。于時公卿設供張，祖道都門外。車數百兩。道路觀者，多歎息泣下，共言其賢。漢史既傳其事，而後世工畫者，又圖其迹。至今照人耳目，赫赫若前日事。

國子司業楊君巨源，方以能詩訓後進。一旦以年滿七十，亦白丞相去，歸其鄉。

世常說古今人不相及，今楊與二疏，其意豈異也？

予忝在公卿後，遇病不能出。不知楊侯去時，城門外送者幾人，車幾兩，馬幾疋，道邊觀者，亦有歎息知其爲賢以否，而太史氏，又能張大其事爲傳，繼二疏蹤跡否，不落莫否。見今世無工畫者，而畫與不畫，固不論也。

然吾聞楊侯之去，丞相有愛而惜之者，白以爲其都少尹，不絕其祿。又爲歌詩以勸之，京師之長於詩者，亦屬而和之。又不知當時二疏之去，有是事否。古今人同不同，未可知也。

中世士大夫，以官爲家，罷則無所於歸。楊侯始冠，

---

[1] Title of a subordinate local official.
[2] Names of a gentleman and his nephew, who were prominent officials in the Han dynasty.
[3] Title of the Chancellor of the Imperial University.
[4] Prefecture in modern Shansi Province.

Farewell Message to Shao-yin[1] Yang

Years ago, when Shu Kuang and Shu Shou[2] retired in their old age, high officials set up curtained canopies outside the city gate of the capital to bid them farewell. There were several hundred carriages in the procession. Most of the spectators by the roadside sighed and shed tears, and all praised the two men for their worthiness. In addition to their biographies in the History of the Han dynasty, skillful painters subsequently depicted the scene, which to this day brightens the eyes and delights the ears of the people, as if it had all happened yesterday.

Yang Chü-yüan, Ssu-yeh[3] of the Imperial University, an accomplished poet well qualified to continue to instruct the younger generation, spoke to the Prime Minister and obtained his consent to his retirement and return home, having reached his seventieth year.

It is commonly said that modern people cannot be compared to the ancients. But in the case of Yang and the two Shus, is there any difference?

As a lesser official, I happened to be taken ill and could not venture abroad. I do not know how many bade him farewell outside the city gate when he left, how many carriages and horses there were, whether among the spectators by the roadside there were some who sighed and who knew that he was worthy, whether the Grand Historian expanded the event into a biography, to follow the example of the two Shus, and whether any coldness was shown him. No skillful painters are in evidence today, but it does not make any difference whether there is a painting.

However, I have heard that the Prime Minister regretted the departure of Shao-yin Yang, that he petitioned the Emperor to appoint Yang the Shao-yin of Hochung[4] so as not to deprive him of his emoluments, and that the Prime Minister composed a poem to give him the veneration he deserved. Similar poetry was written by those in the capital versed in this art. I do not know whether this too happened when the two Shus retired. Indeed it is impossible to know whether the ancients were or were not different from the men of our age.

In recent times, scholars have treated the Civil Service as their home. For they have nowhere to go when they are relieved of their official positions. Shao-yin Yang passed the local examination when he

舉於其鄉，歌鹿鳴而來也。今之歸，指其樹曰：「某樹吾
先人之所種也。某水某丘，吾童子時所釣遊也。」鄉人莫
不加敬，誡子孫以楊侯不去其鄉為法。古之所謂鄉先生沒
而可祭於社者，其在斯人歟？其在斯人歟？

was barely twenty years of age, and came to assume office with that qualification. On his return, he points at some trees and says, "Such and such trees were planted by my ancestors." He goes on to add, "Such a river and such a hill mark the spots where I fished and roamed when I was a boy." The people of the countryside, without exception, show him respect and exhort their children and their children's children to copy the example he set of not leaving his native town lightly. In ancient times, it was said that, when a country squire died, it was proper for him to be worshipped at a local shrine. Will this not also be true of this gentleman?

送石處士序

河陽軍節度御史大夫烏公，爲節度之三月，求士於從事之賢者。有薦石先生者。公曰：「先生何如？」曰：「先生居嵩邙瀍穀之間，冬一裘，夏一葛，食朝夕飯一盂，蔬一盤。人與之錢，則辭。請與出游，未嘗以事辭。勸之仕，不應。坐一室，左右圖書。與之語道理，辨古今事當否，論人高下，事後當成敗，若河決下流而東注，若駟馬駕輕車就熟路，而王良造父爲之先後也，若燭照數計而龜卜也。」

大夫曰：「先生有以自老，無求於人。其肯爲某來邪？」從事曰：「大夫文武忠孝，求士爲國，不私於家。方今寇聚於恒，師環其疆，農不耕收，財粟殫亡。吾所處地，歸輸之塗，治法征謀，宜有所出。先生仁且勇。若以義請，而彊委重焉，其何說之辭？」

於是譔書詞，具馬幣，卜日以授使者，求先生之廬而請焉。先生不告於妻子，不謀於朋友，冠帶出見客，拜受

---

[1] A geographical subdivision covering Mengchow 孟州 and Huaichow 懷州 in modern Honan Province.

[2] Wu Chung-yin 烏重胤 , a high official in the T'ang dynasty.

[3] Shih Hung 石洪 , a native of Loyang 洛陽 .

[4] All in Loyang.

[5] The Yellow River.

[6] Skillful drivers in ancient times.

[7] Chengting 正定 *Hsien*, Hopeh Province.

Preface to Poetry Addressed to Retired Scholar Shih

Three months after he assumed his office as Military Governor of Hoyang Chün,[1] the Honorable Chief Censor Wu[2] asked his worthy subordinates to recommend scholars for suitable positions. Someone submitted the name of Master Shih,[3] about whom the Governor made inquiries. The answer was: "The master makes his home between the Sung and Mang Mountains and between the Ch'an and Ku Rivers,[4] wears one fur garment in winter and one coarse cloth garment in summer, and eats one bowl of rice with one dish of vegetables morning and evening. When money is offered him, he declines it. When he is asked to go out, he never refuses under any pretext. When he is advised to take an official position, he does not respond. He sits in a room with books to both left and right of him. When he reasons with others his eloquence is like the River[5] overflowing and running eastward; when he discusses the right and wrong of ancient and contemporary affairs he is so sure of his ground that it is like a four-horse carriage driven through familiar roads with Wang Liang and Ts'ao Fu[6] taking the reins; and when he assesses the abilities of men and their future success or failure, his prognostication is as clear and revealing as examining under candle-light, counting by numbers or divining with the aid of tortoise shells.

The Chief Censor asked, "Since the master can afford to grow old without seeking the help of others, will he consent to come to me?" The subordinate replied, "With your high civilian and military qualifications and your patriotism and filial piety, you are seeking scholars to work for the country and not for your family. Now that the rebels are gathered at Hengchow,[7] and the region is swarming with troops, there is neither tilth nor harvest, and wealth and grain have been exhausted. The place where we remain is on the grain transport route, and here we should have good government and adopt sound requisition policies. The master is both humane and valiant. If we appeal to his sense of righteousness and invest him with important responsibilities, how can he refuse?"

A letter was therefore prepared, gifts set aside, and a day of good omen chosen and a messenger was dispatched to the house of the master in order to present the request. Without informing his wife and children

書禮於門內。宵則沐浴，戒行李，載書冊，問道所由，告行於常所來往。晨則畢至張上東門外。

　　酒三行，且起。有執爵而言者曰：「大夫眞能以義取人，先生眞能以道自任，決去就。爲先生別。」又酌而祝曰：「凡去就出處何常？惟義之歸。逐以爲先生壽！」又酌而祝曰；「使大夫恒無變其初，無務富其家而飢其師，無甘受佞人而外敬正士，無味於諂言，惟先生是聽，以能有成功，保天子之寵命。」又祝曰：「使先生無圖利於大夫，而私便其身。」

　　先生起拜，祝辭曰：「敢不敬蚤夜以求從祝規？」於是東都之人士，咸知大夫與先生，果能相與以有成也。逐各爲歌詩六韻，遣愈爲之序云。

---

and consulting with his friends, he came out to receive the messenger and bowed as he accepted the letter and gifts at the door. In the evening, he bathed, packed his baggage, and loaded his books; then he inquired about the way and said goodbye to his close associates. The following morning, all his friends gathered outside the eastern gate to see him off.

After drinking three rounds, when the master rose to take leave, someone raised his cup and gave this toast, "The Chief Censor can really secure scholars by his righteousness, and the master can really take it upon himself to observe the Way and decide what to accept or reject. Farewell to the master!" The same man refilled his cup and proposed another toast, "Is there a standard for accepting or rejecting a position and for choosing between employment and retirement? It depends solely on righteousness. Long live the master!" Once more he filled his cup and gave a toast, "Let the Chief Censor not alter his earlier conduct. Let him not engage in enriching his own family and starving his army. Let him not listen to the deceitful man and show superficial respect to the upright gentleman. Let him not be deceived by words of flattery and let him listen only to the master. Thus he will obtain success and fulfill the gracious mandate of the Son of Heaven." And a final toast was given, "Let the master not seek profit from the Chief Censor or further his private ends."

The master rose, bowed and answered the toast in these words, "How dare I refrain from seeking, morning and night, respectfully to comply with the wishes just expressed?"

Then the people of the Eastern Capital[8] all realized that the Chief Censor and the master could really collaborate successfully. Poems containing six rhymes were composed on the subject, and I was designated to write this preface.

送溫處士赴河陽軍序

伯樂一過冀北之野，而馬羣遂空。夫冀北馬多天下，伯樂雖善知馬，安能空其羣邪？解之者曰：「吾所謂空，非無馬也，無良馬也。伯樂知馬，遇其良，輒取之，羣無留良焉。苟無良，雖謂無馬，不爲虛語矣。」

東都固士大夫之冀北也。恃才能深藏而不市者，洛之北涯曰石生，其南涯曰溫生。大夫烏公，以鈇鉞鎮河陽之三月，以石生爲才，以禮爲羅，羅而致之幕下。未數月也，以溫生爲才，於是以石生爲媒，以禮爲羅，又羅而致之幕下。

東都雖信多才士，朝取一人焉，拔其尤，暮取一人焉，拔其尤。自居守河南尹以及百司之執事，與吾輩二縣之大夫，政有所不通，事有所可疑，奚所諮而處焉？士大夫之去位而巷處者，誰與嬉遊？小子後生，於何考德而問業焉？搢紳之東西行過是都者，無所禮於其廬。若是而稱曰：「大夫烏公一鎮河陽，而東都處士之廬無人焉，」豈不可也？

夫南面而聽天下，其所託重而恃力者，惟相與將耳。

[1] Sun Yang 係陽, a connoisseur of horses in the Ch'in dynasty. See page 29.
[2] Modern Hopeh and Shansi Provinces.
[3] Wen Tsao 溫造.
[4] The writer was then Magistrate of Honan *Hsien* 河南縣. The other *hsien* or district under the same governor was Loyang.

Preface to the Poem on Retired Scholar Wen's Departure for Hoyang Chün

After Po-lo[1] visited the wilderness in North Chi,[2] its herd of horses was depleted. Since there were more horses in North Chi than anywhere in the country, how could Po-lo deplete the herd in spite of his thorough knowledge of horses? The explanation is that here the word "deplete" does not mean that there were no longer any horses, but that there were no longer any *good* horses. Because of his knowledge of horses, Po-lo took away the good ones whenever he saw them, thus stripping the herd of its best stock. If there were no good horses left, it may not therefore be far wrong to say that there were no longer any horses.

The Eastern Capital is indeed the North Chi of scholars. Scholar Shih, who lived at the northern end of Loyang, and Scholar Wen,[3] who lived at its southern end, were both secure in their own ability but hiding it from public view and not about to trade on it. Three months after his assumption of office as Military Governor of Hoyang, Chief Censor Wu, recognizing the ability of Scholar Shih, invited him with handsome gifts to join his staff. Scarcely a few months later, also recognizing the ability of Scholar Wen and through the intermediary of Scholar Shih, the Chief Censor invited Wen too, with due ceremony, to join his staff.

The Eastern Capital has indeed an abundance of able men. But, when *one* is taken in the morning and *another* in the evening, both of them outstanding, where can all the officials from the Governor of Honan down, including the secretaries of various offices and the func-tionaries in our two *hsien*,[4] obtain advice in dealing with difficult govern-ment affairs and unresolved problems? With whom will officials who have been relieved of their positions and who live in secluded lanes play and travel? From whom will the younger generation seek advice about virtue and literary pursuits? The gentlemen from east and west, who pass through the capital, will no longer be able to pay their respects to the homes of the two scholars. Can it not therefore be said that, since Chief Censor Wu became Military Governor of Hoyang, there were no talent left in the homes of retired scholars in the Eastern Capital?

In ruling his country, a sovereign relies mainly on his prime ministers and generals. The former recruit for the Son of Heaven his court officials, and the latter, the civilian and military staff. When this task

77

相爲天子得人於朝廷，將爲天子得文武士於幕下，求內外無治，不可得也。愈縻於茲，不能自引去，資二生以待老。今皆爲有力者奪之。其何能無介然於懷邪？

生既至，拜公於軍門。其爲吾以前所稱，爲天下賀，以後所稱，爲吾致私怨於盡取也。

留守相公，首爲四韻詩，歌其事。愈因推其意而序之。

---

[5]Title of a high local official.

is properly discharged, there is no reason why peace and order should not prevail in the capital and in the provinces. Having been appointed to my present post, I am in no position to seek retirement, but I had hoped to associate with the two scholars until my old age. Now that they both have been taken away by the powers that be, how can I help feeling disappointed?

On your arrival, Scholar Wen, to pay your respects to the Chief Censor at his military headquarters, will you not relate to him the idea of the first part of this preface which has been written to congratulate the country, and of the latter part to express my personal regret at the departure of the scholars.

As the Honorable Liu-shou[5] has composed an eight-line poem to commemorate this event, I have expanded his idea and written this preface.

乳 母 墓 銘

　　乳母李，徐州人，號正眞，入韓氏乳其兒愈。愈生未
再周月，孤失怙恃。李憐，不忍棄去，視保益謹，遂老韓
氏。

　　及見所乳兒愈舉進士第，歷佐汴徐軍，入朝爲御史，
國子博士，尚書都官員外郞，河南令，娶婦生二男五女，
時節慶賀，輒率婦孫列拜進壽。

　　年六十四，元和六年三月十八日疾卒。卒三日，葬河
南縣北十五里。愈率婦孫視窆封，且刻其語于石，納諸墓，
爲銘。

---

[1] Prefecture in modern Kiangsu Province.
[2] Title of a ministerial official.
[3] 811, reign of Emperor Hsien-tsung.

Inscription on the Tomb Tablet of My Wet-Nurse

My wet-nurse, whose family name was Li and given name Cheng-chen, was from Hsüchow.[1] She joined the Han family to nurse me, its son. Unfortunately I was bereaved of my parents before I had reached even my second birthday. She took pity on me and stayed on to take even greater care of me, eventually remaining with the Han family until her old age.

She lived to see the baby nursed by her obtain his *chin-shih* degree, become an assistant in the military headquarters of Pienchow and Hsüchow, enter Court as Censor, Doctor of the Imperial University and Yüan-wai-lang[2] of the Ministry of Justice, and serve as Magistrate of Honan. She also lived to see me get married and bring forth two sons and five daughters. In celebration of the festivals of the season, I would bring along my wife and children to pay her respects on our knees and to offer her our toasts.

She lived to the age of sixty-four and died from sickness on the 18th of the 3rd month of the 6th year of Yüan-ho.[3] Three days after her death she was buried fifteen *li* north of Honan *Hsien*. I took my wife and children to attend the burial. I had this inscription engraved on stone and deposited in the tomb.

祭 十 二 郎 文

年月日，季父愈，聞汝喪之七日，乃能銜哀致誠，使建中遠具時羞之奠，告汝十二郎之靈。

嗚呼，吾少孤，及長，不省所怙，惟兄嫂是依。中年，兄歿南方，吾與汝俱幼，從嫂歸葬河陽。既又與汝就食江南。零丁孤苦，未嘗一日相離也。

吾上有三兄，皆不幸早世。承先人後者，在孫惟汝，在子惟吾，兩世一身，形單影隻。嫂常撫汝指吾而言曰：「韓氏兩世，惟此而已。」汝時尤小，當不復記憶，吾時雖能記憶，亦未知其言之悲也。

吾年十九，始來京城。其後四年，而歸視汝。又四年，吾往河陽，省墳墓，遇汝從嫂喪來葬。又二年，吾佐董丞相于汴州，汝來省吾。止一歲，請歸取其孥。明年，丞相薨，吾去汴州，汝不果來。是年，吾佐戎徐州，使取汝者始行，吾又罷去，汝又不果來。

吾念汝從于東，東亦客也，不可以久。圖久遠者，莫如西歸，將成家而致汝。嗚呼，孰謂汝遽去吾而歿乎？吾與汝俱少年，以為雖暫相別，終當久相與處，故捨汝而旅

---

[1] Name of a friend or relative.
[2] Mengch'eng 孟城 *Hsien*, Honan Province.
[3] Prefecture in modern Honan Province.
[4] Prefecture in modern Kiangsu Province.

Funerary Message to Nephew No. 12

On (date, month and year), seven days after hearing of his death, Uncle Yü, with sorrow and sincerity, has been able to ask Chien-chung[1] to arrange a sacrifical feast, with delicacies of the season, for the spirit of Nephew No. 12 and to send him the following message:

Alas, I was bereaved of my parents when I was young! When I grew up, I had to rely on my brother and sister-in-law for their support. My brother died in the South when he was middle-aged. At that time you and I were both very young, and we followed my sister-in-law to bury my brother at Hoyang.[2] Then you and I earned our living south of the Yangtze. As we were both orphaned and alone, we were in each other's company daily and never separated.

Before me there were three brothers, who all unfortunately had died early. You and I were the only ones in our generations to succeed our ancestors, and each of us was the sole male descendant in his generation. On one occasion my sister-in-law, with you in her arms, pointed at us and said, "These are the only ones left in two generations of the Han family!" As you were even younger, most probably you cannot recall. Though I can recall it, I did not realize how sad the remark was.

I did not come to the capital until I was nineteen. Four years later, I went home to see you. Four years after that, I went to Hoyang to visit our ancestral tombs and met you on your way to bury my sister-in-law. Another two years, and I went to Pienchow[3] to assist Prime Minister Tung. It was then that you came to see me. Only one year elapsed before you asked leave to fetch your family. The Prime Minister died in the following year, and I left Pienchow before you could join me there. That year I was an assistant at the military headquarters in Hsüchow.[4] No sooner had I sent for you than I was relieved of my post. Again you were not able to come.

I thought that, when you were in the East, you were a mere visitor and could not stay there long. As a permanent plan, there was nothing like returning to the West. I was thus prepared to make my home there and send for you. Alas, who could have foreseen that you would leave me and die unexpectedly? As we were both young men, I thought that despite our temporary separation we would ultimately live together for

食京師，以求斗斛之祿。誠知其如此，雖萬乘之公相，吾不以一日輟汝而就也。

去年，孟東野往，吾書與汝曰：「吾年未四十，而視茫茫，而髮蒼蒼，而齒牙動搖。念諸父與諸兄，皆康彊而早世。如吾之衰者，其能久存乎？」吾不可去，汝不肯來，恐旦暮死，而汝抱無涯之戚也。孰謂少者歿而長者存，彊者夭而病者全乎？

嗚呼，其信然邪？其夢邪？其傳之非其真邪？信也，吾兄之盛德而夭其嗣乎？汝之純明而不克蒙其澤乎？少者彊者而夭歿，長者衰者而存全乎？

未可以為信也，夢也，傳之非其真也，東野之書，耿蘭之報，何為而在吾側也？嗚呼，其信然矣！吾兄之盛德而夭其嗣矣！汝之純明，宜業其家者，不克蒙其澤矣！所謂天者誠難測，而神者誠難明矣！所謂理者不可推，而壽者不可知矣！

雖然，吾自今年來，蒼蒼者或化而為白矣。動搖者或脫而落矣。毛血日益衰。志氣日益微。幾何不從汝而死也。死而有知，其幾何離。其無知，悲不幾時，而不悲者無窮期矣。

汝之子始十歲，吾之子始五歲。少而彊者不可保，如

---

[5] Roughly equivalent to a peck.

[6] Five *tou*.

[7] Meng Chiao 孟郊 (751-814), one of the great T'ang poets.

[8] Name of a servant.

yet a long time. That is why I left you and lived in the capital to earn a *tou*[5] or *hu*[6] of official rice. Had I known what would happen, I would not have accepted the position of a duke or prime minister that comes with ten thousand carriages and missed you for a single day!

Last year, when Meng Tung-yeh[7] visited you, I took the occasion to write to you in these words: "I am not quite forty, but my sight is getting dim, my hair gray and my teeth shaky. As I recall, my father, uncles and brothers were all hale and healthy but died early. Can someone as infirm as I live long?" At that time I could not leave nor did you consent to come. I was afraid that I might die one day and cause you unbounded grief. Who could expect that the young would die and the elderly live, that the strong would die and the sickly be spared?

Alas, is it true? Or is it all a dream? Is the information passed on not the truth? If it is true, can a man of as great virtue as my brother be deprived of his heir at such an early age? Can someone as bright and pure as you not receive his blessing? Can the young and strong die and the elderly and infirm be spared?

If it could not be believed, if it were a dream and if the information passed on was not the truth, why are the letter of Tung-yeh and the report of Keng Lan[8] at my side? Alas, it *is* true! A man of as great virtue as my brother *did* lose his son at an early age! Someone as bright and pure as you, who should succeed to the family tradition, could *not* receive his blessing! What is called Heaven is hard to predict and the gods are hard to understand! What is called reason cannot be gauged and our life span cannot be known!

Since the start of this year, what was gray has partly become white, and what were shaky have partly fallen out, my hair and blood have steadily weakened and my ambition has daily dwindled. It should not be long before I follow you to the grave! If there is consciousness after death, how can we be separated for any length of time? If there is no consciousness then, my feeling of sadness will not endure, and then for an unlimited time I shall have no sadness at all.

Your son is only ten years old, and mine just five. Since the young and strong cannot be spared, can these children be expected to grow up? Alas, how sad, how sad!

A letter you sent last year said that you had contracted beriberi,

此孩提者，又可冀其成立邪？嗚呼哀哉！嗚呼哀哉！

汝去年書云，比得軟腳病，往往而劇。吾曰，是疾也，江南之人常常有之，未始以為憂也。嗚呼，其竟以此而殞其生乎？抑別有疾而至斯乎？

汝之書，六月十七日也。東野云，汝歿以六月二日，耿蘭之報無月日。蓋東野之使者，不知問家人以月日，如耿蘭之報，不知當言月日。東野與吾書，乃問使者，使者妄稱以應之耳。其然乎，其不然乎？

今吾使建中祭汝，弔汝之孤，與汝之乳母。彼有食，可守以待終喪，則待終喪而取以來。如不能守以終喪，則遂取以來。其餘奴婢，並令守汝喪。吾力能改葬，終葬汝於先人之兆，然後惟其所願。

嗚呼，汝病吾不知時，汝歿吾不知日。生不能相養以共居，歿不得撫汝以盡哀。斂不憑其棺，窆不臨其穴。吾行負神明，而使汝夭，不孝不慈，而不得與汝相養以生，相守以死。一在天之涯，一在地之角。生而影不與吾形相依，死而魂不與吾夢相接。吾實為之，其又何尤？彼蒼者天，曷其有極！

自今以往，吾其無意於人世矣。當求數頃之田於伊潁

---

[9] One hundred *mou* 畝, each of which is about one-sixth of an acre.
[10] Two rivers in Honan Province.

which worsened frequently. In reply I said that people south of the Yangtze often have this disease, and so I did not worry very much about it. Alas, was it just this that killed you, or was it something else that proved fatal?

Your letter was dated the seventeenth of the sixth month. On the other hand, Tung-yeh said that you had died on the second of that month, and the report of Keng Lan was undated. Tung-yeh's messenger had not inquired of our folks about the exact date, while Keng Lan did not know that the report should bear a date. The letter Tung-yeh sent me gave the date he had heard from the messenger, who had answered his query haphazardly. Is this true or is it not?

Now I am asking Chien-chung to offer my sacrifices to you and send my condolences to your bereaved children and your nurse. If they have sufficient food and can afford to wait till the end of the period of mourning, they can be fetched here at that time. On the other hand, if they cannot wait, they may come immediately. As to other male and female servants, I shall see that they remain in mourning for you. When I am able to move your grave, I shall arrange for your reburial in our ancestral cemetery, and only then can I consider my wishes fulfilled.

Alas, when you were sick, I did not know the exact time; and when you died, I did not know the exact date! When you were alive, I could not live with you, so that we could have taken care of each other; and when you died, I could not express my grief in full at your side. When you were dressed for the coffin, I could not witness it; and when you were buried, I was absent from your grave. My acts were unworthy in the gods' eyes and caused you to die young. I am both unfilial to my parents and unkind to the younger generation, so that we could not live together and take care of each other till our death. Now, while one is on the border of Heaven, the other is at the corner of the earth. When you lived, your shadow was seldom beside me, and after your death your soul is not in contact with my dreams. Since I have caused all this, whom can I blame? Oh, Heaven above, is there any end to my grief?

From now on I shall lose all my interest in this world, and I shall seek a few *ch'ing*[9] of farm land on the I and Ying[10] for my remaining

之上，以待餘年。敎吾子與汝子幸其成長，吾女與汝女待
其嫁，如此而已。

　　嗚呼，言有窮而情不可終。汝其知也邪？其不知也邪？
嗚呼哀哉，尚饗！

years. I shall teach your son and mine till they grow up, and I shall take care of your daughter and mine till they are married.

Alas, words are exhaustible but sentiments never end! Do you know or do you not know? Alas, how sad! May you partake of this feast!

柳子厚墓誌銘

子厚諱宗元。七世祖慶，爲拓跋魏侍中，封濟陰公。曾伯祖奭，爲唐宰相，與褚遂良，韓瑗俱得罪武后，死高宗朝。皇考諱鎮，以事母，棄太常博士，求爲縣令江南。其後以不能媚權貴，失御史。權貴人死，乃復拜侍御史。號爲剛直。所與游，皆當世名人。

子厚少精敏，無不通達。逮其父時，雖少年已自成人。能取進士第，嶄然見頭角。衆謂柳氏有子矣。其後以博學宏詞授集賢殿正字。儁傑廉悍，議論證據今古，出入經史百子，踔厲風發，率常屈其座人。名聲大振，一時皆慕與之交。諸公要人，爭欲令出我門下，交口薦譽之。

貞元十九年，由藍田尉拜監察御史。順宗即位，拜禮部員外郎。遇用事者得罪，例出爲刺史，未至，又例貶州

---

[1] Liu Tsung-yüan (773-819). See pp. 99-101 below.
[2] Title of Prime Minister.
[3] Both Po-shih and T'ai-ch'ang were official titles. The former position was that of a scholar under the latter, who was a cabinet minister.
[4] Title of a language officer.
[5] 803, reign of Emperor Teh-tsung 德宗.
[6] A subordinate local official.
[7] Lant'ien *Hsien*, Shensi Province.
[8] Title of an official of one of the ministries.

Inscription on Liu Tzu-hou's Tomb Tablet

Tzu-hou's name was Tsung-yüan.[1] His direct ancestor in the seventh generation back, by the name of Ch'ing, served as Shih-chung[2] during the Northern Wei dynasty, and the title of Duke of Chi-yin was conferred on him. His great-granduncle, named Shih, was one of the T'ang Prime Ministers, who was sentenced to death during the reign of Kao-tsung together with Ch'u Sui-liang and Han Yüan, because they offended Empress Wu. His father, Chen, forsook his position as Po-shih of T'ai-ch'ang[3] and sought to serve as a *Hsien* Magistrate south of the Yangtze, because he wished to take care of his mother. Subsequently, owing to his inability to flatter someone in power, he lost his position as Censor. On this man's death, he was reinstated, and, as Censor, he was noted for his straightforwardness, and those with whom he associated were all celebrities of the time.

When Tzu-hou was young, he was precocious and capable, and there was no subject that he did not pursue thoroughly. When his father was still alive, Tzu-hou, though still young, had matured as an adult. As he succeeded in taking the *chin-shih* degree and proved himself outstanding, the general feeling was that the Liu family had a son of great promise. Later, he passed the extraordinary imperial examination and was designated as the Cheng-tzu[4] of the Chi-hsien Council. He was outstanding, incorruptible and courageous. His discussions on ancient and modern events were profound, and he quoted from the classics, history and the hundred schools with ease. He had forensic ability and could always prevail in a debate. For this reason, he soon became widely known and and had many admirers, who yearned to associate with him. Those who held lofty positions vied to have him as their pupil, and they all praised him highly.

In the nineteenth year of Cheng-yüan,[5] he was promoted from the office of Wei[6] of Lant'ien[7] to a Supervisory Censorship. When Emperor Shun-tsung ascended the throne, he was appointed Yüan-wai-lang[8] of the Ministry of Rites. Because the person who had recommended him committed an offense, Tzu-hou had, according to precedent, to be demoted to Prefect. Before he reached his destination, however, he was, again according to precedent, further demoted to Sub-Prefect of

司馬。居閒，益自刻苦，務記覽，爲詞章，汎濫停蓄，爲深博無涯涘。而自肆於山水間。

元和中，嘗例召至京師，又偕出爲刺史，而子厚得柳州。既至，歎曰：「是豈不足爲政邪？」因其土俗，爲設教禁，州人順賴。其俗以男女質錢，約不時贖，子本相侔，則沒爲奴婢。子厚與設方計，悉令贖歸。其尤貧力不能者，令書其傭，足相當，則使歸其質。觀察使下其法於他州，比一歲，免而歸者且千人。

衡湘以南，爲進士者，皆以子厚爲師。其經承子厚口講指畫，爲文詞者，悉有法度可觀。

其召至京師而復爲刺史也，中山劉夢得禹錫，亦在遣中，當詣播州。子厚泣曰：「播州非人所居，而夢得親在堂，吾不忍夢得之窮，無辭以白其大人。且萬無母子俱往理。」請於朝，將拜疏，願以柳易播，雖重得罪，死不恨。遇有以夢得事白上者，夢得於是改刺連州。

嗚呼，士窮乃見節義。今夫平居里巷相慕悅，酒食游

[9] Prefecture in modern Hunan Province.
[10] 806-820, reign of Emperor Hsien-tsung.
[11] Prefecture in modern Kwangsi Province.
[12] Title of a superior local official.
[13] Prefectures in modern Hunan Province.
[14] A noted poet of the T'ang dynasty (772-842).
[15] Ting Hsien 定縣, Hopeh Province.
[16] Prefecture in modern Kweichow Province.
[17] Liu Yü-hsi's courtesy name.
[18] Prefecture in modern Kwangtung Province.

Yungchow.[9] During the time that he lived there, he worked even harder than before, delving into ancient books and taking notes from them. His writings became voluminous and profound beyond measure, and in between studies he roamed the mountains and rivers.

In the middle of Yüan-ho,[10] he was, according to precedent, recalled to the capital. Once more he was, among others, appointed to a prefecture; this time he was assigned to Liuchow.[11] On his arrival there he sighed, "Is this not a place where good government can prevail?" In keeping with the local customs, he devised various regulations and prohibitions, which the people of the prefecture readily accepted to their benefit. One of the local customs was to use men and women as hostages for loans and to take them as slaves if the debt was not redeemed in time and if the accrued interest equaled the capital. In such cases, Tzu-hou devised ways and means to enable the debtor to effect the redemption. Those who were too poor to do so were permitted to work for the creditors who were required to keep records of their wages. When the wages sufficed for the payment, the hostages were released. The Kuan-ch'a-shih[12] ordered this new rule to apply to other prefectures, which resulted in the release of nearly a thousand hostages by the end of the year.

At that time, all *chin-shih* south of Hengchow and Hsiangchow[13] regarded Tzu-hou as their teacher. Those to whom he lectured showed remarkable ability to comply with the accepted usage in their writings.

When he was recalled to the capital and reappointed Prefect, Liu Yü-hsi[14] of Chungshan[15] was also among those to be placed, and he was assigned to Pochow.[16] Tzu-hou wept when he heard about it and said: "Pochow is not a place for a human being, and, with his mother still living, I cannot bear to see someone as miserable as Meng-teh.[17] I am hard put to it to make a plausible explanation to her. Furthermore, there is absolutely no reason for mother and son to go there together." When he was on the point of submitting a memorial to the throne about his wish to exchange posts with Liu Yü-hsi and express his determination to do so without regrets, even if he should be condemned to death for it, someone appealed to the emperor to reconsider Meng-teh's case, and he was reappointed to Lienchow.[18]

Alas, it is only in adversity that a scholar's integrity and righteousness can ·be seen. Ordinarily, when two persons living in the same neighborhood admire each other, eat, drink and play together, laugh

戲相徵逐，詡詡强笑語以相取下，握手出肺肝相示，指天日涕泣，誓生死不相背負，眞若可信。一旦臨小利害，僅如毛髮，比反眼若不相識，落陷穽，不一引手救，反擠之，又下石焉者，皆是也。此宜禽獸夷狄所不忍爲，而其人自視以爲得計。聞子厚之風，亦可以少媿矣。

子厚前時少年，勇於爲人，不自貴重。顧藉謂功業可立就，故坐廢退。既退，又無相知有氣力得位者推挽，故卒死於窮裔，材不爲世用，道不行於時也。

使子厚在臺省時，自持其身，已能如司馬刺史時，亦自不斥，斥時有人力能舉之，且必復用不窮。然子厚斥不久，窮不極，雖有出於人，其文學辭章，必不能自力以致，必傳於後，如今無疑也。雖使子厚得所願，爲將相於一時，以彼易此，孰得孰失，必有能辨之者。

子厚以元和十四年十一月八日卒，年四十七，以十五年七月十日歸葬萬年先人墓側。子厚有子男二人，長曰周六，始四歲，季曰周七，子厚卒乃生，女子二人，皆幼。

其得歸葬也，費皆出觀察使河東裴君行立。行立有節槩，立然諾，與子厚結交，子厚亦爲之盡，竟賴其力。葬

---

[19] 819, reign of Emperor Hsien-tsung.
[20] Hsienning 咸寧 *Hsien*, Shensi Province.
[21] A geographical subdivision roughly equivalent to modern Shansi Province.

and converse with and show courtesy toward each other, hold hands and lay bare their hearts, and point with tears in their eyes to heaven and the sun, swearing that to the very end of their lives they will not let each other down, it may all seem credible. But, once a small conflict of interests, even as small as a single hair, divides the two, they may turn around as if they had never known each other. When one falls into a pit, the other not only does not pull him out, but pushes him down and even pelts him with stones. This sort of thing happens everywhere. Not even barbarians and animals can bear to act like this, but a man capable of such acts would regard it as perfectly in order. When he hears of Tzu-hou's behavior, he should indeed feel ashamed of himself.

When Tzu-hou was young, he was deeply devoted to others, but attached no importance to himself. Convinced that he could achieve success at once, he endured his demotions with good grace. However, after being demoted, he did not have a good friend in strong enough a position to be able to save him. As a result, he died in a remote part of the country, without being given a chance to use his talents for the benefit of the world and to see his Way prevail in his time.

If, when Tzu-hou was still at court, he had behaved as he did when he was Sub-Prefect and Prefect, he would not have been removed, and, even in the event of his removal, he would have been helped by powerful men and could have been re-employed and spared his poverty. However, if Tzu-hou had not been rejected for a long time and if he had not become extremely poor, it is beyond doubt that, despite his outstanding ability, he would not have been able to devote the same effort to his writings, and make it as certain as it now is that they would be transmitted to posterity. Even if Tzu-hou had become Commander-in-Chief or Prime Minister for a time, as he had wished, it could easily be seen whether it would have been a gain or a loss.

Tzu-hou died on the eighth day of the eleventh month of the fourteenth year of Yüan-ho[19] at the age of forty-seven. His remains were returned on the tenth day of the seventh month of the fifteenth year to be buried in the ancestral cemetery at Wannien.[20] He was survived by two sons, Chou-liu, aged only four, and Chou-ch'i, who was born after Tzu-hou died, and two daughters who were both young.

His burial expenses were met by P'ei Hsing-li of Hotung,[21] the Kuan-ch'a-shih, a man of integrity and magnanimity whose word is his bond. As a friend, Tzu-hou always did what he could for P'ei, and finally he

子厚於萬年之墓者，舅弟盧遵。遵，涿人，性謹愼，學問
不厭。自子厚之斥，遵從而家焉，逮其死不去。既往葬子
厚，又將經紀其家。庶幾有始終者。銘曰：

「是惟子厚之室，既固既安，以利其嗣人。」

---

²²Cho *Hsien* 涿縣 , Hopeh Province.

had to rely on him. The one who made the arrangements for the burial is Lu Tsun, Tzu-hou's cousin from Chochow,[22] a man prudent by nature, who is never tired of pursuing his studies. After Tzu-hou was dismissed, Lu joined Tzu-hou's family and never left him before his death. After burying Tzu-hou, Lu will manage his household; he is indeed a man who is consistent from beginning to end.

The tablet inscription reads:

> Here is a chamber for Tzu-hou,
> A safe and a strong one,
> A blessing to all his descendants,
> Who shall follow him hereafter!

柳
二
州

韓文公評公文云雄深雅健似司馬子長崔蔡不足多也葬時為銘其墓又將其儔
傑瑰悍柳州羅池建廟祀公文公復作碑頌其死而為神云。

Liu Tsung-yüan (773-819)

Liu Tsung-yüan had the courtesy name of Tzu-hou 子厚. His ancestors originally came from Hotung 河東.[1] His great-grand-uncle, Shih 奭, was Prime Minister in the T'ang dynasty and was put to death after offending Empress Wu 武后. His father, Chen 鎮, served as Censor, and during his lifetime moved his family to Wu 吳.[2]

When he was young, Tzu-hou was extremely intelligent, and his writings were outstanding and refined. Even then, he was greatly respected by his contemporaries. After receiving his *chin-shih* degree, he was appointed to the Secretariat. Shortly afterward, he was transferred to Lant'ien 藍田[3] as a subordinate local official. In the 19th year of Chen-yüan,[4] he was attached to the Supervisory Censorship. As his talent was greatly appreciated by Wang Shu-wen 王叔文, who was then in power, he was promoted to the position of Yüan-wai-lang 員外郎[5] in the Ministry of Rites and was earmarked for further advancement. With the eclipse of Wang, however, he was demoted to Prefect, and, even before he arrived at his post, further demoted to Sub-prefect of Yungchow 永州.[6]

Disappointed with his political career and practically exiled to a barren community with little to do, he resigned himself to leisurely travels and to writing. It was during this interval that many of his masterpieces were produced, especially the famous records of his travels. He also imitated the style of the *Li sao* 離騷[7] and wrote profusely on the feelings of

[1] Yungchi *Hsien* 永濟縣, Shansi Province.

[2] Ancient name of Kiangsu Province.

[3] A *hsien* in Shensi Province.

[4] 803, reign of Emperor Teh-tsung.

[5] Title of a ministerial official.

[6] Prefecture in modern Hunan Province.

[7] A great poetic work by Ch'ü Yüan 屈原 of the state of Ch'u 楚 in the Chou dynasty 周.

frustration that were then in his heart. These writings were greatly esteemed by many of his learned friends. But, while they were impressed with his unusual ability, no one went as far as to recommend his services, as there had been some apprehension that his resourcefulness might not prove to be an unmixed asset.

In the 10th year of Yüan-ho 元和 ,[8] Liu Tsung-yüan was transferred to Liuchow 柳州 [9] as Prefect. At the same time, his bosom friend, Liu Yü-hsi 劉禹錫 ,[10] was appointed to Pochow 播州[11] in the same position. "Pochow is not a place for a human being, and, with his mother still living, I cannot bear to see someone as miserable as Meng-teh.[12] I am hard put to it to make a plausible explanation to her. Furthermore, there is absolutely no reason for mother and son to go there together." So he took the liberty of submitting a memorial to the throne, offering to exchange posts with Liu Yü-hsi. By a happy coincidence, however, those in a high position also spoke on Yü-hsi's behalf. As a result, he was reappointed to Lienchow 連州[13] instead.

In Liuchow, the same custom prevailed as in Yüanchow— that of taking human beings as pledges for debts.[14] In case of default, when the amount of accrued interest equaled the principal owed, the person concerned was confiscated as a slave. Liu Tsung-yüan devised a method by which these men and women were released wherever possible. In cases of extreme poverty, he arranged for the work of debtors to count toward their redemption, which was secured when the total wages sufficed to pay the debt. Those who had already defaulted were redeemed at Liu's own expense.

[8] 815, reign of Emperor Hsien-tsung.
[9] Prefecture in modern Kwangsi Province.
[10] A great T'ang poet (772-842).
[11] Prefecture in modern Kweichow Province.
[12] Courtesy name of Liu Yü-hsi.
[13] Prefecture in modern Kwangtung Province.
[14] See p. 26, above.

Southern scholars who had attained their *chin-shih* degree came from several thousand *li* to be tutored by Liu, and derived great benefit from his instruction. He was then already known, as he is now, as Liu Liuchow, this being the name of the prefecture where he held his last post before he died at the age of forty-seven in the fourteenth year of Yüan-ho.

When he was young, Tzu-hou's ambition was to make his services available to the state, and he declared that there was room for his accomplishments. Unfortunately he did not live long enough, and all his life he had to contend against innumerable odds. Though he did not fulfil his expectations, his name was widely known even in his own time, and his writings were especially prized by Han Yü, whom he helped extensively in developing the classical prose movement and who described his works as "vigorous, profound, elegant and robust, like those of Ssu-ma Ch'ien, Grand Historian of the Han dynasty." After his death Liu Tsung-yüan was well remembered, and a shrine was erected to his memory. The inscription on his tomb tablet was composed by the great Han Yü.[15]

[15] See pp. 90-97, above.

桐葉封弟辯

古之傳者有言，成王以桐葉與小弱弟戲，曰：「以封汝。」周公入賀。王曰：「戲也。」周公曰：「天子不可戲。」乃封小弱弟於唐。

吾意不然。王之弟當封耶？周公宜以時言於王，不待其戲而賀以成之也。不當封耶？周公乃成其不中之戲，以地以人，與小弱者爲之主。其得爲聖乎？

且周公以王之言。不可苟焉而已，必從而成之耶？設有不幸，王以桐葉戲婦寺，亦將舉而從之乎？凡王者之德，在行之何若。設未得其當，雖十易之不爲病，要於其當，不可使易也。而況以其戲乎？若戲而必行之，是周公教王遂過也。吾意周公輔成王，宜以道。從容優樂，要歸之大中而已。必不逢其失而爲之辭，又不當束縛之，馳驟之，使若牛馬然，急則敗矣。且家人父子，尚不能以此自克，

[1] r. 1104-1068 B.C.
[2] Shu-yü 叔虞.
[3] T'ang *Hsien* 唐縣, Hopeh Province.

Criticism of the Grant of a Fief by Means
of a Paulownia Leaf

It is recorded in an ancient historical book that King Ch'eng [of the Chou dynasty][1] was playing with one of his younger brothers[2] by holding out to him [as a scepter] a paulownia leaf and saying: "Hereby I confer a fief on you." The Duke of Chou came in and offered his congratulations. When the emperor said that it was just a joke, the duke replied that the Son of Heaven should not speak in jest. As a result, the emperor was compelled to grant his younger brother the fief of T'ang.[3]

To me this does not seem plausible. If the brother had been entitled to the grant, the duke should have recommended it to the emperor at the appropriate time, and should not have waited till a jest was made and then turned it into reality by offering his congratulations. If the brother was not entitled to the grant, how could the Duke of Chou be regarded as a sage when he turned a jest into reality and placed a state and its people under the emperor's younger brother, who was scarcely mature?

Moreover, did the Duke of Chou have the grant confirmed just because he thought that the king should not have spoken lightly? If unfortunately the king had played the same trick on a woman or a eunuch with the same paulownia leaf, would the duke still have followed it up? The virtue of a kingly person depends on his action. If it had not been right, it would not have been improper to change his decision as often as ten times, so as to set it right and render any further change unnecessary. Should this not have been all the more the case when a mere jest was involved? If a jest had had to be taken seriously, the Duke of Chou would have been guilty of advising the king to give complete effect to a mistake.

To my mind, the Duke of Chou, in assisting King Ch'eng, should have guided him in an easy and pleasant manner unto the path of righteousness until he reached the ultimate stage of noble propriety. He could not possibly have tried to cover up a mistake when it took place. Furthermore, it would not have been proper for him to restrain or goad the king like a bull or horse, because such impulsive conduct was bound to cause utter failure. If even members of the same family could not control themselves under so severe a restraint, how could it have

況號爲君臣者耶？

是直小丈夫𡙇𡙇者之事，非周公所宜用，故不可信。或曰，封唐叔，史佚成之。

---

[4] According to the *Records of History* 史記, the one who forced King Ch'eng to make good his jest was Yin-i 尹佚, known as the Annalist I 史佚. The story also appears in the *Shuo Yüan* of Liu Hsiang 劉向説苑, in which the act is attributed to the Duke of Chou.

been expected of people in a prescribed sovereign-subject relationship? This was something which only a small man with petty wisdom would have done, not an act which the Duke of Chou could have committed. Hence it is not credible. Elsewhere it has been alleged that the grant to Shu-yü was effected by the Annalist Yin-i.[4]

伊 尹 五 就 桀 贊

伊尹五就桀。或疑曰，湯之仁，聞且見矣，桀之不仁，聞且見矣。夫胡去就之亟也？

柳子曰：「惡，是吾所以見伊尹之大者也。彼伊尹，聖人也。聖人出於天下，不夏商其心，心乎生民而已。曰：『孰能由吾言？由吾言者爲堯舜，而吾生人堯舜人矣。』退而思曰：『湯誠仁，其功遲。桀誠不仁，朝吾從而暮及於天下，可也。』於是就桀，桀果不可得，反而從湯。既而又思曰：『尚可十一乎？使斯人蚤被其澤也。』又往就桀，桀不可，而又從湯，以至於百一，千一，萬一，卒不可。乃相湯伐桀，俾湯爲堯舜，而人爲堯舜之人。是吾所以見伊尹之大者也。

「仁至於湯矣，四去之，不仁至於桀矣，五就之。大人之欲速其功如此。不然，湯桀之辨，一恆人盡之矣，又奚以憧憧聖人之足觀乎？

「吾觀聖人之急生人，莫若伊尹，伊尹之大，莫若於五就桀。作伊尹五就桀贊。」

---

[1] Prime Minister under Emperor T'ang of the Shang dynasty.
[2] Last ruler of the Hsia dynasty.

Eulogy of I Yin's Five Attempts to Join Emperor Chieh

I Yin[1] made five attempts to join Emperor Chieh.[2] Some have doubted this, saying: "Emperor T'ang's benevolence had been widely known, and Emperor Chieh's lack of it also had been widely known. Why did I Yin try to join one and forsake the other repeatedly?"

"Alas," says the author, "this is where I see the greatness of I Yin. Being a sage, I Yin came forth in the world, not with the Hsia or Shang dynasty at heart, but only thinking of the people. 'He who can take my advice,' he said to himself, 'is an Emperor Yao or Emperor Shun, and his people will be the people of Yao or Shun.' Then he turned and thought, 'T'ang is indeed benevolent, but he can achieve success only slowly. On the other hand, though Chieh lacks benevolence, if I follow him in the morning and the effect may be felt by the people by evening, it will have been a good move.' So he joined Chieh. It so turned out that he could not work for this ruler. Thus he left Chieh for T'ang. Then he thought once more: 'Is there not one chance in ten that the people may get the blessing earlier?' So he joined Chieh again. Failing again, he followed T'ang. Then he took a one-hundredth, a one-thousandth and even a one-ten-thousandth chance, but ultimately he still failed. Then it was that he finally decided to become Prime Minister under T'ang and send his punitive expediton against Chieh, so that T'ang could become a Yao or Shun and his people the subjects of a Yao or Shun. This is where I see the greatness of I Yin.

"Notwithstanding T'ang's benevolence, I Yin forsook him four times, and notwithstanding Chieh's lack of the same, he joined him five times. Such was the anxiety of a great man to achieve his success quickly. Otherwise, how could the distinction between T'ang and Chieh, which was obvious even to an ordinary person, be worth the consideration of a sage and induce him to hesitate?

"As I see it, no sage could be like I Yin in hastening to the service of the people and I Yin was never so great as when he made his five attempts to join Chieh. Hence this eulogy."

捕 蛇 者 說

　　永州之野產異蛇，黑質而白章。觸草木盡死。以齧人，無禦之者。然得而腊之以爲餌，可以已大風，攣踠瘻癘，去死肌，殺三蟲。其始，大醫以王命聚之，歲賦其二。募有能捕之者，當其租入。永之人爭奔走焉。

　　有蔣氏者，專其利三世矣。問之，則曰：「吾祖死於是，吾父死於是。今吾嗣爲之十二年，幾死者數矣。」言之貌若甚慼者。余悲之，且曰：「若毒之乎？余將告于蒞事者，更若役，復若賦。則何如？」

　　蔣氏大戚，汪然出涕，曰：「君將哀而生之乎？則吾斯役之不幸，未若復吾賦不幸之甚也。嚮吾不爲斯役，則久已病矣。自吾氏三世居是鄉，積於今六十歲矣。而鄉鄰之生日蹙。殫其地之出，竭其廬之入，號呼而轉徙，飢渴而頓踣，觸風雨，犯寒暑，呼噓毒癘，往往而死者相藉也。曩與吾祖居者，今其室十無一焉。與吾父居者，今其室十無二三焉。與吾居十二年者，今其室十無四五焉。非死而

[1] A prefecture in modern Hunan Province.

The Snake-Catcher

The wilder parts of Yungchow[1] are infested with strange snakes, whose
skin was black with white stripes. At a mere touch, they kill every type
of plant life. No human being is immune from their bites. But, when
their flesh is dried and preserved as a medicine, it can cure leprosy,
deformities of the limbs, neck scrofula and malignant boils, remove
purulent ulcers and kill the three worms afflicting the body. To start
with, the Imperial Physician collected the snakes by order of the
Emperor, and twice a year they were submitted to the court as tribute.
Now, anyone catching them is allowed to present them in lieu of tax
payment. And so the people of Yungchow vie with one another in
hunting the snakes.

There is a man named Chiang, whose family has enjoyed a monopoly
of the business for three generations. When asked about it, he said: "My
grandfather died of this work, and so did my father. I took over from
them twelve years ago and almost lost my life a number of times." In
uttering these words, he appeared very sad, and I felt sorry for him. So
I said: "Do you dislike the work? I can speak to the competent authorities and get them to change your liability and let you pay your taxes in
cash as before. What do you think about that?"

Chiang was greatly upset at this suggestion and burst into tears. "Can
you take pity on me," he cried, "and let me go on living? Distressing as
my present callings is, it is not as bad as once again making me pay my
taxes in cash. If I had not followed this line of business, I would have
had trouble long ago. It is sixty years since all three generations of my
family settled in the village. With the passage of time, my neighbors
have found it more and more difficult to earn their living. They have
used up the produce of their land and the income from their houses,
appealed for help and finally had to move elsewhere. They suffered
hunger and thirst in their wanderings, weathered storms, endured heat
and cold, and breathed the poisonous plague-laden air. As a result, they
have died in droves. Not one in ten of those who lived at the same time
as my grandfather is still here. Not two or three out of ten who lived at
the same time as my father are still here. Not four or five out of ten
who have lived with me for the past twelve years are still here. They

徙爾。而吾以捕蛇獨存。

「悍吏之來吾鄉，叫囂乎東西，隳突乎南北，譁然而駭者，雖雞狗不得寧焉。吾恂恂而起，視其缶而吾蛇尚存，則弛然而臥。謹食之，時而獻焉，退而甘食其土之有，以盡吾齒。蓋一歲之犯死者二焉，其餘則熙熙而樂。豈若吾鄉鄰之旦旦有是哉？今雖死乎此，比吾鄉鄰之死則已後矣。又安敢毒耶？」

余聞而愈悲。孔子曰：「苛政猛於虎也。」吾嘗疑乎是。今以蔣氏觀之，猶信。嗚呼！孰知賦斂之毒，有甚是蛇者乎？故為之說，以俟夫觀人風者得焉。

have either died or moved away. I alone have survived on account of my snake-catching.

"Cruel court messengers come to my native town, shouting loudly from east to west and causing disturbances from north to south. Even dogs and chickens, frightened by the row, are denied peace and quiet. When I fearfully rise and find my snakes still alive in their jar, I can go back to sleep with my mind at rest. I feed them carefully, and at regular intervals I present them to the court. When I get back home, I sustain myself by enjoying the produce of my land until I breathe my last. I place my life in danger no more than twice in a year; the rest of the time I lead a happy existence. Am I in the position of my neighbors, who face danger every day? Even if I die from my job, it will at least be after my neighbors. How could I ever dislike my work?"

When I heard him talk like this, I became even more sorrowful. Confucius once said: "Oppressive rule is fiercer than a tiger." Though I used to doubt this statement, I now think that it is true, to judge from the case of Chiang. Alas, who knows but that the poison of onerous taxation is worse than that of these snakes? Accordingly, I have written this essay for the reference of those whose duty it is to observe the people's way of life.

種 樹 郭 橐 駝 傳

郭橐駝，不知始何名，病瘻，隆然伏行，有類橐駝者，故鄉人號之駝。駝聞之曰：「甚善，名我固當。」因捨其名，亦自謂橐駝云。

其鄉曰豐樂鄉，在長安西。駝業種樹，凡長安豪富人爲觀游及賣果者，皆爭迎取養。視駝所種樹，或移徙，無不活，且碩茂，蚤實以蕃。他植者雖窺伺傚慕，莫能如也。

有問之，對曰：「橐駝非能使木壽且孳也，能順木之天以致其性焉爾。凡植木之性，其本欲舒，其培欲平，其土欲故，其築欲密。既然已，勿動勿慮，去不復顧。其蒔也若子，其置也若棄。則其天者全，而其性得矣。故吾不害其長而已，非有能碩茂之也。不抑耗其實而已，非有能蚤而蕃之也。

「他植者則不然。根拳而土易，其培之也，若不過焉則不及。苟有能反是者，則又愛之太恩，憂之太勤。且視而暮撫，已去而復顧。甚者爪其膚以驗其生枯，搖其本以觀其疏密。而木之性，日以離矣。雖曰愛之，其實害之。雖

---

[1] A district in modern Shensi Province.

The Tree-Planter, Kuo the Camel

Kuo the Camel, whose real name is unknown, is hunchbacked and walks like a camel with his head drooping. For this reason, he was nicknamed the Camel by his townspeople. When Kuo learned of this, he said, "Very well, this is just the right name for me," and, discarding his own name, he called himself the Camel too.

His native town was in Fenglo, which is west of Ch'angan.[1] Kuo the Camel was a planter of trees. All the powerful families and wealthy people in Ch'angan, who planted trees for their pleasure or who engaged in the fruit trade, vied with one another in welcoming and hiring Kuo. They saw the trees planted or even transplanted by him all lived and flourished, and bore fruit early and could be propagated easily. Although others spied on him and imitated him, none could equal his skill.

When questioned on the point, he replied, "I am by no means capable of making trees live long and flourish, but what I *can* do is to enable them to follow their natural propensities and evolve as nature wishes. In the planting of trees, roots must have plenty of room to breathe, the fillings be level, the soil old and packed dense. When they are planted, trees should not be disturbed or worried over. When they are left behind, there is no looking back. At the time of planting, they should be treated like one's favorite children; once they are left alone, they should be regarded as one's unfilial sons. Thus their nature can be kept intact and their potentials fully developed. What I do is not to harm their growth, but I have no way of making them flourish; I take care not to damage their fruits, but I have no way of causing their early fruition and profuse propagation.

"Not so the other tree-planters. In their case, the roots are crooked, new soil is used and the cultivation is either excessive or insufficient. Those who can avoid these practices, however, love the trees too dearly and worry about them too much. They inspect them in the morning and pamper them in the evening. Everytime they leave the trees behind, they would come back and look over them some more. They even scratch their barks to see whether the trees are alive and shake their roots to find out if they are firm. Thus, they depart farther and farther from the nature of trees. They love them in name but harm them in

113

曰憂之，其實讎之。故不我若也。吾又何能爲哉？」

　　問者曰：「以子之道，移之官理可乎？」馳曰：「我知種樹而已，理非吾業也。然吾居鄉，見長人者，好煩其令，若甚憐焉，而卒以禍。旦暮，吏來而呼曰：『官命促爾耕，勖爾植，督爾穫，蚤繰而緒，蚤織而縷，字而幼孩，遂而雞豚。』鳴鼓而聚之，擊木而召之。吾小人輟飧饗以勞吏者，且不得暇，又何以蕃吾生而安吾性耶？故病且怠，若是，則與吾業者，其亦有類乎？」

　　問者嘻曰：「不亦善夫！吾問養樹，得養人術。傳其事以爲官戒。」

fact; they worry about them in name but are hostile to them in fact. That is why they cannot be like me. What else is there that I can claim to do?"

"Can your method be applied to the art of government?" asked the inquirer. "I know only how to plant trees," Kuo replied, "and government is not my line. But, when I am in the countryside, I see officials who are fond of giving orders, as if they took pity on the people, but in fact they merely do harm in the end. Morning and evening officials come and shout at us, 'Official order: Get started with your ploughing and planting! Tend to your harvest! Spin your silk yarn and weave your cloth early! Take care of your children! Feed your chickens and pigs!' These officials beat their drums to assemble the people and knock on their wooden instruments to call them out. We, the humble people, cannot find the leisure to receive these officials even if we give up our morning and evening meals. How can we find time to increase our production and follow our nature? This is why we become exhausted and lethargic. Can there be anything in this similar to my trade?"

"Wonderful!" said the inquirer smilingly, "I asked about tree-planting and learned about the cultivation of men. Let this story be passed on as a lesson to officials!"

宋清傳

宋清，長安西部藥市人也。居善藥。有自山澤來者，必歸宋清氏，清優主之。長安醫工，得清藥輔其方，輒易讎，咸譽清。疾病疕瘍者亦皆樂就清求藥，冀速已，清皆樂然響應。雖不持錢者，皆與善藥。積券如山，未嘗詣取直。或不識，遙與券，清不為辭，歲終度不能報，輒焚券，終不復言。

市人以其異，皆笑之，曰：「清，蚩妄人也。」或曰：「清其有道者歟？」清聞之曰：「清逐利以活妻子耳，非有道也。然謂我蚩妄者亦謬。」

清居藥四十年，所焚券者百數十人。或至大官，或連數州，受俸博，其餽遺清者，相屬於戶。雖不能立報而以賒死者千百，不害清之為富也。

清之取利遠，遠故大，豈若小市人哉？一不得直，則怫然怒，再則罵而仇耳。彼之為利，不亦翦翦乎？吾見蚩之有在也。清誠以是得大利，又不為妄，執其道不廢，卒以富。

116

Biography of Sung Ch'ing

Sung Ch'ing, a man from the Drug Market in the western part of Ch'ang-an, stocked a wide range of good medicines. People coming from distant mountains and rivers always visited him, and he was always hospitable to them. The doctors in Ch'angan could sell their prescriptions easily when they were accompanied by his drugs. They all praised him highly. People with various illnesses and ailments gladly sought drugs from Sung, and hoped these would heal their sicknesses quickly, and he was always pleased to fill their orders. Even to those who did not pay cash he supplied good drugs. He never collected from those whose unpaid bills piled up mountain-high, and he even extended credit to those who were far away and unknown to him. At the end of the year, when he thought that the debts had no chance of being cleared up, he burned the notes and never mentioned them again.

The people of the town laughed at him because of his strange behavior. "Sung is foolish and preposterous," some said. Others commented, "Is Sung not a man of virtue?" On hearing these remarks, Sung observed, "I seek profit to keep my wife and children live, and I am not a man of virtue. But it is equally wrong to say that I am foolish and preposterous."

In the forty years during which he had stocked medicines, Sung burned the unpaid bills of more than one hundred clients. Some of these later became high officials or governor of several prefectures, whose emoluments were handsome. In consequence, those who came to Sung with gifts practically queued up at his door. Although hundreds died without doing so and without paying their debts, this did not affect Sung's great affluence.

Sung looked to the distant future for his profit, which turned out to be considerable. He was not like a small merchant, who gets very angry when he is not paid and who reviles and harbors hatred against those who repeat the failure. How near-sighted they are in their pursuit of profit! I can see that there are indeed fools like these. Ch'ing, however, gained enormous profit in his own way. He was never preposterous, and unfailingly kept to his virtuous way. Thus he ultimately became a rich man.

117

求者益衆，其應益廣。或斥棄沉廢，親與交視之落然者，清不以怠遇其人，必與善藥如故。一旦復柄用，益厚報清。其遠取利皆類此。

吾觀今之交乎人者，炎而附，寒而棄，鮮有能類清之爲者。世之言，徒曰市道交。嗚呼，清，市人也。今之交，有能望報如清之遠者乎？幸而庶幾，則天下之窮困廢辱，得不死亡者，衆矣。市道交豈可少耶？或曰：「清非市道人也。」

柳先生曰：「清居市，不爲市之道。然而居朝廷，居官府，居庠塾鄉黨，以士大夫自名者，反爭爲之不已，悲夫！然則清非獨異於市人也。」

The number of those who needed his help grew larger and larger, and the extent to which he complied with their wishes was greater and greater. Occasionally some of his costomers were unlucky enough to lose their employment, but while their other friends and relatives gave them the cold shoulder, Sung never ceased to be attentive to them. On the contrary, he provided them with good drugs as before. Once these men were reinstated, they rewarded him even more munificently. These were some of the examples of how Sung gained profits in the long run.

I observe that those who make friends nowadays adhere to them when they prosper and abandon them when they suffer adversity, and that very few can do as Sung did. We have heard them referred to as mere business friends. So far as Sung was concerned, he was also a businessman. But can all business friends of today expect their rewards from such long-range as Sung received? If indeed they can approximate his accomplishment, then many of the poor, distressed, displaced and disgraced can hope to escape death. In this sense, how can we afford to have no business friends? However, some insisted, "Sung was not a man of the market."

"Though living in the market," says the writer, "Sung did not follow the practice of the market. On the other hand, those who are in court, in office, in educational institutions, in local communities, and who pose as scholars and officials, show such keenness at it. How sad! Therefore, Sung was unique, and not just different from men of the market."

河　間　傳

河間，淫婦人也。不欲言其姓，故以邑稱。始婦人居戚里，有賢操。自未嫁，固已惡羣戚之亂尨，羞與爲類。獨深居，爲翦製縷結。

旣嫁，不及其舅，獨養姑，謹甚。未嘗言門外事。又禮敬夫，賓友之，相與爲肺腑者。

其族類醜行者謀曰：「若河間何？」其甚者曰：「必壞之。」乃謀以車衆造門，邀之遨嬉，且美其辭曰：「自吾里有河間，戚里之人，日夜爲餰屬。一有小不善，唯恐聞焉。今欲更其故，以相效爲禮節。願朝夕望若儀狀，以自惕也。」

河間固謝不欲。姑怒曰：「今人好辭來，以一接新婦來爲得師。何拒之堅也？」辭曰：「聞婦之道，以貞順靜專爲禮。若夫矜車服，耀首飾，族出謹鬧，以飲食觀游，非婦人宜也。」姑強之，乃從之游。過市。

或曰：「市少南，入浮圖。有國工吳叟，始圖東南壁，甚怪，可使奚官先壁道。」乃入觀。觀已，延及客位，具

---

[1] A *hsien* in modern Hopeh Province.

Biography of Hochien[1]

Hochien was a lewd woman. Reluctance to disclose her identity caused her to be named after her *hsien* or district. First she lived in a village with some relatives and at that time she was very virtuous. Before she got married, she detested the laxity visible among her relatives and deemed it a disgrace to associate with them. She remained discreetly in the back of her house and attended to her dress designs, spinning, weaving and knitting.

When she was married her father-in-law had died, and she served her mother-in-law very attentively. She never talked about anything that happened outside her house. She was respectful to her husband, treating him like a guest and withal a bosom friend.

Those of her relatives who had a low character got together and plotted against her, asking, "What can we do about Hochien?" The worst amongst them said, "We must try to corrupt her." They procured a carriage, and a group of them rode to her house together. They invited her to go out and enjoy herself with them, but said to her euphemistically: "Since you came to our village, your relatives have all been desperately concerned day and night to behave themselves. When they have committed even a slight misdemeanor they are afraid of its leaking out. Now that we wish to see their ways changed, we intend to have these relatives make a conscientious effort morning and night to emulate your good example."

Hochien politely declined the offer, but her mother-in-law said angrily, "They have come to persuade you courteously to become their teacher. Why are you so firm in rejecting the invitation?" "I have heard," she replied, "that the way of a woman is to be chaste, meek, calm and dedicated. To show off fancy carriages, costumes and jewelry, and go out in noisy gatherings and indulge in food, drink and merriment are not worthy of a woman." Under strong pressure from the mother-in-law, however, she finally consented and went with the company.

After winding through the streets someone said, "If we enter the Buddhist pagoda a short distance southward, we shall find an old man by the name of Wu, a painter-craftsman known throughout the nation, who has just painted the southeastern wall. These paintings are very odd. We

食帷牀之側。聞男子欬者，河間驚，跣走出。召從者馳車歸。泣數日，愈自閉，不與衆戚通。

戚里乃更來謝曰：「河間之遽也。猶以前故，得無罪吾屬耶？向之欬者，爲膳奴耳。」曰：「數人笑於門，如是何耶？」羣戚聞且退。

期年，乃敢復召邀於姑，必致之，與偕行。遂入隄隄州西浮圖兩間。叩檻，出魚鱉食之。河間爲一笑，衆乃歡。俄而又引至食所，空無帷幕，廊廡廓然，河間乃肯入。先壁羣惡少於北牖下。降簾，使女子爲秦聲。倨坐觀之。有頃，壁者出宿。

選貌美陰大者主河間，乃便抱持河間。河間號且泣。婢夾持之，或諭以利，或罵且笑之。河間竊顧，視持己者甚美，左右爲不善者已更得適意，鼻息咈然，意不能無動。力稍縱，主者幸一逐焉，因擁致之房。河間收泣，甚適，自慶未始得也。

至日仄，食具，類呼之食。曰：「吾不食矣。」旦暮

---

can send a servant to guide us there." Then they entered the structure to see its inside. After they had finished viewing, she was invited to the guest room, where food was spread out beside a curtained bed. Suddenly she heard a man's cough. She was so frightened that she ran out without her shoes. Thereupon she ordered an attendant to take her home post-haste in a carriage. She wept for several days, and thereafter she confined herself even more to her own house without communicating with her relatives.

Then they came to offer their apologies, saying, "What came over you? Are you still offended with us because of what happened? The man who coughed that day was only a kitchen hand." "But why did several people laugh near the door?" she queried. Upon hearing this, the relatives withdrew.

It was not until a whole year later that the relatives dared visit Hochien's mother-in-law again and prevailed upon her to urge Hochien to rejoin them. This time they went to another pagoda west of a certain sandbank. They knocked and entered, and were treated to fish and turtle. Hochien smiled, and her companions were pleased. She was soon led to a dining-room without any curtains where the corridors were empty. Hochien consented to enter this room, in which a number of wicked youths had been secreted in the wall under the northern window. Then the curtain was let down and some girls were ordered to play Ch'in[2] music. Hochien and others squatted down to watch them. Shortly afterward, the youths secreted in the wall came out to sleep with the girls.

A handsome man with a good-sized organ was selected to take on Hochien. When he embraced her, she screamed and cried. Then the maids held her, some trying to get her to see what pleasure it would bring to her and others scolding and making fun of her. As she stole a glance at the man who had her in his arms, she found him very handsome. Those around who were indulging in wicked behavior were more and more gratified, breathing heavily. She could not but be affected and as soon as she relaxed her resistance a little, her adversary got what he wanted and took her in his embrace to another room. Hochien stopped crying and began to enjoy herself greatly, and congratulated herself on pleasures she had never experienced before.

When dinner was being served toward evening and she was called to partake of it, she said that she did not care for it. Later, as the carriage

123

駕車，相戒歸。河間曰：「吾不歸矣。必與是人俱死。」
羣戚反大悶，不得已俱宿焉。

夫騎來迎，莫得見。左右力制。明日乃肯歸。持淫夫
大泣，齧臂相與盟，而後就車。既歸，不忍視其夫。閉目
曰：「吾病。」與之百物，卒不食，餌以善藥，揮去。心
怦怦，恆若危柱之絃。夫來，輒大罵。終不一開目。愈益
惡之。夫不勝其憂。數日，乃曰：「吾病且死，非藥餌能
已。爲吾召鬼解除之，然必以夜。」

其夫自河間病，言如狂人，思所以悅其心。度無不爲。
時上惡夜祠甚。夫無所避。既張具，河間命邑臣告其夫召
鬼祝詛。上下吏訊驗笞殺之。將死，猶曰：「吾負夫人，
吾負夫人。」

河間大喜，不爲服。闔門，召所與淫者，倮逐爲荒淫。
居一歲，所淫者衰，益厭，乃出之。

召長安無賴男子，晨夜交於門。猶不慊，又爲酒壚西
南隅。己居樓上，微觀之。鑿小門，以女侍餌焉。凡來飲

was harnessed for her to return home, she said, "I am not going home. I won't be parted from this man until I die." Now her relatives were greatly at a loss what to do, but they had to agree to stay behind at least overnight.

Hochien's husband went to fetch her home, but he did not get to see her. The next day she consented to go home only when she was forced to do so by others. Before she mounted the carriage, however, she grabbed the man with whom she had had the affair and cried bitterly, the two swearing eternal loyalty to each other. On her arrival home, she could not bear to look at her husband. Keeping her eyes closed, she said, "I am sick." She not only refused to eat anything, but even rejected good medicine. Her heart throbbed as tensely as a string on a lute's fret in danger of breaking. Whenever her husband came near her, she berated him severely. She never opened her eyes, and became more and more resentful of her husband. The distress was more than the husband could stand. "I am so sick that I shall soon die!" she said several days later. "I cannot possibly be cured by medicine; summon a spirit to get me released from this condition, but it must be by night."

Immediately after Hochien became sick, her husband raved like a lunatic and was racking his brains to find a way to please her. She reckoned that he was prepared to go to any lengths. At that time the Emperor disliked very much the practice of praying to spirits at night, but the husband was prepared to take the consequences. So he frequented the shrines of darkness dedicated to evil spirits and worshipped there. Hochien had a member of the magistrate's office bring her husband to trial for conjuring up spirits to her injury. As a result of this trumped-up charge, he was hauled into court, tried, whipped and sentenced to death. Even when he was nearing the end of his life, he cried: "I have let my wife down! I have let my wife down!"

Thereupon Hochien was greatly pleased. Without as much as pretending to mourn for her deceased husband, she opened her door wide and sent for the man with whom she had been intimate. She shamelessly resumed her illicit relations with him. But, after the lapse of a year, the man showed signs of flagging. She got tired of him, and drove him out.

Then she called together a group of good-for-nothings from Ch'ang-an, and they engaged in orgies day and night in her house. Not content with this, she set up a wine-store at the southwestern corner of the house, and stayed upstairs herself to watch the goings-on. Through an installed

125

酒，大鼻者，少且壯者，美顏色者，善爲酒戲者，皆上與合，且合且窺，恐失一男子也。猶日呻呼懵懵，以爲不足。

積十餘年，病髓竭而死。自是雖戚里爲邪行者，聞河間之名，則掩鼻蹴頞，皆不欲道也。

柳先生曰：「天下之士，爲修潔者，有如河間之始爲妻婦者乎？天下之言朋友相慕望，有如河間與其夫之切密者乎？河間一自敗於强暴，誠服其利，歸敵其夫，猶盜賊仇讎，不忍一視其面，卒計以殺之，無須臾之戚。則凡以情愛相戀結者，得不有邪利之猾其中耶？亦足知恩之難恃矣。朋友固如此，況君臣之際尤可畏哉？余故私自列云。」

side door, she sought to attract passers-by, using young servant girls as bait. Of the men who went in to drink, she chose only those with big noses, the robust, the young and the handsome, who were most frolicsome after drinking, to be taken upstairs to give her satisfaction. All the time, she would keep an eye open, lest she miss even one man. And yet she never ceased to sigh dreamily, thereby showing her appetites to be still unsatiated.

After more than a decade of dissipation, she fell sick; her spirit and health broke down, and she soon died. Thereafter, even those relatives in the village who led an immoral life turned up their noses and knitted their brows whenever the name of Hochien was mentioned. No one cared to repeat it.

The author comments: "Of the scholars of the world, who can compare in virtue and purity with Hochien when she first became a wife? Of friends who are said to have admired one another, is there any who can be as close as Hochien was to her husband? Once she succumbed to force, she became convinced of the pleasure, and returned home even to oppose her husband, treating him like a robber and an enemy. She could not bear to see his face and finally plotted his death, and did not grieve for him for a moment. Can those, then, who are joined together by affection and love be free from the evil influence of self-interest? We see here that mutual devotion is something difficult to rely upon. This is true of friends; is it not even more terrifyingly so in the relations between a ruler and his subjects? I have therefore taken the liberty to set down this note."

賀進士王參元失火書

　　得楊八書，知足下遇火災，家無餘儲。僕始聞而駭，中而疑，終乃大喜，蓋將弔而更以賀也。

　　道遠言略，猶未能究知其狀。若果蕩焉泯焉而悉無有，乃吾所以尤賀者也。

　　足下勤奉養，寧朝夕。唯恬安無事是望也。乃今有焚煬赫烈之虞，以震駭左右，而脂膏潃瀡之具，或以不給，吾是以始而駭也。

　　凡人之言皆曰，盈虛倚伏，去來之不可常。或將大有為也，乃始厄困震悸。於是有水火之孽，有羣小之慍，勞苦變動，而後能光明。古之人皆然。斯道遼闊誕漫，雖聖人不能以是必信。是故中而疑也。

　　以足下讀古人書，爲文章，善小學。其爲多能若是，而進不能出羣士之上，以取顯貴者，無他故焉。京城人多言足下家有積貨。士之好廉名者，皆畏忌。不敢道足下之善。獨自得之，心蓄之，銜忍而不出諸口。以公道之難明，而世之多嫌也，一出口，則嗤嗤者以爲得重賂。

　　僕自貞元十五年[1]見足下之文章，蓄之者蓋六七年，未嘗言。是僕私一身而負公道久矣，非特負足下也。及爲御

---

[1] 799, reign of Emperor Teh-tsung.

Congratulatory Message to *Chin-shih* Wang Ts'an-yüan on the Burning of His House

A letter from Yang the Eighth brought the news that your house was destroyed by fire, and that nothing was left of its contents. At first I was stunned, then I had my doubts, and finally I felt greatly pleased. I was on the point of expressing my sympathy, when I decided to change my message to one of congratulations.

Owing to the distance and the sketchiness of the information, I am not sure of the details of the accident. If the calamity was extensive and absolutely nothing has been left, I congratulate you all the more.

You have been diligent in taking care of your parents, and morning and night you have remained happy. All you have hoped for is that nothing would happen and that you would live in peace and safety. But the devastating fire must have shocked you and may also have deprived you of your essential culinary facilities. That is why I was at first stunned by the report.

It has commonly been observed that prosperity and adversity are not constant. A man of great promise has to first experience distress and fear. Therefore, there come the disasters of flood or fire, and the abuse of the mob. Only by enduring great hardship and the capricious changes of fortune can one have a bright future. This is true of ancient men. So profound and mystical is the pattern that even sages could not be certain of its meaning. That is why I then had my doubts.

You have read the books of the ancients, can write ably and are well versed in philology. With all these accomplishments, you have nevertheless not surpassed others in official distinction. There is no other explanation than that the people of the capital have often talked about the wealth of your family, so that scholars obsessed with their reputation of incorruptibility are afraid of speaking well of you. As justice is seldom clearly served and the world is full of suspicion, they would rather conceal your merits and make no mention of them, lest they be thought by the scornful to have received a fat bribe from you.

Since I read your writings in the fifteenth year of Chen-yüan,[1] I have borne them in mind but never mentioned them for six or seven years. For this reason, I have long been partial to myself and not only let you down, but also failed to do my duty to justice. Later, when I

129

史尚書郎，自以幸爲天子近臣，得奮其舌，思以發明天下之鬱塞。然時稱道於行列，猶有顧視而竊笑者。僕良恨修己之不亮，素譽之不立，而爲世嫌之所加，常與孟幾道言而痛之。

乃今幸爲天火之所滌盪，凡衆之疑慮，舉爲灰埃。黔其廬，赭其垣，以示其無有。而足下之才能，乃可顯白而不汚，其實出矣。是祝融回祿之相吾子也。則僕與幾道十年之相知，不若茲火一夕之爲足下譽也。宥而彰之，使夫蓄於心者，咸得開其喙。發策決科者，授子而不慄。雖欲如向之蓄縮受侮，其可得乎？於茲吾有望乎爾，是以終乃大喜也。

古者列國有災，同位者皆相弔。許不弔災，君子惡之。今吾之所陳若是，有以異乎古，故將弔而更以賀也。

顏曾之養，其爲樂也大矣，又何闕焉。

---

[2] Title of a ranking official.

[3] A feudal state situated in modern Hsüch'ang 許昌 *Hsien*, Honan Province.

[4] Both were distinguished disciples of Confucius.

became the Shang-shu-lang[2] of the Censorship, I regarded myself as an official near to the Son of Heaven and capable of speaking more freely. I thought of voicing what must have been your latent disappointment. However, whenever I broached the subject to my colleagues, there were some who stared at me and secretly ridiculed me. I truly regret my failure to achieve personal character, my lack of an established reputation, and consequently my susceptibility to the suspicion of the world. I have often spoken of this to Meng Chi-tao with agony.

Now that the heavenly fire has fortunately swept away everything, the misgivings of the multitude have been turned to ashes. Your house has been charred and your walls baked reddish brown; they give abundant evidence of nothing being left. Your talents can at last be dispalyed in the open without embarrassment. The truth is out, thanks to the help of the God of Fire. Thus, the friendship which Chi-tao and I have had for you for ten years has not brought you such recognition as did this fire in one single night. From now on, you will be forgiven and exalted by all. As a result, those who have kept your accomplishments in their hearts will all open their mouths, and those who are in charge of imperial examinations will confer honors on you without fear. How can they remain as reserved as before and risk being blamed for so doing? I have therefore great hopes for you, and so in the end I felt greatly pleased.

In ancient times, when calamities befell the various countries and their sovereigns, those who were of equal station in neighboring states would send their condolences. On one occasion, the State of Hsü[3] failed to do so, and was resented by the man of virtue. The situation to which I have referred is different from the usual one in ancient times. So, though on the point of expressing my sympathy, I have changed my mind and offer you my congratulations instead.

There is no greater pleasure, as in the case of Yen-tzu and Tseng-tzu,[4] than the satisfaction of taking care of one's parents. What more is there for a man to desire?

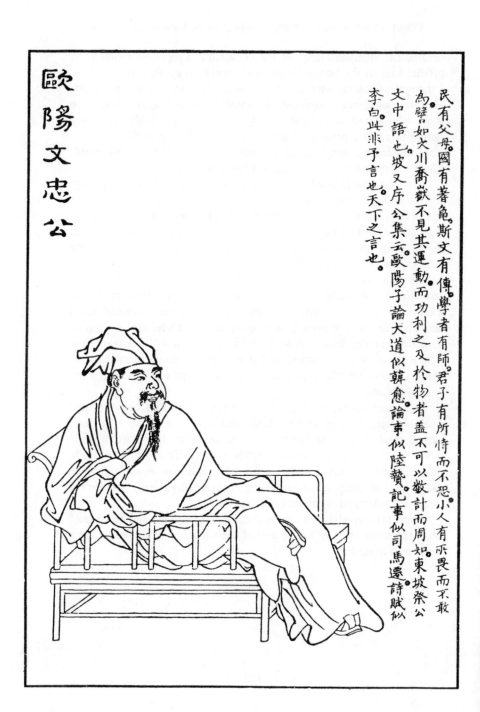

歐陽文忠公

民有父母國有著龜斯文有傳學者有師君子有所恃而不恐小人有所畏而不敢為壁如大川喬嶽不見其運動而功利之及於物者蓋不可以數計而周知東坡祭公文中語也坡又序公集云歐陽子論大道似韓愈論事似陸贄記事似司馬遷詩賦似李白此非予言也天下之言也。

Ou-yang Hsiu (1007-1072)

Through the unswerving efforts of Han Yü, Liu Tsung-yüan and their school, T'ang prose had been restored to the glory and dignity of the ancient classical style. With the passage of time, however, the development of political and social conditions created a growing tendency among scholars to indulge once again in the so-called *p'ien-wen* or rhymed prose, which had been in vogue before. At the same time, not only did traditional poetry tend to be more and more effete and florid, but there arose a new genre of poetry, called *tz'u* 詞, which had similar characteristics. All this helped the revival of the *p'ien-wen*, which reached its culmination in the early part of the Sung dynasty.

It was at this juncture that Ou-yang Hsiu emerged. Although he and all his colleagues had been *p'ien-wen* writers, he saw the need to stem the tide, and to him fell the honor of saving Chinese prose from the degeneration of the Five Dynasties 五代,[1] as Han Yü had before him saved it from eight dynasties of degeneration.

Ou-yang Hsiu, whose courtesy name was Yung-shu 永叔, was a native of Luling 廬陵.[2] He lost his father at the early age of four, and his mother, née Cheng 鄭, swore to live out her life of widowhood and bring up her boy. The family was so poor that she used reeds as pens, and with these she scribbled on the ground to teach him to write. He was a precocious child and outstripped other children in his studies. He had already achieved great fame as a scholar before he came of age.

The Sung dynasty had passed the half-century mark when Ou-yang grew up to be an accomplished student. He had

[1] 907-959.
[2] Chi-an 吉安 *Hsien*, Kiangsi Province.

133

observed the deterioration of the literary style. Though some of his predecessors and contemporaries, who were also eminent scholars, sought to reverse the trend, they met with little success. It happened that, when Ou-yang at an early age was living in Suichow 隨州 ,[3] he accidentally came across a waste-paper basket in which he found some manuscripts left by Han Yü. He studied them, admired them tremendously and immediately came under Han's spell. Thereafter he concentrated his attention on Han's works and vowed to equal his achievements.

This ambition was more than fulfilled, since Ou-yang turned out to be the greatest prose writer of the Sung dynasty. He passed the imperial examination and came out first among all the *chin-shih*. He was appointed to the Eastern Capital, Loyang 洛陽 , as a subordinate prefectural official. His reputation as a scholar steadily grew on a nation-wide basis, and he was transferred to the Court as a literary official. Later, he was assigned to the Censorship.

Even at that early age, he always spoke his mind whenever he found anything wrong. As a result, he had to pay the price of frequently offending those in power, and had to suffer the fate of being demoted to subordinate provincial posts. When he was a censor, he supported Emperor Jen-tsung 仁宗 (r. 1023-1063) in selecting worthy men for prominent positions. His policy thereby encountered the opposition of certain high officials, who regarded him as partial to his friends. This gave him the impetus to write his famous essay "On the Partisanship of Friends,"[4] which was submitted to the throne.

Though his constant and outspoken remonstrances incurred the displeasure and enmity of many unworthy men, the emperor was nevertheless wise enough to appreciate and even praise his frankness. On one occasion, His Majesty personally bestowed on him the uniform of a fifth-grade official as a

[3] Prefecture in modern Hupeh Province.
[4] See pp. 140-143, below.

token of his favor and said to his aides, "Whence have I been able to get a man like Ou-yang Hsiu?" Ou-yang was then given the post of Private Secretary to the Imperial Court and afterward appointed to the Secretariat to draft imperial orders and decrees. This position had traditionally involved a preliminary examination, but he was exempted from it as a special favor.

Subsequently, however, because of his unrestrained expression of views on every possible occasion, he was intermittently demoted to no fewer than six prefectures. In one of these,[5] his administration was so enlightened that the people nicknamed him the "Candle Reflecting the Will of Heaven" 照天蠟燭 . It was in Ch'uchow 滁州[6] that he himself adopted the nickname "Old Drunkard" 醉翁 and built the famous Old Drunkard's Pavilion, the essay on which (醉翁亭記)[7] was one of his masterpieces.

While serving as Magistrate of Iling 夷陵,[8] to which he was first demoted, and having little to do, he ransacked the archives of the district and found to his consternation the innumerable mistakes that had been made by his predecessors. He sighed and said, "Since this is what happens in even a small district such as this, other parts of the country must undoubtedly present the same picture." From then on, he did not dare to overlook anything, however insignificant.

Whenever he came into contact with learned scholars, he was most interested in discussing the affairs of government with them rather than literature, because, while the latter might result in self-improvement, the former could contribute to the betterment of the people's lot. In the several prefectures he headed, he never strained for spectacular success

---

[5] Sungchow 宋州 , in modern Honan Province, designated as the Southern Capital.

[6] Prefecture in modern Anhwei Province.

[7] See pp. 186-189, below.

[8] Ichang 宜昌 *Hsien*, Hupeh Province.

and personal fame, but he laid special stress on magnanimity and simplicity, which proved a boon to the poeple wherever he went. He was sometimes asked how it was that his magnanimity and simplicity did not result in the paralysis of government. "If I meant 'license' by 'magnanimity' and 'negligence' by 'simplicity'," he replied, "then government might be paralysed and the people harmed. But, when I say 'magnanimity' I refer to the absence of tyranny and impulse, and, when I say 'simplicity', I mean the absence of red tape."

In the second year of Chia-yu 嘉祐 ,[9] he was Chief Imperial Examiner, and it was during this examination that three other great masters of prose, Su Shih 蘇軾, his brother Ch'e 轍 and Tseng Kung 曾鞏, won their *chin-shih* degree. At that time, it was still the custom to write in the increasingly discredited style, which was then known as the Imperial University Style 太學體 . Ou-yang made it a point to suppress this style by disqualifying those young men who continued to practice it. This caused such opposition among the unsuccessful candidates that, when he left the examination hall, they booed him on the streets and the situation virtually got out of hand. Nevertheless, the reform adopted by Ou-yang was scrupulously observed in subsequent examinations.

One of the important positions held by him was that of Chief Editor of the *History of the T'ang Dynasty*, which, in contradistinction to the one that already existed, is now known as the *New History of T'ang* 新唐書 . Associated with him was Sung Ch'i 宋祁 , another distinguished scholar and statesman. The traditional practice was that separate articles appearing in the work were never identified by name, only that of the chief editor being given. But in this instance Ou-yang showed his extreme modesty by making an exception and, out of respect for seniority in scholarship, allowed the name of Sung Ch'i to appear under anything written by this associate of his.

[9] 1057, reign of Emperor Jen-tsung.

The highest position held by Ou-yang was that of Vice-Premier. However, the prominence he attained enabled him on many occasions to carry as much weight as a full-fledged prime minister. He also served as Secretary of the Hanlin Academy 翰林侍讀學士 , a position of great distinction in a high state institution composed of eminent scholars. When he was head of two prefectures, he had the exalted titles of Minister of Rites and Minister of War.

As a frequent victim of court jealousy and calumny, Ou-yang petitioned for retirement at as early an age as sixty, and thereafter frequently repeated the request to retire, only to be turned down by the throne. His firm intention to retire was clearly marked in some of his later writings.[10] Though his integrity and loyalty were as a rule amply vindicated, he finally offended Wang An-shih 王安石 , who was then Prime Minister, by opposing some of his reforms. The rebuff he then received from the latter, whom he himself had been instrumental in grooming for promotion, determined him once and for all to insist on leaving the official scene. At last, Emperor Shen-tsung 神宗 , the third sovereign under whom he had served, relieved him from active duty by conferring on him the title of Teacher of the Imperial Household. In the fifth year of Hsi-ning 熙寧 , which was the year after his retirement, he died. The posthumous title of Grand Teacher of the Imperial Household was conferred on him and he was canonized as Wen-chung 文忠.

Ou-yang was a literary genius who wrote in a free and natural style. His statements were brief but clear, reliable and penetrating. He cited examples to substantiate the highest truths, which proved to be so persuasive, lofty and unique that the people reverenced him as their teacher.

As a great teacher, he was never slow to keep open the door to talent, and those of his younger contemporaries of promise were always given his blessing. Thus, scores of them

[10] See pp. 196-199, below.

became prominent as a result of his recognition. The pre-eminent example was that of the five other great Sung masters of prose, Tseng Kung, Wang An-shih, Su Hsün and his two sons, Shih and Ch'e. They had all been poor men living in obscurity, but they were promoted by Ou-yang, because, as he said, they were certain to achieve distinction for themselves in the world.

Besides being an outstanding teacher, he was a staunch friend. There were many who enjoyed his backing during their lifetime and for whose families he cared after their death.

He was a great connoisseur and collector of ancient records. He treasured every bit of writing on ancient metal and stone dating from the Chou 周, Han 漢 and later eras. He carried out the most diligent research on even incomplete and broken chronicles and never tired of demonstrating their authenticity. In addition to the new history of the T'ang dynasty, of which he was the official editor, he compiled, in his private capacity, the *New History of the Five Dynasties* 新五代史. In both instances he displayed accurate scholarship and sound judgment, in strict accordance with the principles underlying the *Spring and Autumn Annals* 春秋 of Confucius.

In commenting on the contributions of this great master, Su Shih, his pupil, said that he was "like Han Yü in his discussion of the Great Way, like Lu Chih 陸贄 [11] in that of human nature, like Ssu-ma Ch'ien 司馬遷 [12] in recording historical events and like Li Po 李白 [13] in writing poetry and *fu.*"[14] This has been commonly regarded as an accurate and fair appraisal.

[11] Prime Minister under Emperor Teh-tsung 德宗 of the T'ang dynasty, who was noted for his masterful memorials to the throne.

[12] See p. 27, note 15.

[13] The great T'ang poet.

[14] An essay usually in rhymed prose.

朋　黨　論

　　臣聞朋黨之說，自古有之。惟幸人君辨其君子小人而已。大凡君子與君子，以同道爲朋，小人與小人，以同利爲朋，此自然之理也。

　　然臣謂小人無朋，惟君子則有之。其故何哉？小人所好者，祿利也，所貪者，財貨也。當其同利之時，暫相黨引以爲朋者，僞也。及其見利而爭先，或利盡而交疏，則反相賊害，雖其兄弟親戚，不能相保。故臣謂小人無朋，其暫爲朋者，僞也。

　　君子則不然，所守者道義，所行者忠信，所惜者名節。以之修身，則同道而相益。以之事國，則同心而共濟，終始如一。此君子之朋也。

　　故爲人君者，但當退小人之僞朋，用君子之眞朋，則天下治矣。堯之時，小人共工讙兜等四人爲一朋，君子八元八凱十六人爲一朋。舜佐堯，退四凶小人之朋，而進元凱君子之朋。堯之天下大治。

　　及舜自爲天子，而皋夔稷契等二十二人並列于朝，更

---

[1] This essay was submitted to the throne, and so the writer referred to himself as the "subject."

[2] Huan-tou 讙兜, Kung-kung 共工, San-miao 三苗 and Kun 鯀.

[3] Po-fen 伯奮, Chung-k'an 仲堪, Shu-hsien 叔獻, Chi-chung 季仲, Po-hu 伯虎, Chung-hsiung 仲熊, Shu-pao 叔豹 and Chi-li 季貍.

[4] Ts'ang-shu 蒼舒, T'ui-ai 隤敳, T'ao-yeh 檮戭, Ta-lin 大臨, Mang-chiang 尨降, T'ing-chien 庭堅, Chung-jung 仲容 and Shu-ta 叔達.

On the Partisanship of Friends

Your subject[1] has heard that the partisanship of friends is traceable to ancient times but it is expected of the ruler to distinguish between gentlemen and unworthy men. The friendship between gentleman and gentleman is based on the Way, and that among unworthy men, on profit. This is a matter of course.

But your subject would add that the unworthy man has no friends and that only the gentleman has friends. Why? What the unworthy man desires is profit and emoluments and what he avidly seeks is wealth. When there is profit enough for all and unworthy men temporarily band together in a party of friends, the friendship thus formed is false. As soon as they vie with one another for the profit, or when the profit is exhausted, they would be estranged and even go so far as to harm one another; though they may be brothers or relatives, they will not look after one another. Your subject therefore says that unworthy men have no friends and that, when they temporarily befriend one another, they are not sincere.

Not so with the gentleman. What he adheres to is honor and righteousness, what he practices is loyalty and honesty, and what he prizes is a good name and integrity. When gentlemen cultivate themselves on such a basis, they share the Way and help improve one another. When they serve the country on this basis, they are of one mind and cooperate from beginning to end. Such is the friendship of gentlemen.

He therefore who is the ruler should merely rid himself of false parties consisting of unworthy men and employ the true associations of gentlemen; then he can bring peace and order to his land. In Emperor Yao's time, four unworthy men[2], including Kung-kung and Huan-tou, formed a group of friends, while sixteen gentlemen, known as the Eight Yüan[3] and Eight K'ai,[4] formed another group of friends. Emperor Shun, then serving under Emperor Yao, helped him get rid of the group consisting of the four evil men and bring to the fore the group of sixteen gentlemen. As a result, peace and order reigned in Yao's empire.

When Shun himself became the Son of Heaven, twenty-two men, including Kao, K'uei, Chi and Hsieh, stood together at court, and they praised and deferred to one another. The twenty-two men formed a

相稱美，更相推讓。凡二十二人爲一朋，而舜皆用之。天下亦大治。

書曰：「紂有臣億萬，惟億萬心；周有臣三千，惟一心。」紂之時，億萬人各異心，可謂不爲朋矣，然紂以亡國。周武王之臣，三千人爲一大朋，而周用以興。後漢獻帝時，盡取天下名士囚禁之，目爲黨人。及黃巾賊起，漢室大亂，後方悔悟，盡解黨人而釋之。然已無救矣。唐之晚年，漸起朋黨之論。及昭宗時，盡殺朝之名士，或投之黃河。曰：「此輩清流，可投濁流。」而唐遂亡矣。

夫前世之主，能使人人異心不爲朋，莫如紂。能禁絕善人爲朋，莫如漢獻帝。能誅戮清流之朋，莫如唐昭宗之世。然皆亂亡其國。更相稱美推讓而不自疑，莫如舜之二十二臣，舜亦不疑而皆用之。然而後世不誚舜爲二十二人朋黨所欺，而稱舜爲聰明之聖者，以辨君子與小人也。周武之世，舉其國之臣三千人，共爲一朋。自古爲朋之多且大，莫如周。然周用此以興者，善人雖多而不猒也。

夫興亡治亂之迹，爲人君者可以鑒矣。

---

[5]Chang Chüeh 張角, a native of Chülu 鉅鹿, in modern Hopeh Province, and a Taoist devotee during the Later Han dynasty, had several hundred thousand followers, who rose in rebellion. Because of their yellow headgear, they were known as "Yellow Caps."

group of friends, who were all employed by Shun. As a result, Shun's empire also enjoyed great peace and order.

The *Book of History* said, "The last emperor of the Yin dynasty had millions of subjects with millions of minds, while the Chou dynasty had three thousand officials with only one mind." With millions having diverse minds there could not be any union; the Yin Emperor lost his country as a result. The three thousand officials of King Wu of Chou formed one large union of friends, and the Chou dynasty was enabled to prosper as a result. During the reign of Emperor Hsien of the Later Han dynasty, all the famous scholars of the land were imprisoned and regarded as partisans. Subsequently, when the Yellow Cap Rebellion[5] broke out, the Han dynasty was in utter chaos. The unwise action taken was then regretted, and all the so-called partisans were released, but it was too late to save the situation. During the later years of the T'ang dynasty, the partisanship controversy began to stir up discussion. In the reign of Emperor Chao-tsung, all the famous scholars at court were either killed or thrown into the Yellow River, with the observation, "These pure men can be consigned to the impure current." This spelled the end of the T'ang dynasty.

Of the rulers who reigned in earlier times, none could compare with Emperor Chou in alienating the minds of men and preventing them from banding together, none could compare with Emperor Hsien of Han in forbidding good men to associate, and none could compare with Emperor Chao-tsung of T'ang in putting to death a whole party of pure and virtuous men. But all these rulers lost their countries. As against this, none could compare with Shun's twenty-two ministers, who praised and deferred to one another without sowing doubts among themselves, and Shun made use of their services with complete confidence. Later generations have not ridiculed Shun for having been deceived by the twenty-two friendly partisans, but praised him instead as an enlightened sage, because he was able to distinguish between gentlemen and unworthy men. During the reign of King Wu of Chou, all three thousand officials banded together as friends. The size of this group had never been equaled from time immemorial, and this was the reason for the rise of the Chou dynasty, because they were all good men, and there could never be too many of these.

The traces of the rise and fall of dynasties and of peace and chaos in past history can be a lesson to all rulers!

143

縱 囚 論

信義行於君子，而刑戮施於小人。刑入于死者，乃罪大惡極，此又小人之尤甚者也。寧以義死，不苟幸生，而視死如歸，此又君子之尤難者也。

方唐太宗之六年，錄大辟囚三百餘人，縱使還家，約其自歸以就死。是以君子之難能，期小人之尤者以必能也。其囚及期而卒自歸無後者，是君子之所難，而小人之所易也。此豈近於人情？

或曰：「罪大惡極，誠小人矣，及施恩德以臨之，可使變而爲君子，蓋恩德入人之深而移人之速，有如是者矣。」

曰：「太宗之爲此，所以求此名也。然安知夫縱之去也，不意其必來以冀免，所以縱之乎？又安知夫被縱而去也，不意其自歸而必獲免，所以復來乎？夫意其必來而縱之，是上賊下之情也。意其必免而復來，是下賊上之心也。吾見上下交相賊，以成此名也。烏有所謂施恩德與夫知信義者哉？

「不然，太宗施德於天下，於茲六年矣。不能使小人不爲極惡大罪，而一日之恩，能使視死如歸而存信義，此又

[1] A.D. 632.

144

On the Release of Prisoners

Honesty and righteousness prevail among gentlemen, and a criminal penalty is the lot of the unworthy men. Those who deserve punishment by death are the most wicked among criminals; they are the most unworthy among men. On the other hand, it takes the rarest of gentlemen to die in the cause of righteousness rather than live on ignominiously, and to face death calmly as though going home.

In the sixth year of the reign of Emperor T'ai-tsung of the T'ang dynasty,[1] more than three hundred prisoners condemned to death had their cases reviewed and permitted to go home, and a date was set for them to return for their execution. This was tantamount to expecting the most unworthy among men to carry out what would be difficult even for the gentleman. Strangely enough, all the prisoners ultimately returned on time, none of them missing the roll call. What was difficult for the gentlemen thus became apparently easy for unworthy men. Was this at all consistent with human nature?

Some say that, although those who have committed the most wicked crimes are truly unworthy men, yet when humaneness is shown them, they can be transformed into gentlemen; so deeply can humaneness move people and so quickly can it change them.

I feel that Emperor T'ai-tsung did this to seek fame. How do we know that he did not order the prisoners released because he assumed they would return in the hope of a pardon? And how do we know that the prisoners did not return because they were sure they would be pardoned if they returned voluntarily? If the emperor released the prisoners because he was sure they would return, it would be a case of the ruler taking advantage of his subjects' condition. If the prisoners returned because they were sure of their pardon, it would be a case of the subjects' taking advantage of the emperor's intentions. In either case, I see the ruler and the ruled conspiring together in an act calculated to bring praise. Where do we find humaneness on the one side and honesty and righteousness on the other?

Were it not so, it would be untenable to say that, while after six years of humane rule Emperor T'ai-tsung had failed to prevent unworthy men from committing the most wicked crimes, one day's favor could have

145

不通之論也。」

「然則何爲而可?」曰:「縱而來歸, 殺之無赦, 而又縱之, 而又來, 則可知爲恩德之致爾。然此必無之事也。」若夫縱而來歸而赦之, 可偶一爲之爾。若屢爲之, 則殺人者皆不死。是可爲天下之常法乎? 不可爲常者, 其聖人之法乎?

是以堯舜三王之治, 必本於人情, 不立異以爲高, 不逆情以干譽。

---

[2] Emperor of the ancient T'ang dynasty, who reigned *circa* 2333-2234 B.C.

[3] Emperor of the Yü dynasty, who reigned *circa* 2233-2184 B.C.

[4] Emperor Yü 禹 of the Hsia dynasty, who reigned *circa* 2183-2177 B.C., Emperor T'ang 湯 of the Shang dynasty, r. *circa* 1751-1739, and King Wen 文王 of the Chou dynasty, who did not in fact rule as king but who was canonized as such by his son, King Wu 武王, the first ruler of the Chou dynasty.

caused them to adhere to the path of honesty and righteousness and face death without flinching.

What, then, would be the proper course to take? My belief is that, if a group of prisoners were released and came back, they should be executed, and if later another group were released and still they came back, then it can be taken as the result of the emperor's humaneness. But such a thing can hardly happen. On the other hand, to release prisoners and pardon them upon their return is something that can be done only once in a while. If it is repeated and all those guilty of murder would not have to die, could it be accepted as the universal law of the land? Could anything not universal be in conformity with the law handed down by the sages?

The rule of Yao,[2] Shun[3] and the Three Sovereigns[4] was therefore always based on human nature. They never performed anything extraordinary merely to put on the appearance of magnanimity, nor did they ever act against human nature in the search for fame.

論臺諫官言事未蒙聽允書

　　臣聞自古有天下者，莫不欲爲治君，而常至於亂，莫不欲爲明主，而常至於昏者，其故何哉？患於好疑而自用也。夫疑心動於中，則視聽惑於外。視聽惑，則忠邪不分，而是非錯亂。是非錯亂，則舉國之臣皆可疑。盡疑其臣，則必自用其所見。夫以疑惑錯亂之意而自用，則多失。失，則其國之忠臣，必以理而爭之。爭之不切，則人主之意難回。爭之切，則激其君之怒心，而堅其自用之意。然后君臣爭勝，於是邪佞之臣，得以因隙而入，希旨順意，以是爲非，以非爲是，惟人主之所欲者，從而助之。

　　夫爲人主者，方與其臣爭勝，而得順意之人，樂其助己，而忘其邪佞也，乃與之，並力以拒忠臣。夫爲人主者，拒忠臣而信邪佞，天下無不亂，人主無不昏也。

　　自古人主之用心，非惡忠臣而喜邪佞也，非惡治而好亂也，非惡明而欲昏也，以其好疑自用，而與下爭勝也。使爲人主者，豁然去其疑心，而回其自用之意，則邪佞遠而忠言入。忠言入，則聰明不惑，而萬事得其宜，使天下尊

Memorial on the Refusal to Accept the Remonstrances of the Censor

Your subject has heard that, from time immemorial, those who have exercised dominion over a country have invariably sought to bring about peace and serve as able and wise rulers, but have frequently ended up causing disorder and showing lack of wisdom. How can this be accounted for? The source of the trouble lies in suspicion and overweening pride. When suspicion is aroused in one's mind, one's sight and hearing are deluded. Then it is not possible to distinguish between loyalty and wickedness, and there is confusion between right and wrong. In these circumstances, all the subjects of the country are open to suspicion. Since all are suspect, the ruler is bound to be overweening. Coupled with suspicion and confusion, this overweening pride leads to many mistakes, which cause loyal subjects to remonstrate. When the remonstrance is not strong enough the ruler's mind cannot be changed, and when the remonstrance is strong enough the ruler is angered and his overweening pride reinforced. There then ensues a contest between ruler and subject to gain the upper hand. It is at such a juncture that wicked and deceitful subjects seize the opportunity for cajolery and fawning obeisance, treating right as wrong and wrong as right and catering to the ruler's every desire.

When the ruler is battling with his subjects for the upper hand and finds men who bow to his wishes, he is happy in their support and disregards their wickedness and deceit. As a result, he co-operates with them in repelling loyal subjects. When a ruler repels his loyal subjects and places his confidence in the wicked and deceitful, the country can never be free from disorder nor the ruler from unwisdom.

From ancient times, rulers have never at heart disliked loyal subjects and preferred the wicked and deceitful, never disliked peace and chosen disorder, never disliked wisdom and desired unwisdom. The trouble is that they have been obsessed with suspicion and overweening pride and used to struggling with their subjects for the upper hand. If a ruler open-mindedly gets rid of his suspicion and overweening pride, the wicked and deceitful can be kept at a distance and loyal advice accepted. With the acceptance of loyal advice, wisdom is not beclouded and everything proceeds in orderly fashion. The country will then reverence him as a

爲明主，萬世仰爲治君。豈不臣主俱榮而樂哉？與其區區
自執，而與臣下爭勝，用心益勞，而事益惑者，相去遠矣。

臣聞書載仲虺稱湯之德曰:「改過不恡,」又戒湯曰:「自
用則小。」成湯，古之聖人也。不能無過，而能改過，此
其所以爲聖也。以湯之聰明，其所爲不至於繆戾矣，然仲
虺猶戒其自用。則自古人主，惟能改過，而不敢自用，然
後得爲治君明主也。

臣伏見宰臣陳執中，自執政以來，不叶人望，累有過
惡，招致人言，而執中遷延，尙玷宰府。陛下憂勤恭儉，
仁愛寬慈，堯舜之用心也。推陛下之用心，天下宜至於治
者，久矣。而紀綱日壞，政令日乖，國日益貧，民日益困，
流民滿野，濫官滿朝。其亦何爲而致此？由陛下用相不得
其人也。

近年宰相多以過失因言者罷去。陛下不悟宰相非其人，
反疑言事者好逐宰相。疑心一生，視聽旣惑，遂成自用之
意。以謂宰相當由人主自去，不可因言者而罷之。故宰相
雖有大惡顯過，而屈意以容之。彼雖惶恐自欲求去，而屈

---

wise ruler, and numberless generations uphold him as a sovereign of peace. Would this not be an honor and a pleasure for both ruler and subject? Indeed he would be far above the overweening sovereign who battles with his subjects with increasing anxiety and confusion.

Your subject has heard that according to the *Book of History* Chung Hui[1] exalted as a virtue Emperor T'ang's alacrity in correcting his own mistakes, and that he admonished the emperor that "overweening pride is petty". Though Emperor T'ang, who was an ancient sage, was not infallible, he was able to correct his mistakes, and that is why he was a sage. With his wisdom and his freedom from wrong-doing, he was nevertheless warned by Chung Hui against overweening pride. Down through the ages, therefore, only those sovereigns who have been able to correct their mistakes and who have not dared to be overweening have succeeded in being able and wise rulers.

Your subject humbly submits that Prime Minister Ch'en Chih-chung,[2] since he assumed office, has not lived up to the expectations of the people and that his repeated mistakes and wrong-doings have caused them to complain. Nevertheless he has continued to remain in office and bring disgrace to it. Your Majesty, with the heart of Yao and Shun, has evinced solicitude, diligence, politeness, frugality, benevolence and generosity. With Your Majesty's elevated intentions, the country should have achieved peace and order long ago. As it is, day by day the institutions of the state have been deteriorated, laws and orders become lax, the country has been increasingly impoverished, the people distressed, society filled with vagabonds and the Court with undeserving officials. How has this come about? It has been due to Your Majesty's unfortunate selection of a Prime Minister.

In recent years, prime ministers have mostly been removed from office as a result of remonstrances against their mistakes. Your Majesty, without realizing that your prime minister is not the right man, nevertheless suspects that those who make remonstrances are bent on getting rid of him. With the rise of suspicion, Your Majesty's sight and hearing are deluded and overweening pride asserts itself, as it is maintained that a prime minister should be removed only by the ruler himself and not as a result of remonstrances. Though the prime minister has committed serious offenses and made glaring mistakes Your Majesty has condescended to tolerate them; though he himself wanted to retire Your Majesty has condescended to retain him. In spite of the fact that

意以留之。雖天災水旱，饑民流離，死亡道路，皆不暇顧，而屈意以用之。其故非他，直欲沮言事者爾。言事者何負於陛下哉？

使陛下上不顧天災，下不恤人言，以天下之事委一不學無識，諂邪狠愎之執中，而甘心焉。言事者本欲益於陛下，而反損聖德者，多矣。然而言事者之用心，本不圖至於此也。由陛下好疑自用而自損也。

今陛下用執中之意益堅，言事者攻之愈切。陛下方思有以取勝於言事者，而邪佞之臣得以因隙而入。必有希合陛下之意者，將曰：「執中宰相不可以小事逐，不可使小臣動搖。」甚者，則誣言事者欲逐執中而引用他人。陛下方患言事者上忤聖聰，樂聞斯言之順意，不復察其邪佞而信之，所以拒言事者益峻，用執中益堅。

夫以萬乘之尊，與三數言事小臣角必勝之力。萬一聖意必不可回，則言事者亦當知難而止矣。然天下之人與後世之議者，謂陛下拒忠言，庇愚相。以陛下為何如主也？

前日御史論梁適罪惡，陛下赫怒，空臺而逐之。而今

---

[3] Prime Minister under Emperor Jen-tsung.

flood and drought and other natural disaster persist and famine renders the people homeless and causes death on the road, and the Prime Minister spends no time to attend to their distress, Your Majesty reluctantly has kept him in office. For this state of affairs there is no other explanation than the deliberate attempt to obstruct remonstrances. But in what way have the remonstrators failed Your Majesty?

If Your Majesty is to ignore the natural calamities, turn a deaf ear to remonstrances and be content to entrust the affairs of the country to Ch'en, who is uneducated, ignorant, obsequious, wicked, cruel and obstinate, it means that the remonstrances, though initially seeking to be of some help to you, have had the effect of detracting immensely from Your Majesty's virtue. But this has never been their intention, and the damage has been done by Your Majesty's own suspicion and overweening pride.

The greater Your Majesty's determination to retain the services of Ch'en, the stronger will be attacks by the remonstrators. As Your Majesty is anxious to win your battle with them, wicked and deceitful subjects can take the opportunity to work their mischief. There must be some who seek to comply with Your Majesty's wishes and say, "Prime Minister Ch'en should not be removed for a minor cause, nor should his position be shaken by minor officials." They may even falsely accuse the remonstrators of wishing to get rid of Ch'en and recommend someone else in his place. Troubled by the effrontery of the remonstrators as regards your wisdom, Your Majesty is happy to hear these remarks, which are agreeable to you, and, without taking cognizance of their wickedness and deceit, believes in them. As a result, the rejection of the remonstrators is all the sterner and the wish to keep Ch'en in office all the firmer.

Now that Your Majesty, in the exalted position of the Son of Heaven, is engaged in a battle to certain victory with some of your subjects who make remonstrances, they should be aware of their handicap and stop short in the event Your Majesty's will is shown to be irrevocable. However, the people of the country and the critics in future generations will say that Your Majesty has rejected loyal advice and protected a stupid prime minister. What kind of a ruler will they take Your Majesty to be?

The day before yesterday, when censors discussed the offences committed by Liang Shih,[3] Your Majesty was so angry that you expelled

153

日御史又復敢論宰相，不避雷霆之威，不畏權臣之禍，此乃至忠之臣也，能忘其身而愛陛下者也。陛下嫉之惡之，拒之絕之。

執中為相，使天下水旱流亡，公私困竭，而又不學無識，憎愛挾情，除改差繆，取笑中外，家私穢惡，流聞道路，阿意順旨，專事逢君，此乃諂上傲下，愎戾之臣也。陛下愛之重之，不忍去之。

陛下睿智聰明，羣臣善惡，無不照見，不應倒置如此，直由言事者太切，而激成陛下之疑惑爾。

執中不知廉恥，復出視事，此不足論。陛下豈忍因執中上累聖德，而使忠臣直士，卷舌於明時也？臣願陛下廓然回心，釋去疑慮，察言事者之忠，知執中之過惡，悟用人之非，法成湯改過之聖，遵仲虺自用之戒，盡以御史前後章疏出付外廷，議正執中之過惡，罷其政事，別用賢材，以康時務，以拯斯民，以全聖德，則天下幸甚。

everyone from the Censorship. But today censors are still audacious enough to criticize the Prime Minister. Not dodging the power of the throne nor fearing the catastrophe that can be inflicted on them by those in power, these censors are Your Majesty's most loyal subjects. They are selfless in their love for Your Majesty, and yet Your Majesty hates, loathes, rejects and turns them away.

On the other hand, while Ch'en is Prime Minister, the whole country is suffering from flood and drought, the people are left homeless, and everywhere distress and impoverishment prevail. Moreover, he is uneducated and ignorant, his likes and dislikes are based on sentiment, his reforms are ill-conceived and a laughing-stock throughout the country, his filthy family secrets are notorious, and he knows nothing but to be obsequious to Your Majesty. We have a minister who is cringing to his superior, haughty to his subordinates and obstinate and offensive to all. But Your Majesty cherishes him and respects him and cannot bear to get rid of him.

With your great wisdom, Your Majesty has been able to see through the merits and flaws of all your subjects, and there should not have been the topsy-turvy condition that has prevailed. This must have been due to the excessess to which the remonstrators have gone and which have stimulated the suspicion and delusion of Your Majesty.

Oblivious to any sense of shame, Ch'en has re-assumed his office. Though this is unworthy of comment, can Your Majesty bear to see loyal subjects and outspoken scholars hold their tongues in a time of enlightenment, just because Ch'en has tarnished Your Majesty's virtue? Your subject hopes that Your Majesty will change your mind, do away with your suspicion, recognize the loyalty of the remonstrators, realize Ch'en's faults and offences and the error of keeping him in office, emulate the sageness of Emperor T'ang in correcting his mistakes, heed the admonition of Chung Hui with regard to overweening pride, refer all memorials by censors to a review board of the competent authorities, recitify Ch'en's faults and offences, remove him from office and replace him with a worthy successor, so that the affairs of the times may be set aright, the people delivered from their plight, and Your Majesty's virtuousness sustained. This done, it will be a great blessing for the country.

Having received favored treatment from Your Majesty and being entrusted with the deliberative duties, your subject has ventured to

臣以身叨恩遇，職在論思，意切言狂，罪當萬死。

express his heartfelt thoughts with unrestrained frankness. For this unpardonable offence he deserves the death penalty ten thousand times.

爲 君 難 論 下

嗚呼，用人之難，難矣，未若聽言之難也。夫人之言，非一端也。巧辯縱橫而可喜，忠言質樸而多訥，此非聽言之難，在聽者之明暗也。諛言順意而易悅，直言逆耳而觸怒，此非聽言之難，在聽者之賢愚也。

是皆未足爲難也，若聽其言則可用，然用之有輒敗人之事者。聽其言若不可用，然非如其言，不能以成功者。此然後爲聽言之難也。請試舉其一二。

戰國時，趙將有趙括者，善言兵，自謂天下莫能當。其父奢，趙之名將，老於用兵者也。每與括言，亦不能屈，然奢終不以括爲能也。歎曰：「趙若以括爲將，必敗趙事。」

其後奢死，趙遂以括爲將。其母自見趙王，亦言括不可用。趙王不聽，使括將而攻秦。括爲秦軍射死，趙兵大敗，降秦者四十萬人，阬於長平。蓋當時未有如括善言兵，亦未有如括大敗者也。此聽其言可用，用之輒敗人事者，趙括是也。

[1] This was the topic of the first part of the essay.
[2] A district in modern Shansi Province.

On the Difficulty of Being a Ruler (II)

Alas, the difficulty of selecting personnel is great indeed![1] But it is not so great as that of judging advice. This is varied in nature. Some of it, being brilliantly eloquent and presenting all sides of each question, gives delight. Some of it, being faithful counsel, is straightforward and plain but mostly deliberate. It is not difficult to judge either, but it depends on the enlightenment, or the lack of it, on the part of the listener. Flattering advice complies with the wishes of the man to which it is offered and thus is disposed to please. On the other hand, frank advice, which is displeasing to the listener, can provoke anger. It is not difficult to judge either, but it depends on the wisdom or stupidity of the listener.

All this does not present any really serious difficulty. But some advice, while appearing to be acceptable, is liable to cause discomfiture when followed. Other advice may appear to be unacceptable, but there can be no success without acting in accordance with it. Herein lies the difficulty of assessing advice. Let me cite an example or two.

In the period of the Warring States, there was in the state of Chao a general, Chao Kua, who was well versed in military science and who bragged about being irresistible throughout the whole empire. His father, Sheh, was a general famous in Chao as an experienced soldier. In his discussions with Kua, Sheh could never get the better of him, but he never regarded the young man as a capable soldier. He even said with a sigh, "If Chao employed Kua as one of its generals, it would be doomed to defeat."

After the death of Sheh, Kua became general. Even his mother went to the King of Chao and said that recourse should not be had to Kua's services. The king rejected this advice, and dispatched Kua against the state of Ch'in. In the end, Kua was shot to death by the Ch'in army, with the result that the Chao army suffered a disastrous defeat. Four hundred thousand men surrendered to Ch'in, and they were all slaughtered at Ch'angp'ing.[2] At that time, no one was so well versed in military science as Kua, but no one had suffered such a crushing defeat as he. This was an instance where advice appeared to be acceptable, but what followed upon its acceptance was failure.

　秦始皇欲伐荊,問其將李信用兵幾何。信方年少而勇,對曰:「不過二十萬,足矣。」始皇大喜,又以問老將王翦,翦曰:「非六十萬不可。」始皇不悅,曰:「將軍老矣。何其怯也?」因以信為可用,即與兵二十萬,使伐荊。王翦遂謝病退老於頻陽。已而信大為荊人所敗,亡七都尉而還。

　始皇大慚,自駕如頻陽謝翦。因強起之,翦曰:「必欲用臣,非六十萬不可。」於是卒與六十萬而往,遂以滅荊。夫初聽其言,若不可用,然非如其言,不能以成功者,王翦是也。

　且聽計於人者,宜如何? 聽其言若可用,用之宜矣,輒敗事。聽其言若不可用,捨之宜矣,然必如其說,則成功。此所以為難也。

　予又以謂秦趙二主,非徒失於聽言,亦由樂用新進,忽棄老成,此其所以敗也。大抵新進之士喜勇銳,老成之人多持重。此所以人主之好立功名者,聽勇銳之語則易合,聞持重之言則難入也。

　若趙括者,則又有說焉。予略考史記所書,是時趙方遣廉頗攻秦。頗,趙名將也,秦人畏頗,而知括虛言易與也。因行反間於趙,曰:「秦人所畏者,趙括也,若趙以

---

[3] An old *hsien* or district in Shensi Province.

[4] High local military commanders.

[5] Written by Ssu-ma Ch'ien 司馬遷, the Grand Historian of the Han dynasty.

When the First Emperor of Ch'in planned to invade the state of Ching, he asked his general, Li Hsin, how many troops would be required. Being young and brave, Li replied, "No more than 200,000 will suffice." The emperor was greatly pleased and consulted Wang Chien, an old general, whose opinion was that fewer than 600,000 would not do. The emperor frowned and commented tartly, "You must be getting old! How you are losing your nerve!" The emperor, thinking that Li Hsin could be trusted, assigned 200,000 troops to him and dispatched him against Ching. Thereupon, Wang Chien asked for sick leave and retired to P'inyang.[3] Li, as it turned out, was badly defeated by the men of Ching and lost seven Tu-wei.[4]

Greatly embarrassed, the First Emperor drove his own chariot to P'inyang to offer his apologies to Wang and drag him out of retirement. Said Wang, "If Your Majesty must employ my humble services, I still say that fewer than 600,000 troops will not suffice." A force of this size was finally assigned to him, and he soon annihilated Ching. In this instance, Wang's advice had appeared unacceptable, but it turned out that only by acting in accordance with it was success possible.

Moreover, with regard to the art of taking advice, what are the guidelines? If a piece of advice sounds feasible, it would be sensible to follow it. But once adopted, it may turn out to be destructive. Another piece of advice may sound infeasible; yet to ensure success, it must be followed. This is where the dilemma lies.

Again, my view is that the rulers of Ch'in and Chao were defeated, not only because they failed to take the correct advice, but also because they were prone to make use of those who are newly advanced and neglect and forsake those who are old and experienced. As a rule, his new advisers tend to be bold and rash, while the old and experienced are more prudent. A ruler seeking success and fame is, therefore, likely to take the advice of the former and reject that of the latter.

In the case of Chao Kua, there is another explanation. In my random study of *Shih-chi*,[5] I find that at that time the state of Chao was considering the dispatch of Lien P'o to attack Ch'in. As Lien was a famous Chao general, the men of Ch'in were afraid of him; they knew, too, that Chao Kua was merely a braggart and easy to cope with. A campaign of counter-propaganda was conducted by them in Chao, asserting that Chao Kua was the man feared by them and that, were Chao to appoint him commanding officer, Ch'in would be terrified. Not realizing that

161

爲將，則秦懼矣。」趙王不悟反間也，遂用括爲將，以代頗。藺相如力諫，以爲不可。趙王不聽，遂至於敗。

由是言之，括虛談無實，而不可用，其父知之，其母亦知之，趙之諸臣藺相如等亦知之，外至敵國亦知之，獨其主不悟爾。夫用人之失，天下之人皆知其不可，而獨其主不知者，莫大之患也。前世之禍亂敗亡由此者，不可勝數也。

---

[6]Famous prime minister of the state of Chao in the Warring States period.

this was counter-propaganda, the King of Chao selected Chao Kua in place of Lien P'o. Despite the energetic remonstrances of Lin Hsiang-ju,[6] the king insisted on his own choice, and was defeated as a result.

The unfounded boast of Chao Kua and his unfitness for service, then, were known to his father, to his mother, to the high officials of Chao, including Lin Hsiang-ju, and even to the enemy, but only his ruler failed to realize this. In the selection of personnel, a mistake visible to the whole country but not to the ruler is the greatest danger. There are innumerable instances in history where disorder, disaster, defeat and downfall have resulted from such an error.

論禁止無名子傷毀近臣狀

右臣竊見前年宋庠等出外之時，京師先有無名子詩一首傳於中外，尋而庠罷政事。

近又風聞外有小人欲中傷三司使王堯臣者，復作無名子詩一篇，略聞其一兩句。臣自聞此詩，日夕疑駭，深思事理，不可不言。

伏以陛下視聽聰明，外邊事無小大，無不知者。竊恐此詩流傳漸廣，須達聖聰。臣忝爲陛下耳目之官，不欲小人浮謗之言上惑天聽，合先論列，以杜姦讒。

況自兵興累年，繼以災旱，民財困竭，國帑空虛。天下安危，繫於財用虛實。三司之職，其任非輕。近自姚仲孫罷去之後，朝廷以積年蠹弊，貧虛窘乏之三司，付與堯臣，仰其辦事。乃是陛下委信責成之日，堯臣多方展效之時。

臣備見從前任人，率多顧惜祿位，寧可敗事於國，不肯當怨於身。如堯臣者，領職以來，未及一月，自副使以下，不才者悉請換易。足見其不避嫌怨，不徇人情，竭力

Memorial on the Prohibition of the Anonymous Slandering of Trusted Court Officials

Your subject has seen that, the year before last, when Sung Hsiang[1] and others left the capital, first there had been an anonymous poem against Sung circulated in the capital and in other parts of the country. Subsequently Sung retired from the government.

Recently it has been reported that another anonymous poem has been circulated outside the capital by unworthy men wishing to discredit Wang Yao-ch'en, Minister of Finance. One or two lines of the poem have been read to your subject. Since learning of this composition, he has been astonished, has had serious doubts and has devoted himself to profound meditation. As a result, he has found it impossible to remain silent.

Given Your Majesty's wisdom, there is no event, big or small, outside the palace that can escape your attention. It is feared that the circulation of this poem will gradually expand and that it should be drawn to Your Majesty's attention. As Your Majesty's eyes and ears, your subject does not wish the slander of unworthy men to cloud your judgment. To obviate the harmful effect of the defamation, he has chosen to discuss the matter first.

Moreover, for many years the country has been afflicted with armed conflict and with drought, resulting in great poverty and distress for the people and the depletion of the national coffers. As the safety of the country is dependent on sound finances, the responsibility of the Minister of Finance is by no means light. After the recent dismissal of Yao Chung-sun, the Court entrusted to Wang the reform of the Ministry of Finance, which has for years been riddled with corruption, insolvency and destitution. Given Your Majesty's trust in him, this is indeed the time for Wang to render good service in every possible way.

Your subject has observed that, in making appointments, officials used to be most concerned with the maintenance of the emoluments and positions of those already in office, and that they would rather let the state suffer than incur the displeasure of their subordinates. In the case of Wang, however, less than a month after his assumption of office, those under him, from the Vice Commissioner down, who have been found to be incapable, have been replaced. This is ample proof that he

救時，以身當事。今若下容讒間，上不主張，則不惟材智之臣，無由展效，亦恐忠義之士，自茲解體。

臣思作詩者雖不知其姓名，竊慮在朝之臣，有名位與堯臣相類者，嫉其任用，故欲中傷，只知爭進於一時，不思沮國之大計。

伏自陛下罷去呂夷簡，夏竦之後，進用韓琦，范仲淹以來，天下欣然，皆賀聖德。君子既蒙進用，小人自恐道消，故共喧然，務騰讒口，欲惑君聽，欲沮好人。不早絕之，恐終敗事。

況今三司，蠹弊已深，四方匱乏已極，堯臣必須大有更張，方能集事，未容展效，已被謗言。臣近日已聞浮議紛然，云堯臣更易官吏，專權侵政。今又造此詩語，搖惑羣情。若不止之，則今後陛下無以使人，忠臣無由事主。讒言罔極，自古所患，若一啓其漸，則扇惑羣小，動搖大臣。貽患朝廷，何所不至？

伏望特降詔書，戒勵臣下，敢有造作言語，誣搆陰私者，一切禁之，及有轉相傳誦，則必推究其所來，重行朝

---

[2] Prime Minister under Emperor Jen-tsung.
[3] A military governor under Emperor Jen-tsung.
[4] Both Han and Fan were distinguished prime ministers under the same emperor.

is not afraid of causing discontent and does not yield to personal pressure, but rather shoulder his responsibilities and do his best to rectify the deficiencies of the times. If slander is tolerated below and no action is taken above to curb it, not only will talented and enlightened officials be unable to render proper service, but loyal and righteous men will henceforth be disheartened.

Your subject feels that, though the author of the poem is not known by name, he may possibly be someone at Court in a position similar to that of Wang, who is jealous of his appointment and who therefore is out to harm him. What such a man cares about is simply to get the better of his rival without concern as to the obstruction he may cause to the weighty plans of the state.

Since Your Majesty removed Lü I-chien[2] and Hsia Sung[3] and promoted Han Ch'i and Fan Chung-yen,[4] the whole country has expressed its gratification and gratitude for your wisdom. Now that men of virtue have been given advancement, unworthy men, apprehensive of eclipse, have panicked and resorted to slander in order to mislead Your Majesty and obstruct the rise of good men. If these unworthy men are not got rid of at an early stage, they will cause serious trouble.

Furthermore, the Ministry of Finance at present is deeply mired in corruption and inefficiency, and the country is experiencing extreme poverty. Wang must therefore make radical changes before he can discharge his functions successfully. But hardly has he been given the time to do anything to prove himself, he is already subjected to slander. Your subject has recently heard numerous unfounded criticisms of him, to the effect that he has replaced many public functionaries, arrogated dictatorial powers to himself, and encroached on government authority. On top of these hostile comments, this poem is circulated in order to incite the people. If it is not stopped, Your Majesty will from now on be unable to use anyone, nor will loyal subjects be able to serve their sovereign. There is no limit to slander, which has been a source of trouble from the earliest times. If its gradual spread is permitted, unworthy men themselves will be incited and important ministers shaken. There is no telling how much harm it will do the Court.

Your Majesty is humbly implored to cause a special decree to be issued, prohibiting all Your Majesty's subjects from making false accusations regarding the private conduct of others and tracking down the authors of those in circulation, with a view to securing the renewed

典，所貴禁止讒巧，保全善人。謹具狀奏聞，伏候勅旨。

enforcement of the law. What is important is to prohibit slander and protect good men. This memorial is respectfully submitted, and the imperial decree humbly awaited.

論大理寺斷冤獄不當劄子

臣風聞大理寺近奏斷德州公案一道，爲一班行王守度謀殺妻事，止斷杖六十私罪。其守度所犯情理極惡，本因踰濫，欲誘一求食婦人爲妻，自持戎杖，恐逼正妻阿馬，令其誣以姦事，髡截頭髮，又自以繩索付與阿馬，守度持刀在旁，逼令自縊，其命垂盡，只爲未有棺器，卻且解下。其後又與繩索，令自縊，阿馬偶得生逃。

臣略聞此大概，其他守度兇惡之狀，備於案牘，人不忍聞。阿馬幽苦冤枉如此，而法吏止斷誣姦，降以杖罪。

竊以刑在禁惡，法本原情。今阿馬之冤，於情可憫，守度所犯，其惡難容。若以法家斷罪舉重而論，則守度誣姦不實之罪輕，迫人以死之情重。

原其用意，合從謀殺。凡謀殺之罪，其類甚多。或有兩相爭恨，理直之人，因發忿心殺害理曲之人者，死與未死，須被謀殺之刑。豈比守度曲在自身，阿馬本無所爭，備極陵辱，迫以自裁，虐害之情，深於謀殺遠矣。

臣嘗伏讀眞宗皇帝賜諫臣之詔曰：「冤枉未申，賞刑

---

[1] Prefecture in modern Shantung Province.

Memorial on a Wrongful Decision of
the Ministry of Justice

Your subject has received a report that the Ministry of Justice has recently submitted the decision on a Tehchow[1] case—that of a colleague, Wang Shou-tu, who was sentenced to only sixty lashes for plotting the murder of his wife. The acts committed by Shou-tu were dastardly. Overstepping the due bounds of propriety and seducing a beggarwoman into marrying him, Shou-tu threatened his own wife, Ah Ma, with a sword and club, compelled her to admit adultery, shaved off her hair and handed her a rope, stood beside her with a sword in hand and forced her to hang herself. When she was dying, she was temporarily released only for lack of a coffin. Then the rope was handed to her once more, and she was again forced to hang herself. Somehow, however, she managed to escape alive.

This was the gist of what your subject heard. Shou-tu's cruelty is detailed in the dossier, which no one can bear to read. Despite the heinous wrong done to Ah Ma, the judgment of the court was confined to the husband's trumped-up charge of adultery and the punishment to flogging.

In your subject's opinion, the penalty should be aimed at the deterrence of wrongdoing, and the law must be based on human feeling. Now the injustice done to Ah Ma arouses feelings of pity, and the wrong committed by Shou-tu is hardly to be tolerated. So far as the weight of judicial opinion is concerned, Shou-tu's false charge of adultery was of little importance, but his attempt to force someone to die was much more serious.

It was a case of malice prepense, and the object was to commit murder. The crime of murder is of many kinds. When two persons are involved in a dispute, the one who is in the right but who out of rage attempts to kill the other party, is guilty of murder, irrespective of whether the latter dies. In the case of Shou-tu, the wrong was on his side, and, though Ah Ma provoked no quarrel with him, she was subjected to every form of torture and humiliation and forced to commit suicide. The cruel injury done to her was far worse than a mere attempt to commit a murder.

Your subject has respectfully read the decree of His Majesty Emperor

171

踰度者，皆許論列。」今之冤婦，臣職當言者也。豈有聖
主在上，國法方行，而令強暴之男，而敢逼人以死？臣恐
守度不誅，則自今強者陵弱，疎者害親，國法邃墮，人倫
敗矣。

　　其王守度一宗公案，伏望聖慈特令中書細詳。情理果
如臣之所聞，即乞行刑法，以止姦凶。取進止。

Chen-tsung to the Censors, which stated, "Cases may be submitted which involve unrighted wrongs and excessive rewards and penalties." Here is a wronged woman, whose case your subject deems it his duty to discuss. When our enlightened emperor is on the throne and the laws of the country are enforced, how can a man of violence be permitted to force someone to die? Your subject apprehends that, if Shou-tu is not put to death, the strong will oppress the weak, outsiders will harm members of the family, the nation's laws will fall into disuse and human relationships will ultimately collapse.

It is humbly requested that Your Majesty refer the case of Wang Shou-tu to the Prime Minister's Office for a detailed review. If what your subject has heard is the truth, I humbly implore you to mete out the penalty required by law, so that an end may be put to treachery and cruelty.

畫 錦 堂 記

仕宦而至將相，富貴而歸故鄉，此人情之所榮，而今
昔之所同也。蓋士方窮時，困阨閭里，庸人孺子，皆得易
而侮之。若季子不禮於其嫂，買臣見棄於其妻。一旦高車
駟馬，旗旄導前，而騎卒擁後，夾道之人，相與駢肩累迹，
瞻望咨嗟。而所謂庸夫愚婦者，奔走駭汗，羞愧俯伏，以
自悔罪於車塵馬足之間。此一介之士，得志當時，而意氣
之盛，昔人比之衣錦之榮者也。

惟大丞相魏國公則不然。公相人也。世有令德，為時
名卿。自公少時，已擢高科，登顯仕。海內之士，聞下風
而望餘光者，蓋亦有年矣。所謂將相而富貴，皆公所宜素
有。非如窮阨之人，僥倖得志於一時，出於庸夫愚婦之不
意，以驚駭而夸耀之也。

[1] Hsiang Yü 項羽, King of Ch'u 楚霸王, once said: "Not to return to one's native town after achieving wealth and official distinction is like being dressed in brocade and parading at night." For this reason Han Ch'i 韓琦, a great political figure in the Sung dynasty, gave the name "Daylight Brocade Hall" to a structure he had built when he became wealthy and officially distinguished and served as the administrative head of his native town.

[2] Chi-tzu was the courtesy name of Su Ch'in 蘇秦, a great strategist in the Warring States period. Having failed to convince King Hui of the state of Ch'in 秦惠王 after memorializing him ten times, Su returned home in distress. Upon his arrival, his sister-in-law refused to cook him a meal.

[3] Chu Mai-ch'eng 朱買臣, a prominent official in the Han dynasty, was divorced by his wife while he was a poor man. When he returned home after distinguishing himself, she failed to win him back and committed suicide.

[4] Being dressed in brocade signifies returning home after achieving wealth and official distinction.

[5] Modern Anyang 安陽, Honan Province.

The Daylight Brocade Hall[1]

To rise to prominence as Commander-in-Chief or as Prime Minister and to return to one's native town on achieving wealth and official distinction—these are ambitions cherished by human nature alike in modern and ancient times. When a scholar is poor and lives in distress in his own village, even vulgar people and children find it easy to insult him. Chi-tzu,[2] for example, was snubbed by his sister-in-law, and Mai-ch'eng[3] abandoned by his wife. Once a scholar rides in a high carriage drawn by four horses, with flag-bearers leading in front and a mounted escort bringing up the rear, a crowd of spectators would gather on both sides of the road to watch and sigh, and ordinary men and stupid women rush forward in great excitement and shamefacedly prostrate themselves in the dust stirred up by the carriage and the horses. Such is the elation coming to a scholar when his ambition is fulfilled—an honor which was compared by the ancients to that of being dressed in brocade.[4]

However, the case of His Excellency the Duke of Wei, the great Prime Minister, is altogether different. His Excellency is a native of Hsiangchow.[5] For generations, his family has been noted for its great virtue and a number of its members have distinguished themselves as officials in their time. Since his youth, as an outstandingly successful candidate in the imperial examination, His Excellency has served as a high official. Scholars within the country have for years looked up to him in awe. The prominence of a commander-in-chief or prime minister and its attendant wealth and official distinction are what His Excellency has always deserved; he is unlike the man who once lived in poverty and distress and who by a stroke of good luck achieved momentary success, contrary to the expectations of ordinary men and stupid women and astonishing them and filling them with admiration and envy.

175

然則高牙大纛，不足爲公榮，桓圭袞裳，不足爲公貴。惟德被生民，而功施社稷，勒之金石，播之聲詩，以耀後世，而垂無窮。此公之志，而士亦以此望於公也。豈止夸一時，而榮一鄉哉？

公在至和中，嘗以武康之節，來治於相。乃作畫錦之堂於後圃。既又刻詩於石，以遺相人。其言以快恩讎，矜名譽爲可薄。蓋不以昔人所夸者爲榮，而以爲戒。於此見公之視富貴爲如何，而其志豈易量哉？

故能出入將相，勤勞王家，而夷險一節。至於臨大事，決大議，垂紳正笏，不動聲色，而措天下於泰山之安。可謂社稷之臣矣。其豐功盛烈，所以銘彝鼎而被弦歌者，乃邦家之光，非閭里之榮也。

余雖不獲登公之堂，幸嘗竊誦公之詩。樂公之志有成，而喜爲天下道也，於是乎書。

---

[6] 1054-1055, reign of Emperor Jen-tsung.
[7] In modern Chekiang Province.
[8] A mountain range extending through Shantung Province.

For this reason, his swaying standards are not a sufficient honor for him, nor his official ivory tablet and embroidered cloak a sufficient distinction for him. But the many good deeds he has done for the people and his great achievements throughout the country, engraved on metal and stone and revered in song and verse, will cast their splendor on future generations and live in memory without end—this is what His Excellency cherishes and what all scholars expect of him. How much greater is this than to be the pride of a single age and to have the honor of a single locality?

In the reign of Chih-ho,[6] as Military Governor of Wuk'ang,[7] His Excellency was simultaneously assigned to Hsiangchow, his native town, as its administrative head. In the back-yard of his official residence, he has had the Daylight Brocade Hall constructed. Subsequently he has caused his poetry to be engraved on stone as a legacy to the people of Hsiangchow. In his composition he deprecates the gratification of one's feelings of friendship or hatred and the stress of reputation alone. This shows that, rather than consider as an honor what was the pride of men of former times, he guards against it. Thus do we see in what light he regards wealth and official distinction and how lofty his ambition is.

He has therefore been able to serve as Commander-in-Chief and as Prime Minister, rendering signal services to the reigning dynasty because of his assiduity, and acquitted himself equally well in times of peace and of danger. When he was confronted with important affairs of state and had to make weighty decisions, he performed his duties solemnly and calmly and made the country as safe as the T'ai Mountains.[8] He is indeed a Minister of State in the true sense. His great accomplishments, which are inscribed on historical monuments and sung to music, redound to the honor of the entire country, and are not the glory of his own village alone.

Though I have not had the privilege of visiting the hall built by His Excellency, I have read his poetry and am gratified at the achievement of his ambition. As I am happy to tell the story to the people of the whole country, I have committed it to writing.

177

峴 山 亭 記

峴山臨漢上，望之隱然，蓋諸山之小者。而其名特著
於荆州者，豈非以其人哉？其人謂誰？羊祜叔子，杜預元
凱是已。方晉與吳以兵爭，常倚荆州以爲重，而二子相繼
於此，遂以平吳，而成晉業，其功烈已蓋於當世矣。至於
流風餘韻，藹然被於江漢之間者，至今人猶思之，而於思
叔子也尤深。

蓋元凱以其功，而叔子以其仁，二子所爲雖不同，然
皆足以垂於不朽。余頗疑其反自汲汲於後世之名者，何哉？

傳言，叔子嘗登茲山，慨然語其屬，以謂此山常在，
而前世之士，皆已湮滅於無聞，因自顧而悲傷。然獨不知
茲山待己而名著也。

元凱銘功於二石，一置茲山之上，一投漢水之淵，是知
陵谷有變，而不知石有時而磨滅也。豈皆自喜其名之甚，
而過爲無窮之慮歟？將自待者厚，而所思者遠歟？

山故有亭，世傳以爲叔子之所遊止也。故其屢廢而復
興者，由後世慕其名而思其人者多也。

熙寧元年，余友人史君中煇以光祿卿來守襄陽。明年，

---

[1] A hill south of Hsiangyang *Hsien* 襄陽縣, Hupeh Province.
[2] Prefecture in modern Hupeh Province.
[3] Great generals in the Tsin dynasty.
[4] 1068, reign of Emperor Shen-tsung 神宗.

The Hsien Hill Pavilion

The Hsien Hill[1] is on the Han River. It is hardly visible when viewed from afar. Though it is one of the smallest hills, its name is especially well known all over Chingchow[2] because of the men once identified with it. Who were these men? They were Yang Hu and Tu Yü.[3] When the Tsin dynasty fought the state of Wu, Chingchow was relied on as a great fortress, and, with the two men successively in control of it, the regime of Wu was brought to an end and the Tsin dynasty completed its conquest, which was the greatest achievement of the age. The rich legacy and fine tradition handed down by the two men have left their traces throughout the Yangtze and the Han River region. To this day, the people still hark back to them, especially to Yang Hu.

Tu Yü was noted for his meritorious service and Yang Hu for his humaneness. Though they differed in their conduct, immortality was equally their due. However, I rather suspect that both of them were not free from anxiety about achieving such celebrity.

It is alleged that Yang once climbed the hill and remarked with feeling to his subordinates that, despite the eternal presence of the hill, those scholars who had lived before had been totally lost to memory. So he mourned for himself, not realizing that the hill had to wait for him to make its name more illustrious.

Tu recorded his exploits on two stones, placing one of them on the hill and throwing the other into the Han River. Though convinced of the possible changes to be wrought on the hill, he failed to realize that the carving on the stone could also one day wear off. Did the two gentlemen love their own names so much that they could not cease to be anxious lest they be not known to posterity? Did they think of themselves so highly that they projected their thoughts far into the future?

On the hill, there stood a pavilion, which was remembered by many generations to have been a place of rest for Yang. From time to time, this building has fallen into disrepair and been restored, which reflected the large number of people who admired the man and thought of him in later ages.

In the first year of Hsi-ning,[4] my friend, Shih Chung-hui, came to

179

因亭之舊，廣而新之，既周以回廊之壯，又大其後軒，使與亭相稱。君知名當世，所至有聲。襄人安其政而樂從其遊也，因以君之官名其後軒，爲光祿堂。又欲紀其事于石，以與叔子元凱之名並傳于久遠。君皆不能止也，乃來以記屬於余。

余謂君知慕叔子之風，而襲其遺迹，則其爲人，與其志之所存者，可知矣。襄人愛君而安樂之如此，則君之爲政於襄者，又可知矣。此襄人之所欲書也。

若其左右山川之勝勢，與夫草木雲煙之杳靄，出沒於空曠有無之間，而可以備詩人之登高，寫離騷之極目者，宜其覽者自得之。至於亭屢廢興，或自有記，或不必究其詳者，皆不復道。熙寧三年十月二十有二日六一居士歐陽脩記。

---

[5] Title of a high official in the central government.

Hsiangyang as Prefect, with the title of Kuang-lu-ch'ing.[5] A year later he had the old pavilion widened and renovated. In addition to surrounding the structure with magnificent galleries, he enlarged its rear hall to bring its proportions in line with the pavilion. Shih was a man of renown in his time, and enjoyed great popularity wherever he went. Pleased with his administration and happy to follow in his footsteps, the people of Hsiangyang have named the rear hall after his official designation as the Kuang-lu Hall. They have also decided to record the event on a monument, so that his name might be handed down with those of Yang and Tu to posterity. As Shih failed to stop them, he has assigned the task of writing to me.

Since Shih admires Yang's personality and emulates his example, it is plain what kind of a man he is and what his ambition is. Since the people of Hsiangyang love him so much and are so pleased and happy with him, it is also clear what his administration has meant to the prefecture. All this the people wish to have recorded.

As to the imposing sights of the surrounding mountains and rivers and the appearance and disappearance of hazy grasses and trees, clouds and mist, which may be discerned in the distance and which may provide poets with the inspiration for their compositions and serve as a source of their emotions, these can well be left to the appreciation of the visitors themselves. Nor is it for me to say anything about the intermittent disrepair and restoration of the pavilion, since separate records may already exist or it may be unnecessary to describe them in detail.

> By the Retired Scholar Liu-i, Ou-yang Hsiu,
> the twenty-second day of the tenth month
> of the third year of Hsi-ning

豐 樂 亭 記

脩既治滁之明年，夏始飲滁水而甘。問諸滁人，得於州南百步之近。其上豐山聳然而特立，下則幽谷窈然而深藏，中有清泉滃然而仰出。俯仰左右，顧而樂之。於是疏泉鑿石，闢地以爲亭，而與滁人往遊其間。

滁於五代干戈之際，用武之地也。昔太祖皇帝嘗以周師破李景兵十五萬於清流山下，生擒其將皇甫暉姚鳳於滁東門之外，遂以平滁。脩嘗考其山川，按其圖記，升高以望清流之關，欲求暉鳳就擒之所，而故老皆無在者，蓋天下之平久矣。

自唐失其政，海內分裂，豪傑並起而爭。所在爲敵國者，何可勝數？及宋受天命，聖人出而四海一。嚮之憑恃險阻，剗削消磨。百年之間，漠然徒見山高而水清。欲問其事，而遺老盡矣。

今滁介於江淮之間，舟車商賈，四方賓客之所不至。民生不見外事，而安於畎畝衣食，以樂生送死。而孰知上

---

[1] Prefecture in modern Anhwei Province.
[2] Mountains south of Ch'u *Hsien* 滁縣.
[3] First Emperor of the Sung dynasty.
[4] One of the rulers of the Southern T'ang dynasty 南唐.
[5] Mountains northwest of Ch'u *Hsien*.

The Pavilion of Prosperity and Happiness

The year after my appointment to Ch'uchow[1] as its prefect, I drank the water there in the summer and found it sweet. Upon inquiry, I learned from the people that it comes from as near as one hundred paces south of the prefecture. Above are the Feng Mountains,[2] which soar to the skies, and below is a deep valley which is hidden in a hollow and from which spring water bubbles up. Looking above and below, left and right, I was enraptured. It was therefore decided to cut through the stones in order to get at the water and break the ground for a pavilion, so that I could visit the surroundings with the people of the prefecture.

During the warring times of the Five Dynasties, Ch'uchow was a battleground. With the forces of the Later Chou dynasty, Emperor T'ai-tsu[3] routed one hundred and fifty thousand troops of Li Ching[4] below the Ch'ingliu Mountains[5] and captured alive his two generals, Huang-fu Hui and Yao Feng, outside the eastern gate of Ch'uchow, whereupon peace was restored to this prefecture. I have studied the mountains and rivers of the area and, with the aid of maps and records, ascended the heights to survey the Ch'ingliu Pass in order to locate the place of Huang-fu's and Yao's capture. But a long time has elapsed since the peace of the country was restored, and none of those who lived then were around to guide me.

After the T'ang dynasty came to an end, the country was divided. Many valiant men were involved in the struggle; many states faced one another as adversaries. With the conferment of the heavenly mandate on the Sung dynasty, an enlightened emperor emerged and the country was reunited. Difficult terrains of strategic importance, on which the various contestants once relied as their bases, were levelled and worn away. In these one hundred years, only the lofty mountains and the placid rivers were left untouched. Though I wished to inquire into the facts, no one has survived the old regime and lived to tell the tale.

Today, Ch'uchow lies between the Yangtze and Huai Rivers, to which boats, vehicles, merchants and visitors from the four corners do not resort. The people, unconcerned with what goes on outside their boundaries, are devoted to peaceful farming and the search for food and clothing, in order to enjoy a happy life and give their dead a decent burial.

之功德，休養生息，涵煦百年之深也？

　　脩之來此，樂其地僻而事簡，又愛其俗之安閑。既得斯泉于山谷之間，乃日與滁人仰而望山，俯而聽泉，掇幽芳而蔭喬木，風霜冰雪，刻露清秀，四時之景，無不可愛。又幸其民，樂其歲物之豐成，而喜與予遊也。因爲本其山川，道其風俗之美，使民知所以安此豐年之樂者，幸生無事之時也。夫宣上恩德，以與民共樂，刺史之事也。遂書以名其亭焉。

They hardly realize that their peace and prosperity have been nurtured for a century by the benevolence of their ruler.

Since my arrival here I have been pleased with the secluded location and the light business, and loved the calm and leisurely pace of the people. Since I have made the spring water accessible to all mountains and valleys, I am able in the daily company of the people of Ch'uchow to look at the mountains above, listen to the murmur of the spring below, breathe the delightful perfumed air and enjoy the shade of towering trees. Even when wind, frost, snow and ice arrive, the environment is at its most picturesque. The beauty of all four seasons is admirable. Moreover it is fortunate that the people are happy in the enjoyment of their yearly rich harvests, and are glad to wander round with me. I have for these reasons traced the history of the mountains and rivers and spoken of the admirable local customs, so that the people may know that they can enjoy their good years because they have had the good fortune of living in untroubled times. Since it is the duty of the prefect to extol the favors of the ruler and share in the happiness of the people, I have written this account and given the pavilion its name.

醉翁亭記

環滁，皆山也。其西南諸峯，林壑尤美。望之蔚然而深秀者，琅邪也。山行六七里，漸聞水聲潺潺而瀉出于兩峯之間者，釀泉也。峯回路轉，有亭翼然臨于泉上者，醉翁亭也。作亭者誰？山之僧曰智僊也。名之者誰？太守自謂也。太守與客來飲于此，飲少輒醉，而年又最高，故自號曰醉翁也。

醉翁之意不在酒，在乎山水之間也。山水之樂，得之心而寓之酒也。

若夫日出而林霏開，雲歸而巖穴暝，晦明變化者，山間之朝暮也。

野芳發而幽香，佳木秀而繁陰，風霜高潔，水清而石出者，山間之四時也。朝而往，暮而歸，四時之景不同，而樂亦無窮也。

至於負者歌于塗，行者休于樹，前者呼，後者應，傴僂提攜，往來而不絕者，滁人遊也。

臨谿而漁，谿深而魚肥。釀泉爲酒，泉香而酒冽。山肴野蔌，雜然而前陳者，太守宴也。宴酣之樂，非絲非竹，

---

[1] Ch'u *Hsien,* Anhwei Province. The author was Prefect of Ch'uchow at the time.

[2] Mountain ten *li* southwest of Ch'uchow.

[3] Equivalent to one-third of a mile.

186

The Old Drunkard's Pavilion

Ch'uchow[1] is surrounded by mountains; the woods and valleys to the southwest are particularly beautiful. One of the ranges, the Langya,[2] which can be seen from a long way off, is thickly covered with tall and graceful vegetation. After journeying on the mountainside for six or seven *li*,[3] one begins to hear the sound of flowing water. It is the Niang Spring rushing out from between two peaks. Placed amidst surrounding elevations and winding roads is a pavilion which juts out over the spring like the wing of a bird. This is the Old Drunkard's Pavilion, which was built by the monk Chih-hsien and named by the Prefect with an allusion to himself. He frequently comes here and drinks with his guests. He gets drunk on a few cups, and he is the oldest of all the topers. Hence the self-imposed nickname—Old Drunkard.

However, Old Drunkard's heart is not set on the wine, but lies somewhere betwixt the mountains and the rivers. The delight of mountains and rivers comes from the heart, and is derived from wine.

When the sun rises, the atmosphere in the woods clears up. When the clouds come home, the mountain caves grow dark. This coming of brightness and darkness spells the arrival of morning and evening respectively in the mountains.

Now the wild grass emits a refreshing perfume; now exquisite trees grow luxuriantly and cast a deep shade; now wind and frost, high and pure, go their rounds; now the water becomes clear and the pebbles are exposed to view. These are the four seasons in the mountains. If we make our outings in the morning and come back in the evening, the landscapes of the four seasons are different and the pleasures they afford are unlimited.

People carrying burdens sing as they go, travelers pause to rest under the trees, those walking in front give a shout and those following behind respond. The travelers, with their backs bent, carry their children and come and go incessantly. These are the people of Ch'uchow journeying on the road.

When we angle in the deep brook, we catch fat fish. When we make wine with the sweet spring water, it is clear and smooth to the palate. Other mountain food and wild vegetable are assembled with these and

射者中，弈者勝，觥籌交錯，起坐而諠譁者，衆賓懽也。蒼顏白髮，頹然乎其間者，太守醉也。

已而夕陽在山，人影散亂，太守歸而賓客從也。樹林陰翳，鳴聲上下，遊人去而禽鳥樂也。然而禽鳥知山林之樂，而不知人之樂。人知從太守遊而樂，不知太守之樂其樂也。醉能同其樂，醒能述以文者，太守也。太守謂誰，廬陵歐陽脩也。

---

[4]A game which is no longer in vogue and in which the participants threw arrows into a pot.

[5]Chi-an 吉安 , Kiangsi Province.

set on the table before us when the Prefect gives his feast. Even without wind or stringed instruments, the revelries become intense with arrow-throwing[4] and chess, with drinking and wine games. Now seated, now standing up, the guests utter loud noises, and have a marvelous time. Little by little, the Prefect, sitting in the center with his wrinkled face and gray hair, is seen drooping under the effect of the wine.

Shortly after, the sun sets over the mountains, the shadows of the revelers are scattered around and the guests follow the Prefect as he returns home. A pall of darkness covers the trees, while the birds warble here and there as the guests leave. However, while the birds know the delights of mountains and trees, they do not know those of men; and while men know the delights of traveling with the Prefect, they do not know how the Prefect enjoys their pleasures. It is the Prefect who can share their pleasures while drunk and write about them while sober. Who is the Prefect? It is none other than Ou-yang Hsiu from Luling.[5]

王 彦 章 畫 像 記

太師王公諱彥章，字子明，鄆州壽張人也。事梁爲宣
義軍節度使，以身死國，葬於鄭州之管城。晉天福二年始
贈太師。

公在梁，以智勇聞。梁晉之爭，數百戰，其爲勇將多
矣，而晉人獨畏彥章。自乾化後，常與晉戰，屢困莊宗於
河上。及梁末年，小人趙巖等用事，梁之大臣老將，多以
讒不見信，皆怒而有怠心。而梁亦盡失河北，事勢已去，
諸將多懷顧望。獨公奮然自必，不少屈懈，志雖不就，卒
死以忠。公旣死，而梁亦亡矣，悲夫！

五代終始，纔五十年，而更十有三君，五易國，而八
姓。士之不幸而出乎其時，能不汙其身，得全其節者，鮮
矣。公本武人，不知書。其語質，平生嘗謂人曰：「豹死
留皮，人死留名。」蓋其義勇忠信，出於天性而然。

予於五代書，竊有善善惡惡之志。至於公傳，未嘗不

---

[1] Prefecture in modern Shantung Province.

[2] A geographical subdivision covering parts of Honan, Shantung and Anhwei.

[3] Prefecture in modern Honan Province.

[4] 937, reign of Emperor Kao-tsu of the Later Tsin dynasty 後晉高祖.

[5] 911-914, reign of Emperor T'ai-tsu 太祖 and the Last Emperor 末帝 of the Later Liang dynasty 後梁.

[6] The reign of this emperor lasted from 923 to 925.

[7] A high official under the Last Emperor of the Later Liang dynasty.

[8] Ou-yang Hsiu was the unofficial editor of the *New History of the Five Dynasties* 新五代史.

The Portrait of Wang Yen-chang

Wang Yen-chang, Grand Teacher of the Imperial Household, who had the courtesy name of Tzu-ming, was a native of Shouchang, Yünchow.[1] As a subject of the Liang dynasty, he served as Military Governor of Hsüan-i Chün.[2] He died for his country and was buried in Kuanch'eng, Chengchow.[3] It was only in the second year of T'ien-fu[4] of the Tsin dynasty that the title of Grand Teacher was posthumously conferred on him.

In the Liang dynasty, Wang was known for his wisdom and valor. The war between the Liang and Tsin regimes involved several hundred battles. Of the many brave Liang generals, Wang was the most feared by the men of Tsin. After Ch'ien-hua,[5] he had many engagements with the Tsin forces and caused repeated distresses to Emperor Chuang-tsung[6] on the Yellow River. Toward the end of the Liang dynasty, Chao Yen,[7] a mean man, and others like him were in power; most of the great statesmen and old generals, having lost the confidence of the emperor through slander, were disaffected and indolent. In the meantime, the government had lost all its territory north of the Yellow River. The situation was out of hand, and the military leaders adopted the attitude of watchful waiting. Wang was the only man who was sure of himself and continued to forge ahead unswervingly. Though he died without fulfilling his wishes, he was a man of loyalty. With his death, the Liang dynasty also came to an end, an extremely sad conclusion.

The Five Dynasties lasted only fifty years, during which there were five administrations and thirteen rulers, belonging to eight different families. Of the scholars who were unfortunate enough to emerge in this period, few could keep their integrity intact even if they could manage to avoid complete personal degradation. Originally a military man, Wang was unschooled and always outspoken. He had once said to others: "When a leopard dies, it leaves its skin; when a man dies, he leaves his name." He was by nature a righteous, valiant, loyal and sincere man.

In dealing with the history of the Five Dynasties,[8] I harbored the secret wish of exalting the good and condemning the evil. When it came to the biography of Wang, I always sighed with emotion and regretted

感憤歎息，惜乎舊史殘略，不能備公之事。康定元年，予
以節度判官來此，求於滑人，得公之孫睿所錄家傳，頗多
於舊史，其記德勝之戰尤詳。又言敬翔怒末帝不肯用公，
欲自經於帝前，公因用笏畫山川，爲御史彈而見廢。又言
公五子，其二同公死節。此皆舊史無之。又云公在滑，以
讒自歸於京師，而史云召之。是時梁兵，盡屬段凝，京師
羸兵，不滿數千。公得保鑾五百人之鄆州，以力寡敗於中
都，而史云將五千以往者，亦皆非也。

公之攻德勝也，初受命於帝前，期以三日破敵，梁之
將相，聞者皆竊笑。及破南城，果三日。是時莊宗在魏，
聞公復用，料公必速攻，自魏馳馬來救，已不及矣。莊宗
之善料，公之善出奇，何其神哉？

今國家罷兵四十年，一旦元昊反，敗軍殺將，連四五
年，而攻守之計，至今未決。予嘗獨持用奇取勝之議，而

---

[9] 1040, reign of Emperor Jen-tsung.

[10] Subordinate official under the Military Governor.

[11] Prefecture in modern Honan Province.

[12] A strategic town in modern Hopeh Province, where more than 100 engagements were fought between the Liang and Chin regimes.

[13] A high official in the Later Liang dynasty.

[14] Modern Wenshang *Hsien* 汶上縣, Shantung Province.

[15] King of Hsia 夏, a state on the northwestern border, which rebelled during the reign of Emperor Jen-tsung.

that the old history books were incomplete as regards his deeds. In the first year of K'ang-ting,[9] I was appointed to the Military Governor's office as P'an-kuan.[10] After inquiring of the people of Huachow,[11] I obtained a copy of the family history compiled by Wang's grandson, Jui, which goes into greater detail than the old history books. The family history is especially detailed as to the Battles of Tehsheng.[12] It also states that, angered by the Last Emperor's refusal to make use of Wang's services, Ching Hsiang[13] threatened to commit suicide in the presence of the sovereign. It tells of Wang's impeachment by the Censorship and his subsequent dismissal for drawing a map of the country with his official emblem. It mentions that of his five sons two died on duty with him. All these have been left out from the old history books. It also relates that he had to return to the capital after he was slandered in Huachow, but the official history asserts that he was summoned there. At that time, the men who served the Liang dynasty were all under Tuan Ning, and the troops in the capital, a weak and decimated force, amounted to scarcely a few thousand. Wang was only able to secure five hundred palace guards, with whom he went to Yünchow. With this insufficient force, he was defeated at Chungtu.[14] There is equally little substance in the allegation of the official history that five thousand troops were under his command on this occasion.

Before proceeding to attack Tehsheng, Wang had received orders personally from the emperor and pledged that he would accomplish his mission of annihilating the enemy within three days. All the high officials of the Liang dynasty, civilian and military, who had got wind of this pledge, laughed at him behind his back. As it turned out, however, the capture of the southern city took only three days. At the time, Emperor Chuang-tsung of the Tsin dynasty was in Wei. Having heard of Wang's reinstatement, the emperor expected him to make a precipitate attack. Though the emperor rode at full speed from Wei to the rescue of the beleaguered town, it was too late. How uncanny the prescience of Emperor Chuang-tsung and the unusual strategy of Wang!

Our country has been at peace for forty years. With the outbreak of Yüan-hao's[15] rebellion, for four or five years government forces have sustained defeats and many of their commanding officers were killed. Nevertheless, plans for offense and defense have not yet been formulated. I have been alone in suggesting recourse to an unusual strategy for victory, and I have often regretted that border commanders have missed

歎邊將屢失其機。時人聞予說者，或笑以爲狂，或忽若不聞，雖予亦惑，不能自信。

及讀公家傳，至於德勝之捷，乃知古之名將，必出於奇，然後能勝，然非審於爲計者不能出奇。奇在速，速在果，此天下偉男子之所爲，非拘牽常筭之士可到也。每讀其傳，未嘗不想見其人。

後二年，予復來，通判州事。歲之正月，過俗所謂鐵槍寺者，又得公畫像而拜焉。歲久磨滅，隱隱可見。亟命工完理之，而不敢有加焉，懼失其眞也。

公善用槍，當時號王鐵槍。公死已百年，至今俗猶以名其寺，童兒牧豎，皆知王鐵槍之爲良將也。一槍之勇，同時豈無？而公獨不朽者，豈其忠義之節使然歟？

畫已百餘年矣，完之復可百年，然公之不泯者，不繫乎畫之存不存也。而予尤區區如此者，蓋其希慕之至焉耳。讀其書，尚想乎其人，況得拜其像，識其面目，不忍見其壞也。畫既完，因書予所得者于後，而歸其人，使藏之。

all their opportunities. Those who have heard of my suggestions have either ridiculed them as senseless or pretended to pay no attention to them. As a result, even I myself have begun to have misgivings and lose my self-confidence.

However, after reading in the family history of Wang the account of his victory at Tehsheng. I learned that famous generals in olden times had to depend on an unusual strategy for their victories, but that this strategy could only be resorted to after careful deliberation. Success hinges on speed, and speed, in turn, on determination. This is the typical action of the great men of the world, unattainable by those who are confined within the narrow bounds of normal calculations. Whenever I read Wang's family history, I cannot help thinking of the man.

Two years later, I was again appointed to the prefecture as T'ung-p'an. In the first month, I passed what was popularly known as the Iron Spear Temple, where I obtained Wang's portrait before which I did homage. After years of wear and tear, the image was almost effaced but still faintly visible. At once I ordered an artisan to restore it without, however, adding to the features, lest the true likeness be lost.

A skillful spearman, Wang was known at the time as Iron Spear Wang. Even now, a century after his death, the temple still bears his nickname, and children and herdsmen are aware that Iron Spear Wang was a gifted commander. Wang could not have been unique among his contemporaries merely by virtue of his prowess with the spear, but only he has been immortalized. Is not this perhaps due to his loyalty and righteousness?

The portrait has endured for more than a century, and, having been restored, it can last another century. But Wang's immortality does not hinge on the existence of the portrait, and my special regard for him is due to my unbounded admiration and devotion. Since the story has brought back his memory to us, how much more will we think of him now that we have his portrait before us! Having become familiar with his features, I cannot bear to see the portrait in bad shape. Now that it has been restored, I have set down as a postscript what I have learned, and returned the painting to its owner for safekeeping.

六 一 居 士 傳

六一居士初謫滁山[1]，自號醉翁。既老而衰且病，將退休於潁水[2]之上，則又更號六一居士。

客有問曰：「六一何謂也？」居士曰：「吾家藏書一萬卷，集錄三代以來金石遺文一千卷[3]，有琴一張，有碁一局，而常置酒一壺。」客曰：「是爲五一爾。奈何？」居士曰：「以吾一翁老於此五物之間。是豈不爲六一乎？」

客笑曰：「子欲逃名者乎？而屢易其號。此莊生[4]所謂畏影而走乎日中者也。余將見子疾走大喘渴死，而名不得逃也。」

居士曰：「吾固知名之不可逃，然亦知夫不必逃也。吾爲此名，聊以志吾之樂爾。」

客曰：「其樂如何？」

居士曰：「吾之樂可勝道哉？方其得意於五物也，泰山[5]在前而不見，疾雷破柱而不驚，雖響九奏於洞庭[6]之野，閱大戰於涿鹿[7]之原，未足喻其樂且適也。然常患不得極吾

---

[1] A mountain in Ch'uchow, a prefecture in modern Anhwei Province, where Ou-yang Hsiu was once demoted as Prefect.

[2] A river flowing from Honan to Anhwei Province.

[3] Subdivision of a book, usually containing (in those days) less than a volume.

[4] A great philosopher of the Chou dynasty belonging to the Taoist school.

[5] A mountain range in Shantung Province.

[6] A lake in Central China.

[7] A mountain southeast of Cholu *Hsien* 涿鹿縣 , Hopei Province.

Biography of Retired Scholar Liu-i

When Retired Scholar Liu-i was first relegated to the Ch'u Mountain,[1] he gave himself the nickname of Old Drunkard. When he grew old, infirm and sick and on the point of retiring on the Ying River,[2] he gave himself the further nickname of Retired Scholar Liu-i (six-one).

When a friend asked him, "What does Liu-i stand for?" he said, "In my house I have a collection of ten thousand *chüan*[3] of books, a hand-copied collection in one thousand *chüan* of extant bronze and stone rubbings from the Three Dynasties, together with a lyre, a chess set and an ever-ready pot of wine." "That makes only five units," said the friend; "what about the sixth one?" The retired scholar said, "There is an old man, aging among these five things; does that not make six units?"

The friend smiled and replied, "In changing your nickname repeatedly, are you trying to escape from your real name? This is what Chuang-tzu[4] had in mind when he said that one walks under the center of the sunlight to avoid one's shadow. I can see that you will never succeed in escaping from your name even when you are running fast, gasping ceaselessly and dying from thirst."

"I know indeed," said the retired scholar, "that I cannot escape from my name, nor do I deem it necessary. I gave myself this nickname only to show my pleasure."

"Pleasure at what?" asked the friend.

"How can I exhaust the subject? When I am enraptured with the five treasures, I would not see the T'ai Mountains[5] even if they were right in front of me; I am not perturbed by the quick thunderclap which shatters a pillar; and the most magnificent music played in the wildernesses of the Tungt'ing[6] and the observation of a battle on the plains by Cholu[7] cannot compare with the pleasure and gratification afforded by these five things. But I cannot always extract the most out of them

197

樂於其間者，世事之爲吾累者衆也。其大者有二焉。軒裳
珪組，勞吾形於外。憂患思慮，勞吾心於內。使吾形不病
而已悴，心未老而先衰。尚何暇於五物哉？雖然，吾自乞
其身於朝者三年矣。一日，天子惻然哀之，賜其骸骨，使
得與此五物偕返於田廬，庶幾償其夙願焉。此吾之所以志
也。」

　　客復笑曰：「子知軒裳珪組之累其形，而不知五物之
累其心乎？」

　　居士曰：「不然，累於彼者，已勞矣，又多憂。累於
此者，既佚矣，幸無患。吾其何擇哉？」

　　於是與客俱起，握手大笑曰：「置之。區區不足較也。」
已而歎曰：「夫士少而仕，老而休，蓋有不待七十者矣。
吾素慕之。宜去一也。吾嘗用於時矣，而訖無稱焉。宜去
二也。壯猶如此，今既老且病矣，乃以難彊之筋骸，貪過
分之榮祿，是將違其素志，而自食其言。宜去三也。吾負
三宜去，雖無五物，其去宜矣。復何道哉？」

　　熙寧三年九月七日六一居士自傳。

---

[8]A.D. 1070, in the reign of Emperor Shen-tsung.

because of the many mundane affairs on my mind. There are in particular two. First, my official position burdens my body with hard work externally, and, secondly, my anxiety and deliberations strain my mind internally. As a result, my body, though not sick, is infirm, and my mind has become feeble even before I grow old. What leisure do I have to enjoy the five things? However, for three years I have asked to be allowed to retire from the court. If one day the Son of Heaven takes pity on me and relieves me, so that I may return to my farm house with the five things, I shall fulfill the wish I have long entertained. This is what I really look forward to."

The friend smiled again and said, "Very well, you know that your official position burdens your body, but do you not also know that the five things can burden your mind?"

"No, Sir," replied the retired scholar. "What troubles my body gives me not only physical fatigue but also endless mental anxiety, but what troubles my mind can be shrugged off and cause no distress. Is it not clear what my choice should be?"

Both of them rose. "Let us leave these things alone," said the retired scholar, laughing loudly and holding hands with his friend. "They are mere trifles, and not worth considering." Then he sighed, and added, "Scholars serve as officials when young, and retire when aged, some even before they are seventy. I have always longed for that. This is the first reason why I should retire. My services have been used in my time, but I have as yet made no name for myself. This is the second reason why I should retire. Since I did not make good in my youth, now that I am old and sick, I may run counter to the ambition I have always had and fail to keep my word, if I continue to seek excessive honors and emoluments with a body that can hardly become stronger. This is the third reason why I should retire. In view of these three reasons, I should go even without the five things. What more is there to be said?"

> Autobiography of Retired Scholar Liu-i,
> the seventh day of the ninth month of the
> third year of Hsi-ning.[8]

瀧　岡　阡　表

　　嗚呼，惟我皇考崇公，卜吉于瀧岡之六十年，其子脩始克表於其阡。非敢緩也，蓋有待也。

　　脩不幸，生四歲而孤，太夫人守節自誓。居窮自力於衣食，以長以教，俾至于成人。太夫人告之曰：

　　「汝父爲吏，廉而好施與，喜賓客。其俸祿雖薄，常不使有餘。曰：『毋以是爲我累。』故其亡也，無一瓦之覆，一壟之植，以庇而爲生。吾何恃而能自守邪？吾於汝父，知其一二，以有待於汝也。

　　「自吾爲汝家婦，不及事吾姑，然知汝父之能養也。汝孤而幼，吾不能知汝之必有立，然知汝父之必將有後也。吾之始歸也，汝父免於母喪方逾年。歲時祭祀，則必涕泣曰：『祭而豐，不如養之薄也。』間御酒食，則又涕泣曰：『昔常不足，而今有餘。其何及也？』

　　「吾始一二見之，以爲新免於喪適然耳。既而其後常然，至其終身，未嘗不然。吾雖不及事姑，而以此知汝父之能養也。

[1] The Fenghuang Mountain 鳳凰山 , Yungfeng *Hsien* 永豐縣 , Kiangsi Province.

Inscription on the Memorial Tablet for the Passage to the Shuangkang[1] Tomb

Alas, sixty years after the burial of my revered father, the Duke of Ch'ung, at Shuangkang, I am at last able to erect this tablet for the passage to his tomb! The reason for the long delay is not that I have ventured to procrastinate, but that I have been obliged to wait.

Unfortunately I was bereaved of my father at the age of four. My mother vowed to live out her life as a widow, though she had to maintain a poor family by working to earn food and clothing. She reared and taught me until I grew up, when she told me:

"Your father was an incorruptible official, but he was fond of giving to others and extending hospitality to his guests. Though his emoluments were few, he always saw to it that nothing was left. 'Let not this be a source of embarrassment to me!' he would say. And so he died without leaving even a house with a single tile on its roof, or a single piece of cultivated land on which the family could have depended for its living. What was it, then, that I counted on to sustain me? I knew one or two things about your father, which gave me reason to wait for you to grow up.

"When I married into your family, I was not in time to serve my mother-in-law. But I knew that your father was a filial son. You lost your father when you were young, and I could not be sure that you would one day stand on your own feet. But I knew that your father was destined to have worthy offspring. When I was first joined with your father, he had hardy passed the mourning period for his mother a little over a year earlier. Whenever memorial services were held, he would say with tears: 'Sacrificial offerings, however abundant, cannot compare with even scanty food for parents when they are still alive.' Occasionally, when he had something to eat and drink, he mourned tearfully. 'Before, we scarcely had enough,' he said, 'and now there is always something left. But is it not too late?'

"When I witnessed this expression of grief once or twice, I thought that it was only because he had recently passed the mourning period. Later, I observed that his grief was always the same and that it was no different for the rest of his life. That is why I knew that your father was a filial son though I was not in time to serve my mother-in-law.

201

「汝父爲吏，嘗夜燭治官書，屢廢而歎。吾問之，則曰：『此死獄也。我求其生不得爾。』吾曰：『生可求乎？』曰：『求其生而不得，則死者與我皆無恨也。矧求而有得邪？以其有得，則知不求而死者有恨也。夫常求其生，猶失之死，而世常求其死也。』

「回顧乳者抱汝而立于旁，因指而歎曰：『術者謂我歲行在戌將死。使其言然，吾不及見兒之立也。後當以我語告之。』其平居教他子弟，常用此語。吾耳熟焉，故能詳也。

「其施於外事，吾不能知。其居于家，無所矜飾，而所爲如此。是眞發於中者邪？嗚呼，其心厚於仁者邪？此吾知汝父之必將有後也。汝其勉之。夫養不必豐，要於孝。利雖不得博於物，要其心之厚於仁。吾不能敎汝，此汝父之志也。」

脩泣而志之，不敢忘。

先公少孤力學，咸平三年，進士及第。爲道州判官，泗綿二州推官，又爲泰州判官。享年五十有九，葬沙溪之瀧岡。

太夫人姓鄭氏，考諱德儀，世爲江南名族。太夫人恭儉仁愛而有禮。初封福昌縣太君，進封樂安，安康，彭城

[2] One of the twelve characters forming the second part of the customary designation of a Chinese calendar year.

[3] A.D. 1000, in the reign of Chen-tsung 眞宗.

[4] Title of a subordinate official.

[5] Prefecture in modern Hunan Province.

[6] Title of a subordinate official.

[7] Prefecture in modern Anhwei Province.

[8] Prefecture in modern Szechwan Province.

[9] Prefecture in modern Kiangsu Province.

"When your father was an official, once he burnt candles at night to read his documents. Repeatedly he stopped and sighed. I asked him why. 'This is a case calling for the death penalty,' he said, 'and I cannot seek to make the criminal live.' '*Can* you seek to make a criminal live?' I asked him. 'If I seek and fail,' he replied, 'both the criminal to be condemned and I have no regrets. Can there be any regrets if I succeed? Since success is something possible, we know how much it is regretted when one has not sought to make the criminal live. Though I always try, I fail at times. Yet the world always seeks the death of such a criminal!'

"Turning around, he saw the wet-nurse at our side, holding you in her arms. He pointed at you and sighed. 'The fortune-teller warns me,' he said, 'that I shall die in the year of Hsü.[2] If he is right, I shall not see the boy grow up. Remember to tell him what I have just said to you.' When he had occasion to teach other youngsters of the family, he always made the same remark. I heard it so many times that I am very familiar with it.

"I know nothing about what he did outside the family, but at home he was never boastful or pretentious. Truly, was the way he conducted himself not all initiated from his inner self? Was his heart not filled with humaneness? This is why I knew that your father was destined to have worthy offspring. Exert yourself! In serving one's parents, abundance is not always essential, but filial love is. Although not everyone can be expected to share in all benefits, the important thing is a deeply humane heart. I am incapable of teaching you. This was the will of your father."

I sobbed, kept all this in my memory, and never dared to forget it.

My father was also bereaved of his father at an early age. He devoted himself diligently to his studies. In the third year of Hsien-p'ing,[3] he won his *chin-shih* degree. He then served successively as P'an-kuan[4] of Taochow,[5] T'ui-kuan[6] of Ssuchow[7] and Mienchow,[8] and P'an-kuan of Taichow.[9] He died at the age of fifty-nine and was buried at Shuangkang, Shach'i.

My mother was the daughter of Cheng Teh-i and came from a family south of the Yangtze, which had been well-known for generations. She was respectful, frugal and benevolent, and observed all the tenets of propriety. She was first given the title of Lady of Fuch'ang *Hsien* and promoted to Lady of Lo-an, Ank'ang and P'engch'eng *Chün*. Ever since

203

三郡太君。自其家少微時，治其家以儉約，其後常不使過之。曰：「吾兒不能苟合於世。儉薄所以居患難也。」其後脩貶夷陵，太夫人言笑自若，曰：「汝家故貧賤也，吾處之有素矣。汝能安之，吾亦安矣。」

自先公之亡二十年，脩始得祿而養。又十有二年，列官于朝，始得贈封其親。又十年，脩爲龍圖閣直學士尚書吏部郎中，留守南京。太夫人以疾終于官舍，享年七十有二。

又八年，脩以非才入副樞密，遂參政事。又七年而罷。

自登二府，天子推恩，襃其三世。故自嘉祐以來，逢國大慶，必加寵錫。皇曾祖府君，累贈金紫光祿大夫，太師，中書令。曾祖妣累封楚國太夫人。皇祖府君，累贈金紫光祿大夫，太師，中書令兼尚書令。祖妣累封吳國太夫人。皇考崇公，累贈金紫光祿大夫，太師，中書令兼尚書令。皇妣累封越國太夫人。今上初郊，皇考賜爵爲崇國公，太夫人進號魏國。

於是小子脩泣而言曰：

「嗚呼，爲善無不報，而遲速有時，此理之常也。惟我祖考，積善成德，宜享其隆。雖不克有於其躬，而賜爵

---

[10] As Magistrate of Iling, now Ichang 宜昌 *Hsien*, Hupeh Province.

[11] Sungchow 宋州, modern Shangch'iu 商邱 *Hsien*, Honan Province.

[12] 1056-1063, reign of Emperor Jen-tsung.

[13] Title of Prime Minister.

[14] Title of another Prime Minister.

she was young, she had run her house frugally, and even in her later life she never exceeded the limits set earlier. "My son." she said to me, "you cannot loosely conform to the way of the world. Frugality is what one needs in adverstiy." Subsequently, when I was demoted to Iling,[10] my mother talked and smiled as always. "Your family has always been poor," she said. "So I am accustomed to it. If you can feel unperturbed, so can I."

It was twenty years after the decease of my father that I began to receive official emoluments for the support of my family. It was twelve more years later that I became an official at court and was able to bring honor to my parents. Ten more years elapsed before I became Secretary of the Lung-t'u Library and Division Director of the Personnel Ministry in the Cabinet. I was detailed to serve in the Southern Capital.[11] It was then that my mother died at the age of seventy-two in my official residence.

Eight years later, despite my humble talent, I was appointed Vice Premier and given the opportunity to participate in the important affairs of state. I served in this capacity for seven years, at the end of which I vacated the post.

Since the time when I was invested with the Vice Premiership, Their Majesties have extended favors to my family by posthumously honoring three generations of my immediate forbears. In particular, since the reign of Chia-yu,[12] on the occasion of every national celebration, rare honors have been conferred on them. My great-grandfather was given the First Rank and the titles of Grand Teacher of the Imperial Household and Chung-shu-ling;[13] my great-grandmother, the title of Elder Lady of Ch'u; my grandfather, the First Rank and the titles of Grand Teacher of the Imperial Household, Chung-shu-ling and Shang-shu-ling,[14] my grandmother, the title of Elder Lady of Wu; my father, the Duke of Ch'ung, the First Rank and the titles of Grand Teacher of the Imperial Household, Chung-shu-ling and Shang-shu-ling; and my mother, the title of Elder Lady of Yüeh. On the occasion of his first offerings to Heaven, His reigning Majesty conferred on my father the title of Duke of Ch'ung and promoted my mother to Elder Lady of Wei.

I cannot help being moved to tears when I say this:

"Good deeds are never unrewarded, although it may be early or late. This is a truism. My grandfather accumulated many good deeds and had great virtue. He deserved indeed a rich reward. Although he did not

205

受封顯榮襃大，實有三朝之錫命。是足以表見於後世，而
庇賴其子孫矣。」

乃列其世譜，具刻于碑。既又載我皇考崇公之遺訓，
太夫人之所以教人而有待於脩者，並揭于阡，俾知夫小子
脩之德薄能鮮，遭時竊位，而幸全大節，不辱其先者，其
來有自。

receive it in his lifetime, yet posthumous titles and honors have been bestowed on him and have been sanctified by the solemn mandates of three imperial reigns. This is an illustrious example for future generations and a blessing for his own children and children's children."

Wherefore I have set down the tabular history of the family and caused it to be engraved on the tablet. I have also recorded in it my father's testaments and the manner in which my mother taught me and waited for me to grow up. I have done this to make known that there is ample reason why I have been so fortunate as to be able to keep my integrity intact and brought no disgrace on my ancestors, though, with my modest virtue and limited ability, I have merely been favored by the times and never deserved the positions I have held.

七 賢 畫 序

　　某不幸少孤。先人爲錦州軍事推官時，某始生。生四歲，而先人捐館。某爲兒童時，先妣嘗謂某曰：

　　「吾歸汝家時，極貧，汝父爲吏至廉，又於物無所嗜。惟喜賓客，不計其家有無，以具酒食。在錦州三年，他人皆多買蜀物以歸，汝父不營一物，而俸祿待賓客，亦無餘。已罷官，有絹一匹，畫爲七賢圖六幅。此七君子，吾所愛也。此外無蜀物。」

　　後先人調泰州軍事判官，卒於任。比某十許歲時，家益貧。每歲時設席祭祀，則張此圖於壁。先妣必指某曰：「吾家故物也。」

　　後三十餘年，圖亦故闇。某忝立朝，懼其久而益朽損，遂取七賢命工裝軸之。更可傳百餘年，以爲歐陽氏舊物，且使子孫不忘先世之清風，而示吾先君所好尚，又以見吾母少寡而子幼，能克成其家，不失舊物。蓋自先君有事後二十年，某始及第，今又二十三年矣。事迹如此，始爲作贊並序。

---

[1] Title of a subordinate official.
[2] Prefecture in modern Szechwan Province.
[3] Prefecture in modern Kiangsu Province.

On the Portraits of the Seven Worthy Men

I had the misfortune of losing my father at a very early age. I was born when he was Military T'ui-kuan[1] of Mienchow,[2] and I was only four when he died. In my childhood, my mother said to me:

"When I married into your family, we were very poor. Your father was an incorruptible official. He had no liking for anything material, and he was only fond of his friends, whom he entertained with food and drinks irrespective of his financial condition. While others mostly bought products of Szechwan and took them home, your father never collected a single item in his three years' stay there. After defraying the expenses of entertainment, he had nothing left from his emoluments. When he gave up his post, he had only a roll of silk, which was cut into six scrolls and on which were painted the portraits of seven worthy men. I have always admired these seven gentlemen, but apart from these paintings we had nothing from Szechwan."

Later, my father was transformed to T'aichow,[3] also as Military P'an kuan. It was in that office that he died. When I was a little over ten years old, my family became even poorer. At New Year, when we made offerings to our ancestors, the scrolls were always hung on the walls. On such occasions, my mother was in the habit of pointing at me and saying: "The scrolls are our family mementoes."

More than thirty years elapsed, and the paintings became very faint from age. I was then an official at Court. Lest they should deteriorate further with the passage of time, I had them remounted by an artisan, so that they could be kept for another century or more as an heirloom of the Ou-yang family, to enable our children and children's children not to forget their immaculate ancestral tradition, and to show them the taste and preferences of my deceased father and the ability of my mother to maintain the family without losing its treasured heritage, despite her early widowhood, with a young son to bring up. It was more than twenty years after my father's death that I passed the imperial examination, and now it is again twenty-three years since that time. Such were the facts, and I take this opportunity to set them down in writing as a eulogy.

209

蘇

文公

公常嘆曰知我者惟吾父與歐陽公也歐陽公作公墓誌銘述其語而美公文博辯宏偉又謂為純明篤實君子且又其善與人交急難臨死之賢

Su Hsün (1009-1066)

Three of the eight great masters came from the Su family, consisting of Hsün and his two sons, Shih 軾 and Ch'e 轍. Hsün's courtesy name was Ming-yün 明允, but he was also called Lao-ch'üan 老泉, a name by which he is better known. The family came from Meishan 眉山 in Szechwan Province.

Lao-ch'üan was not hard-working as a student. In fact, he had never been studious until he reached the age of twenty-seven. Having failed more than once to pass the imperial examination, he went home, burnt all his writings and shut himself up in his study. As a result, he became well versed in the six classics and the hundred schools of philosophy.

During the reign of the Sung emperor Jen-tsung 仁宗, he accompanied his two sons to the capital, where he submitted twenty-two of his writings to Ou-yang Hsiu. The great man appreciated and praised them very highly, and regarded them as unexcelled, even by the works of such famous Han authors as Chia I 賈誼 and Liu Hsiang 劉向.[1] He in turn submitted the works to the throne, whereupon Lao-ch'üan was summoned to take a special examination, which he declined. He was then appointed to the Secretariat as one of its editors. Later, he was ordered by imperial decree to collect all the books on rites written since the inauguration of the dynasty. Finally he was assigned as Chu-pu 主簿[2] to Wen-an 文安 *Hsien*, Pachow 覇州,[3] and cooperated with Yao P'i 姚闢, Magistrate of Hsiangch'eng 項城, Ch'enchow 陳州,[4] in editing the dynastic book of rites.

No sooner were one hundred *chüan* of the work completed than Lao-ch'üan passed away, even before the report on it

[1] Great prose writers of the Han dynasty.
[2] Title of a subordinate local official in charge of archives.
[3] Prefecture in modern Hopei Province.
[4] Prefecture in modern Honan Province.

could reach the throne. The news grieved the emperor, who conferred on him a posthumous title and ordered the competent authorities to send his remains by boat to Szechwan to be buried. Lao-ch'üan left twenty *chüan* of his collected works（嘉祐集）and three *chüan* of *Rules on Canonization* 諡法 .

Prime Minister under Duke Huan of Ch'i 齊桓公, who reigned in 685-643 B.C.

A favorite minister under Duke Huan.

A culinary expert.

Another favorite minister under Duke Huan, who was a prince of Wei.

One of the later rulers of Ch'i.

Pao Shu-ya 鮑叔牙, a bosom friend of Kuan Chung.

Hsan-fou 弦父, Kung-kung 共工, San-miao 三苗 and Kun 鯀.

A high official in the state of Lu, where Confucius served as Minister of Justice

管　仲　論

　　管仲相桓公，霸諸侯，攘戎狄。終其身，齊國富彊，諸侯不叛。

　　管仲死，豎刁，易牙，開方用。桓公薨於亂，五公子爭立，其禍蔓延。訖簡公，齊無甯歲。

　　夫功之成，非成於成之日，蓋必有所由起。禍之作，不作於作之日，亦必有所由兆。則齊之治也，吾不曰管仲，而曰鮑叔。及其亂也，吾不曰豎刁，易牙，開方，而曰管仲。

　　何則？豎刁，易牙，開方三子，彼固亂人國者，顧其用之者，桓公也。夫有舜而後知放四凶。有仲尼而後知去少正卯。彼桓公何人也？顧其使桓公得用三子者，管仲也。仲之疾也，公問之相。當是時也，吾以仲且舉天下之賢者以對，而其言乃不過曰：「豎刁，易牙，開方三子，非人情不可近而已。」嗚呼，仲以爲桓公果能不用三子矣乎？

　　仲與桓公處幾年矣。亦知桓公之爲人矣乎？桓公聲不絕乎耳，色不絕乎目，而非三子者，則無以遂其欲。彼其

---

[1] Prime Minister under Duke Huan of Ch'i 齊桓公, who reigned in 685-643 B.C.
[2] A favorite minister under Duke Huan.
[3] A culinary expert.
[4] Another favorite minister under Duke Huan, who was a prince of Wei.
[5] One of the later rulers of Ch'i.
[6] Pao Shu-ya 鮑叔牙, a bosom friend of Kuan Chung.
[7] Huan-tou 驩兜, Kung-kung 共工, San-miao 三苗 and Kun 鯀.
[8] A high official in the state of Lu, where Confucius served as Minister of Justice.

On Kuan Chung[1]

Kuan Chung served as the Prime Minister under Duke Huan and helped him bring under control the other feudal lords and keep the barbarians out. Throughout Kuan's lifetime, the state of Ch'i was rich and strong; the other feudal lords did not dare to rise against it.

When Kuan Chung died, Shu Tiao,[2] I Ya[3] and K'ai Fang[4] jointly took his place. Duke Huan perished at a time when his state was in disorder. His five princes contended for the throne, and there was widespread trouble. Up to the reign of Duke Chien[5] there was not a year of peace.

Success is not achieved in a day, but its origins can be traced. Likewise, catastrophe is not generated in a day, but has its omens. I therefore attribute the good government of Ch'i, not to Kuan Chung, but to Pao Shu.[6] On the other hand, I ascribe the disorder, not to Shu Tiao, I Ya and K'ai Fang, but to Kuan Chung.

True, Shu Tiao, I Ya and K'ai Fang were bound to bring disaster on any state, and Duke Huan himself was responsible for their appointment. However, it took an Emperor Shun to banish the four evil men,[7] and it took a Confucius to get rid of Shao-cheng Mao.[8] After all, who was Duke Huan [compared with these two sages]? The responsibility was indeed that of Kuan Chung in inducing the duke to obtain the services of the three men. When Kuan Chung was ill, Duke Huan asked him who could succeed him as prime minister. To my mind, Kuan could have recommended one of the deserving men in the empire. Instead, he merely observed that the three men lacked the human touch and that they should not be permitted to become intimate with the duke. Alas, how could Kuan really believe that the duke was sure to reject the three men?

Since Kuan had been with Duke Huan for several years, how could he have been ignorant of the duke's character? Duke Huan's ears could never be closed to music nor could his eyes miss beauty. Without the three men, he could not have satisfied these desires. It was only because Kuan was still there that the duke had not at first availed himself of the

215

初之所以不用者，徒以有仲焉耳。一日無仲，則三子者可以彈冠相慶矣。仲以爲將死之言，可以縶桓公之手足邪？

夫齊國不患有三子，而患無仲。有仲，則三子者，三匹夫耳。不然，天下豈少三子之徒？雖桓公幸而聽仲，誅此三人，而其餘者，仲能悉數而去之邪？嗚呼，仲可謂不知本者矣。

因桓公之問，舉天下之賢者以自代，則仲雖死，而齊國未爲無仲也。夫何患三子者？不言可也。

五霸莫盛於桓文。文公之才，不過桓公，其臣又皆不及仲。靈公之虐，不如孝公之寬厚。文公死，諸侯不敢叛晉。晉襲文公之餘威，得爲諸侯之盟主者百有餘年。何者？其君雖不肖，而尚有老成人焉。

桓公之薨也，一敗塗地，無惑也。彼獨恃一管仲，而仲則死矣。夫天下未嘗無賢者，蓋有有臣而無君者矣。桓公在焉，而曰天下不復有管仲者，吾不信也。

仲之書，有記其將死，論鮑叔，賓胥無之爲人，且各疏其短。是其心以爲是數子者，皆不足以託國，而又逆知其將死。則其書誕謾，不足信也。

---

[9] Ruler of the state of Tsin, who reigned in 636-628 B.C.

[10] A later ruler of Tsin, who was murdered in 607 B.C.

[11] A later ruler of Ch'i.

[12] Kuan Chung's philosophical work.

[13] One of the officials of Ch'i.

[14] Hsi P'eng's death. Hsi P'eng 隰朋 was a minister of the state of Ch'i, whom Kuan Chung recommended to Duke Huan. His death was correctly predicted by Kuan Chung. See *Kuan-tzu*, Book X, Ch. 26, *Chieh*.

services of the three men. But, once Kuan was gone, they could be sure of their appointment and congratulate themselves on it beforehand. Did Kuan really think that words spoken on his deathbed could bind Duke Huan hand and foot?

The cause of Ch'i's trouble was not so much the presence of the three men as the absence of Kuan. When he was there, the three were men of no consequence. Furthermore, were there not plenty of others in the world like them? Even if Duke Huan had fortunately listened to Kuan by going so far as to put the three men to death, could Kuan have removed all the rest of their ilk? Alas, must it not be said that Kuan overlooked the essence of the matter?

If, in answer to Duke Huan, he had recommended one of the sages in the empire to take his place, the situation would have remained the same as if he had continued to live. In that event, what difference would the three men have made? Kuan could just as well have said nothing about them at all.

Of the five powerful feudal lords at the time, the most successful were Dukes Huan and Wen.[9] Wen did not surpass Huan in ability, and none of Wen's ministers could equal Kuan. In addition, Duke Ling's[10] cruelty was set against the magnanimity of Duke Hsiao.[11] But, after the death of Duke Wen, no feudal lord dared to rise against Tsin. With the power handed down from him, Tsin continued to be the overlord of the feudal states for more than a century, because there were still elderly and experienced men to guide it, though the rulers themselves were unworthy of their predecessors.

When Duke Huan died, his country suffered the most crushing defeats. This was nothing to be wondered at, because Kuan Chung, on whom he had relied entirely, was dead. There is no lack of worthy men in this world, but it can happen that, when there are good subjects, there is no ruler to make use of them. However, I cannot believe that as long as Duke Huan was at the helm, another Kuan Chung could not have been found.

The *Book of Kuan-tzu*[12] records that, when Kuan Chung approached the end of his life, he commented on Pao Shu and Pin Hsü-wu's[13] character together with their shortcomings. He evidently thought that these men could not be trusted with the task of running the state, although he could foresee his approaching death.[14] The book must have been delusive and untrustworthy.

吾觀史鰌，以不能進蘧伯玉而退彌子瑕，故有身後之諫。蕭何且死，舉曹參以自代。大臣之用心，固宜如此也。

夫國以一人興，以一人亡。賢者不悲其身之死，而憂其國之衰，故必復有賢者，而後可以死。彼管仲者，何以死哉？

---

[15] A gentleman from the state of Wei.

[16] A favorite minister under Duke Ling of Wei.

[17] Ta-fu, a high official, of the state of Wei.

[18] Because of his failure, Shih Ch'iu left this will to his sons: "While I lived, I could not rectify my ruler's mistakes. Hence, when I die, let there be no funeral ceremony, but place my body under the window in our house." When Duke Ling went to express his condolences, he was surprised and asked for an explanation of this arrangement. When Shih Ch'iu's sons told him the reason, Duke Ling honored Ch'ü Po-yü and dismissed Mi Tzu-hsia.

[19] When this Prime Minister (under Emperor Kao-tsu and Emperor Hui of the Han dynasty) was sick, Emperor Hui went to inquire about his health and asked who would be a suitable successor. "No one," replied Hsiao, "knows his subjects better than the ruler." "What about Ts'ao Shen 曹參?" asked the Emperor. "Your Majesty has the right man in mind," answered Hsiao with a bow.

I note that, because he had failed in his attempt to recommend Ch'ü Po-yü[15] for office and to oust Mi Tzu-hsia,[16] Shih Ch'iu[17] left a remonstrance after his death,[18] and that, when Hsiao Ho[19] was dying, he recommended Ts'ao Shen to replace him. Such should have been the thoughtfulness of great statesmen.

A country often rises to great heights because of one man and comes to a sad end for the same reason. Worthy men are not sorry for their own death, but are worried about the decline of their country after they are gone. They should therefore die only when there are worthy successors. Why did Kuan Chung die as he did?

與 梅 聖 兪 書

聖兪足下：睽間忽復歲晚。昨九月中，嘗發書，計已達左右。洵閒居經歲，益知無事之樂。舊病漸復散去，獨恨淪廢山林，不得聖兪，永叔相與談笑，深以嗟惋。

自離京師，行已二年。不意朝廷尚未見遣，以其不肖之文，猶有可者。前月承本州發遣，赴闕就試。聖兪自思，僕豈欲試者？惟其平生不能區區附合有司之尺度，是以至此窮困。今乃以五十衰病之身，奔走萬里以就試，不亦爲山林之士所輕笑哉？

自思少年嘗舉茂才，中夜起坐，裹飯攜餅，待曉東華門外，逐隊而入，屈膝就席，俯首據案。其後每思至此，即爲寒心。今齒日益老，尚安能使達官貴人，復弄其文墨，以窮其所不知邪？

且以永叔之言，與夫三書之所云，皆世之所見。今千里召僕而試之，蓋其心尚有所未信，此尤不可苟進以求其榮利也。

昨適有病，遂以此辭。然恐無以答朝廷之恩，因爲上

---

[1]Courtesy name of Mei Yao-ch'eng 梅堯臣, a great scholar and poet of the Sung dynasty.

[2]Courtesy name of Ou-yang Hsiu 歐陽修.

[3]The first degree conferred on successful candidates in the lower-level local examination.

Letter to Mei Sheng-yü[1]

Dear Sheng-yü:

So soon after our separation it is again the end of the year. I sent you a letter in the middle of the ninth month, which you must have received. After staying home for over a year doing nothing, I am all the more conscious of the pleasure of idleness. My old ailment is gradually disappearing, and my only regret now is that I live confined in the mountains and woods and cannot talk and jest with you and Yung-shu.[2]

Two years have already passed since I left the capital. It gives me unexpected pleasure to learn that the court has not yet forsaken me and does not consider my unworthy writings unacceptable. Last month, the prefecture here urged me to go to the capital for an examination. Just think, Sheng-yü, am I the kind of men who longs to sit the examination? All my life I have been unable to comply with the requirements of the competent authorities, which is the cause of my being in such straits. Today, when I have passed my fiftieth year and my health is declining, would I not become the laughingstock of all those scholars who have withdrawn to the mountains and woods if I traveled ten thousand *li* to sit the examination?

I recall what, when I was young and took the examination for the *mao-ts'ai* degree,[3] I had to get up in the middle of the night, pack my rice and carry my cakes, wait outside the Tung-hua Gate till dawn and join other candidates to enter the hall. There I had to sit at my desk with knees bent and my head bowed. Later, whenever I have thought of this, it has dampened my spirits. Now that I am much older, how can I permit those prominent officials to test my literary ability again and expose my ignorance in the greatest detail?

Moreover, the world must have taken note of what Yung-shu had said and the contents of my three messages. The fact that I am summoned from afar to take the examination shows that the authorities still have no confidence in me. It is all the more inappropriate for me to seek honor and advancement with such a lack of scruples.

As I happened to be sick yesterday, I declined on that pretext. But, lest I give offense by failing to show appreciation of the court's high

221

皇帝書一通以進，蓋以自解其不至之罪而已。不知聖俞當
見之否？

冬寒，千萬加愛。

favor, I have submitted a memorial to the emperor to explain my remissness in answering the summons. I do not know whether you, Sheng-yü, happened to see it.

Since the winter cold is again upon us, be sure to take good care of yourself.

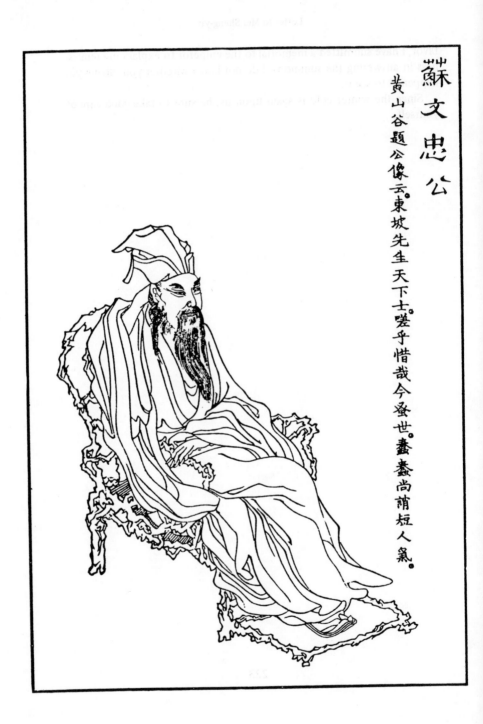

蘇文忠公

黄山谷題公像云東坡先生天下士嗟乎惜哉今蓋世盡盡尚萌短人氣

Su Shih (1037-1101)

Su Shih, the great prose writer, poet, statesman, philosopher, calligrapher and painter, whose courtesy name was Tzu-chan 子瞻, was the elder son of Lao-ch'üan. When he was demoted to Huangchow 黃州,[1] he had a villa built on the Eastern Slope 東坡. This gave him another name, Tung-p'o, and it is by this sobriquet that he is most frequently referred to today.

For ten years after his birth, his father had to travel far and wide, thus leaving the child to be educated by his mother, née Ch'eng 程. As a boy, he showed a remarkable understanding of whatever he was taught, and in his evaluation of men and events of past ages, he formed startlingly mature judgments.

When he was still very young, a scholar from his native town, who had been to the capital, brought back a poem written by Shih Chieh 石介 on the "Imperial Virtues of Ch'ing-li."[2] Tung-p'o asked his teacher about the great men mentioned in the poem, and the teacher was so astonished by his curiosity that he told the boy all about them. "These," said Tung-p'o thereupon, "are the men whom I have been wanting to meet in person." Thus, at that early age, he already harbored the ambition of emulating the examples set by the distinguished men of the time.[3]

Before he came of age, he traveled with his father and brother Ch'e 轍 to the capital, where the two young scholars took the imperial examination together in the second year of Chia-yu.[4] Both won their *chin-shih* degree. The Chief Examiner, Ou-yang Hsiu, who was anxious to restore the classical style of prose writing, was so impressed by Tung-

---

[1] Prefecture in modern Hupeh Province.
[2] 1041-1048, reign of Emperor Jen-tsung.
[3] See p. 275, below.
[4] 1057, reign of Emperor Jen-tsung.

p'o's essay on "The Most Gracious Penalties and Rewards"[5] that he intended to give it first place. On thinking the matter over, however, Ou-yang suspected that no one except Tseng Kung 曾鞏, one of his pupils who was also taking the examination, could have produced the work; and, evidently to ward off the possible charge of favoritism to Tseng, he contented himself with awarding second place to the unsigned paper which was actually written by Su Shih.

After the examination, Tung-p'o paid his respects to the learned statesman, who was so impressed with him that he subsequently declared to one of his prominent friends that even he, the great Ou-yang, recognized in him a rival. When this causal observation went the rounds, those who heard it were surprised, but they were later able to confirm the prescience of the old master.

The first post Tung-p'o ever held outside the capital was that of Chu-pu 主簿[6] of Fuch'ang 福昌.[7] At that time, Ou-yang recommended him to the throne as one "rich in both talent and judgment," whereupon he was given another advanced examination at the Imperial Library. He passed it with flying colors. As a result, he was appointed one of the Associate Judges of the Supreme Court and later transferred to Feng-hsiang 鳳翔[8] as one of the prefect's principal assistants. At that time, the prefecture was being rehabilitated after the disturbances caused by a serious revolt, and the people, a considerable number of whom were engaged in the shipment of lumber, were still suffering from the impoverishment resulting from the burdensome services connected with the hostilities. On arriving at this post, Tung-p'o looked into the position and introduced refroms, which permitted participation in the river traffic and improved the people's lot considerably.

[5] See pp. 232-235.
[6] Title of a subordinate official in charge of archives.
[7] Iyang 宜陽 Hsien, Honan Province.
[8] Prefecture in modern Shensi Province.

During the brief reign of Emperor Ying-tsung 英宗 (1064-1067) Tung-p'o held various posts, one in the council in charge of the people's petitions and one on the Board of History. Shortly after Emperor Shen-tsung 神宗 ascended the throne, Wang An-shih 王安石 became Prime Minister. On account of his divergences of opinion with Wang. Tung-p'o fell into great disfavor and was given leave of absence. In the fourth year of Hsi-ning 熙寧,[9] An-shih proposed changes in the examination system. After Tung-p'o presented his views to the throne, His Majesty exclaimed that his doubts were all resolved. Tung-p'o was immediately summoned for an audience and encouraged to speak freely on the merits and defects of the administration, including the mistakes committed by the emperor himself. He once again made pertinent criticisms without beating about the bush, and the emperor forthwith undertook to give special consideration to them. When An-shih got wind of this, he was even more displeased and had Tung-p'o demoted to a subordinate position in K'aifeng Prefecture 開封府.[10]

At that time, Wang An-shih was introducing his well-known program of reforms, which was found unsatisfactory by Tung-p'o and to which he objected strongly. On one occasion, in a question put to candidates in the imperial examination, Tung-p'o hinted at the autocratic nature of Wang An-shih's administration, which naturally offended the Prime Minister more than ever. Wang felt the insinuation so very keenly that he egged on one of the censors to go out of his way to find fault with Tung-p'o. But, as all this was of no avail, Tung-p'o himself asked for a transfer, and he was sent to Hangchow 杭州[11] as a subordinate official.

Other positions held by him at court were those of Lang-chung 郎中[12] in the Ministry of Rites, Imperial Private

[9] 1071, reign of Emperor Shen-tsung.
[10] Prefecture where the then capital was situated.
[11] Prefecture in modern Chekiang Province.
[12] Title of a member of the ministerial staff.

Secretary, Chung-shu Sheh-jen 中書舍人, ranking official in the Prime Minister's Office, Secretary of the Tuan-ming Hall 端明殿學士 and Secretary and Reader of the Hanlin Academy. In the latter post, he had occasion to read history to Emperor Cheh-tsung 哲宗, who was then still a boy. Great pains were taken to explain to the prince the causes of the rise and fall of former dynasties and rulers. The future emperor nodded frequently, though he kept silent most of the time. When it came to the reading of the ancestral teachings of the imperial household, Tung-p'o took the opportunity to relate them to current events.

Once, while on night duty in the palace, Tung-p'o was given a special audience by the empress dowager, who reigned in place of Emperor Cheh-tsung before he attained his majority. "The year before last," the empress asked the scholar, "what office did you hold?" "I was Deputy Commissioner of Military Training at Ch'angchow 常州 ,"[13] he replied. "What are you now?" he was asked again. "Secretary of the Hanlin Academy," was the answer. "Why such a rapid advancement?" "Because I have had the good fortune of coming under Your Majesty and His Majesty the Emperor." "No," said the empress. "Maybe," Tung-p'o went on, "it was due to the recommendation of someone in power?" Once more the empress denied the suggestion. "Though I am unworthy," Tung-p'o said then with astonishment, "I have not sought my advancement by any other means!" "It was none other than His late Majesty[14] who ordered your promotion," the empress remarked. "Whenever he read your writings, he could not refrain from sighing and exclaiming, 'An extraordinary genius, an extraordinary genius!' But somehow he never got round to availing himself of your service." Tung-p'o was so touched that he wept unashamedly, and both the empress and emperor, and indeed everyone else in attendance,

[13] Prefecture in modern Kiangsu Province.
[14] Emperor Shen-tsung.

228

started sobbing.

In the third year of Emperor Cheh-tsung's reign, Tung-p'o served as Chief Imperial Examiner. It was a cold winter in the capital, and the scholars had to sit at their desks in the open hall to write their examination when it was snowing heavily. As a special act of grace, Tung-p'o relaxed the regulations in such a way that the candidates could take certain liberties in order to alleviate their suffering. Those attendants who found fault with the candidates or accused them unjustifiably of violating the rules were all relieved at Tung-p'o's instance.

Su Tung-p'o was appointed to three cabinet positions— those of Minister of Personnel, which post he did not assume, Minister of War and Minister of Rites.

As in the case of Ou-yang Hsiu and other great scholars and loyal statesmen, the price Tung-p'o had to pay for his frankness was banishment from the court and assignment to regional posts outside the capital. But, of all these men, few suffered the same fate as Tung-p'o, who was off and on demoted to more than ten prefectural offices, including those at Huangchow, Hsü-chow 徐州,[15] Huchow 湖州,[16] Ch'angchow, Hangchow, Ying-chow 潁州,[17] Yangchow 揚州,[18] Huichow 惠州, Lienchow 廉州, and Chiungchow 瓊州.[19] In each of these localities, he left a record of good and efficient administration but, before some remarkable examples are given, here is an interesting anecdote about the man and his extraordinary diligence.

When he was in Huangchow as Deputy Commissioner of Military Training, to which post he had been demoted because certain of his poems were considered objectionable, he was visited one day by a Minister of Finance 司農 by the name of Chu, who had to wait a long time before Tung-p'o emerged. The scholar apologized for his tardiness. "I have just finished

[15] Prefecture in modern Kiangsu Province.
[16] Prefecture in modern Chekiang Province.
[17] Prefecture in modern Anhwei Province.
[18] Prefecture in modern Kiangsu Province.
[19] These three prefectures in modern Kwangtung Province.

my daily exercise," he said, "and I regret that I was not promptly informed of your presence." "May I ask you what your so-called daily exercise consists of?" said the visitor. "Copying the *History of Han* 漢書," was the reply. "With your genius," said Chu, "you can doubtless remember everything for life after one reading. What need is there for you to copy anything by hand?" "This is the third time I have copied the *History of Han*," answered Tung-p'o. "Would you mind showing me some of the copies you have made?" Chu inquired further. Whereupon Tung-p'o ordered one of the old soldiers in attendance to bring a volume from the table. "Please pick out any word you like," he said to Chu. When the latter complied, Tung-p'o recited several hundred words following the one mentioned by Chu. The visitor tried the same thing over and over again, each time with the same result. "You are really a genius sent from heaven above," he sighed. Subsequently, he told his children this story. "Even Su Tung-p'o," he said, "studies like this. How much harder should those of us work who have only an average intelligence?"

In his administrative work, one field in which Tung-p'o distinguished himself in particular was that of flood control. In at least three prefectures, Hsüchow, Hangchow and Yingchow, he had great success in combatting the scourge. In Hangchow he built a dike on the West Lake, to which the people gave the name of Su-kung-t'i 蘇公堤 or the Honorable Su's Dike. It is still standing today.

When he first arrived in Hangchow, there was a serious drought and widespread famine. Tung-p'o petitioned the throne to exempt the prefecture from one-third of its normal rice tribute. He also obtained a special allocation of revenue, which was used for purchase of rice to feed the starving. The following spring, he relieved the shortage by selling the rice in the prefectural granary at a reduced price. In addition, rice soup and drugs were provided by the local government to the sick, many of whom were thereby saved. The prefect himself drew on his own funds to help establish sick-rooms.

Many years later, Tung-p'o revisited Hangchow. Because of his excellent government and his many favors to the people, he found that they worshiped him like a god, hanging up his portrait, making offerings before it, and in some cases erecting shrines in his honor even while he was still alive.

Tung-p'o died at the age of sixty-six in the first year of the reign of Emperor Hui-tsung 徽宗 (1101). In his writings, he followed in the footsteps of his own father, whose unfinished work on the *Exposition of the Book of Changes* 易傳 he completed. In addition, he has left to posterity a work *On the Analects* 論語說, the *Exposition of the Book of History* 書傳, forty *chüan* of the *Collected Works of Tung-p'o* 東坡集, twenty *chüan* of *Collected Works Continued* 東坡續集, fifteen *chüan* of *Memorials* 奏議, ten *chüan* of *Internal Decrees* 內制, three *chüan* of *External Decrees* 外制 and four *chüan* of *Adaptations to the Poems of Tao Yüan-ming* 和陶詩 .

Like Ou-yang Hsiu, Su Tung-p'o was a great patriot. All his life, he was devoted to his country and emperor, and there were few who could match him for loyalty and integrity. Unfortunately, he was not tolerated by some of the men in power who were jealous of him, and for this reason he could not give his undivided attention to the workings of the central government, which could well have benefited from his genius much more than it did.

Long after his death, posthumous honors were heaped on him by a subsequent ruler in the person of Emperor Kao-tsung 高宗, who reigned from 1127 to 1162. This emperor was so impressed with the writings of Su Tung-p'o that he always had them at hand and read them untiringly day in and day out, and personally composed a eulogy of Tung-p'o's collected works. The posthumous titles conferred on the great man included those of Grand Teacher of the Imperial Household and Secretary of the Tzu-cheng Hall 資政殿學士 , and he was canonized as Wen-chung 文忠.

刑賞忠厚之至論

堯舜禹湯文武成康之際，何其愛民之深，憂民之切，而待天下之以君子長者之道也！有一善，從而賞之，又從而詠歌嗟歎之，所以樂其始而勉其終。有一不善，從而罰之，又從而哀矜懲創之，所以棄其舊而開其新。故其吁俞之聲，歡忻慘戚，見於虞夏商周之書。

成康既沒，穆王立，而周道始衰。然猶命其臣呂侯，而告之以祥刑。其言憂而不傷，威而不怒，慈愛而能斷，惻然有哀憐無辜之心。故孔子猶有取焉。傳曰：「賞疑從與，所以廣恩也。罰疑從去，所以謹刑也。」

當堯之時，皋陶爲士，將殺人，皋陶曰殺之三。堯曰宥之三。故天下畏皋陶執法之堅，而樂堯用刑之寬。四岳曰：「鯀可用。」堯曰：「不可，鯀方命圮族。」既而曰：「試之。」何堯之不聽皋陶之殺人，而從四岳之用鯀也？然則

---

[1] Rulers respectively of the ancient T'ang 唐, Yü 虞, Hsia 夏 and Shang 商 dynasties.

[2] Rulers of the Chou 周 dynasty.

[3] A notoriously evil character, who was the father of Emperor Yü of the Hsia dynasty.

[4] Chief feudal lords in the four corners of the empire.

The Most Gracious Penalties and Rewards

How warmly Emperors Yao, Shun, Yü and T'ang,[1] and Kings Wen, Wu, Ch'eng and K'ang[2] loved their people, how deeply they were concerned with them, and they treated them according to the principles of gentlemen and elders! Even when a single good deed was done, it was rewarded, songs were sung about it, and it was extolled far and wide. The rejoicing was over the good beginning made and to encourage further effort consistent to the very end. Even when a single evil deed was performed, it was penalized, but there was understanding compassion and well-intentioned interdiction mixed with the hope that a veil would be drawn over the past and a new vista opened up. Thus, mixed expressions of approval and disapproval, praise and disappointment, are found in all the books of the Yü, Hsia, Shang and Chou dynasties.

Only with the death of Kings Ch'eng and K'ang and the accession of King Mu did the ideal government of Chou begin to decline. But even then Marquis Lü, Minister of Justice, was ordered to make public a just, but lenient, penal code. The message was sympathetic but not sentimental, authoritative but not wrathful, benignant but decisive, filled with understanding compassion for the innocent. This is why Confucius also had a good word to say for this state of affairs. It is stated in an exegesis: "When there is doubt as to rewards, they should be granted so as to afford a wider range of favors. When there is doubt as to penalties, they should rather be avoided as a manifestation of prudence in the dispensation of criminal justice."

In Emperor Yao's time, Kao-yao was the chief gaoler. Each time a death sentence was to be carried out, Kao-yao had to make three pleas for the criminal's execution, which were reversed by Yao with three pardons. The country therefore feared the firmness with which Kao-yao enforced the law and was happy at Yao's leniency in the administration of criminal justice. "The services of Kun,"[3] said the Four Yüehs,[4] "can be enlisted." Emperor Yao denied this, because Kun was disobedient and was a disgrace. But sometime later, the emperor said that he could try the man out. And why did Emperor Yao, on the one hand, refuse to listen to Kao-yao's advice to put criminals to death, but, on the other hand, yield to the suggestion of the Four Yüehs to employ Kun?

聖人之意，蓋亦可見矣。

書曰：「罪疑惟輕，功疑惟重。與其殺不辜，寧失不經。」嗚呼，盡之矣。可以賞，可以無賞，賞之過乎仁。可以罰，可以無罰，罰之過乎義。過乎仁，不失為君子；過乎義，則流而入於忍人。故仁可過也，義不可過也。

古者賞不以爵祿，刑不以刀鋸。賞以爵祿，是賞之道，行於爵祿之所加，而不行於爵祿之所不加也。刑以刀鋸，是刑之威，施於刀鋸之所及，而不施於刀鋸之所不及也。先王知天下之善不勝賞，而爵祿不足以勸也；知天下之惡不勝刑，而刀鋸不足以裁也。是故疑則舉而歸之於仁，以君子長者之道待天下，使天下相率而歸於君子長者之道。故曰忠厚之至也。

詩曰：「君子如祉，亂庶遄已。君子如怒，亂庶遄沮。」夫君子之已亂，豈有異術哉？時其喜怒，而無失乎仁而已矣。春秋之義，立法貴嚴，而責人貴寬，因其褒貶之義以制賞罰，亦忠厚之至也。

---

[5] One of the Confucian classics.

Here we can see the intention behind the judgment of a sage.

"The benefit of the doubt," said the *Book of History*, "should be given to lighten crime and add to merit. Rather fail to punish the extraordinary crime than put the innocent to death." Alas, this is the utmost that can be said! When a man may or may not be rewarded, to reward him is excessive benevolence. When a man may or may not be penalized, to penalize him is carrying justice to excess. Excessive benevolence makes a gentleman, but carrying justice to excess tends to create callousness. Better, therefore, excessive benevolence than carrying justice to excess.

In ancient times, rewards did not take the form of official rank and emoluments, nor was criminal justice administered with swords and saws. Though the conferment of official rank and emoluments is a proper form of reward, the effect of official rank and emoluments reaches only those on whom they are conferred, and not beyond. Though swords and saws are proper instruments to ensure respect for the authority of the law, the effect of swords and saws reaches only those who are punished, and not beyond. Ancient rulers knew that the good deeds of the world are too numerous to be rewarded and encouraged by grants of official rank and emoluments and that the evil acts of the world are also too numerous to be punished and deterred by swords and saws. They therefore chose the path of benevolence in case of doubt, and treated the people of the country according to the principles of gentlemen and elders, so that they could all rally to the principles of gentlemen and elders. That is why these rulers were said to be most gracious.

"If a gentleman is pleased," says the *Book of Songs*, "disorder comes to a quick end. If a gentleman is angry, disorder is stopped in no time." Is there a different way by which a gentleman puts an end to disorder? There is none other than expressing his pleasure and anger at the proper time without ever losing sight of benevolence. The essence of the *Spring and Autumn Annals*[5] is that it prizes severity in law-making but leniency in the condemnation of people. In that book, rewards and penalties take the form of praise and censure. This also exemplifies graciousness at its utmost.

范 蠡 論

越既滅吳，范蠡以謂勾踐爲人，長頸鳥喙，可與共患難，不可與共安樂。乃以其私徒屬浮海而行。至齊，以書遺大夫種曰：「蜚鳥盡，良弓藏，狡兔死，走狗烹。子可以去矣。」

蘇子曰：「范蠡獨知相其君而已。以吾相蠡，蠡亦鳥喙也。夫好貨，天下賤士也。以蠡之賢，豈聚斂積實者？何至耕于海濱，父子力作，以營千金，屢散屢積。此何爲者哉？豈非才有餘而道不足，故功成，名遂，身退，而心終不能自放者乎？使勾踐有大度，能始終用蠡，蠡亦非清淨無爲，以老於越者也。吾故曰：『蠡亦鳥喙也。』

「魯仲連既退秦軍，平原君欲封連，以千金爲壽。連笑曰：『所貴乎天下士者，爲人排難解紛而無所取也。即有取，是商賈之事，連不忍爲也。』遂去，終身不復見，逃隱於海上，曰：『吾與富貴而詘於人，寧貧賤而輕世肆志焉。』使范蠡之去，如魯仲連，則去聖人不遠矣。

---

[1] A general who served Kou Chien, King of Yüeh, for more than twenty years and who succeeded in helping him recover his own state and destroy his conqueror, the King of Wu.

[2] A state covering parts of modern Kiangsu, Anhwei and Chekiang Provinces.

[3] A state, which after the destruction of Wu covered parts of modern Kiangsu, Chekiang and Shantung Provinces.

[4] King of Yüeh.

[5] A state located in Shantung Province.

[6] Wen Chung 文種 , another high official, Ta-fu, under Kou Chien.

[7] A strategist from the state of Ch'i 齊 .

[8] A prince of the state of Chao 趙 .

On Fan Li[1]

After the destruction of Wu[2] by Yüeh,[3] Fan Li thought that Kou Chien,[4] having a long neck and a mouth like a bird's beak, was the kind of person who could share distress with others, but not happiness. For this reason Fan went to sea with his followers. When he arrived in the state of Ch'i,[5] he wrote to Ta-fu Chung,[6] saying, "The flying birds having been exhausted, the good bows are packed away; the crafty rabbits having been killed, the running dogs are cooked. Therefore, you had better go."

"Fan Li," says this writer, "could only read the physiognomy of his ruler. As I see it, Fan himself had a mouth like a bird's beak. Only ignoble men love riches. Fan, being a worthy man, should not have taken to amassing material wealth for himself. And yet he and his son worked hard at a plantation on the coast to acquire one thousand pieces of gold, which were lost and regained more than once. Why did he do this? Was it not because he had more ability than virtue that he retired after achieving fame, but ultimately could not set his mind at rest? Had Kou Chien been magnanimous enough to retain his services to the very end, Fan would not have stuck to his quiet life and spent his old age in Yüeh. That is why I say that Fan also had a mouth like a bird's beak.

"When Lu Chung-lien[7] succeeded in holding back the forces of Ch'in, Prince P'ing-yüan[8] intended to confer a feudal grant on him and first gave him one thousand pieces of gold. 'What,' said Lu with a smile, 'is prized in a scholar of the empire is his ability to settle a conflict without seeking reward. To take anything would stamp a person as a mere merchant. It is not my conception of proper behavior.' So saying, he left without seeing the prince again for the rest of his life. He retired to the sea. 'I would rather,' he said, 'be poor and lowly and be able to look down on the world and do as I please than be rich and distinguished and yield to others.' Had Fan Li departed as Lu Chung-lien did, he would not have been far from being a sage.

237

「嗚呼，春秋以來，用舍進退，未有如蠡之全者也！而不足於此，吾是以累歎而深悲焉。」

---

[9] A period (722-481 B.C.) in the history of the Chou dynasty.

238

"Alas, ever since the Spring and Autumn period,[9] no one has had such a perfect record as Fan Li in accepting and rejecting, entering and retiring from, public service, and yet he has had the shortcomings described above. That is why I have often sighed and grieved deeply for him."

范 增 論

漢用陳平計，間疏楚君臣。項羽疑范增與漢有私，稍奪其權。增大怒曰：「天下事大定矣。君王自爲之。願賜骸骨歸卒伍。」歸未至彭城，疽發背死。

蘇子曰，增之去善矣。不去，羽必殺增。獨恨其不早耳。

然則當以何事去？增勸羽殺沛公，羽不聽，終以此失天下。當以是去耶？曰，否。增之欲殺沛公，人臣之分也，羽之不殺，猶有君人之度也。增曷爲以此去哉？

易曰：「知幾其神乎？」詩曰：「相彼雨雪，先集維霰。」增之去，當於羽殺卿子冠軍時也。陳涉之得民也，以項燕扶蘇。項氏之興也，以立楚懷王孫心，而諸侯之叛之也，以殺義帝。且義帝之立，增爲謀主矣。義帝之存亡，豈獨爲楚之盛衰，亦增之所與同禍福也。未有義帝亡而增獨能久存者也。

---

[1] The statesman who aided Hsiang Yü in achieving his hegemony among the feudal lords.

[2] Prime Minister under Emporer Hui 惠帝 and Emporer Wen 文帝 of Han.

[3] The dictator-general who became king of the state of Ch'u 楚霸王 but who was eventually defeated by Emperor Kao-tsu 高祖 of the Han dynasty.

[4] T'ungshan 銅山 *Hsien*, Kiangsu Province.

[5] Liu Pang 劉邦, who later became Emperor Kao-tzu of the Han dynasty.

[6] Sung I 宋義 under Emperor I of the state of Ch'u 楚義帝.

[7] One of the rebels who made himself king of the state of Ch'u and fought against the Ch'in dynasty.

[8] Hsiang Yen was a general in the State of Ch'u; Fu-su was the crown prince of the Ch'in regime. Both were popular among their respective peoples.

[9] Emperor I 義帝.

On Fan Tseng[1]

Adopting Ch'en P'ing's[2] stratagem, the Han dynasty sought to sow the seeds of discord between the ruler of Ch'u and his ministers. Hsiang Yü[3] suspected Fan Tseng of plotting with the Han administration, and deprived him on some of his powers. This angered Fan greatly. "Now," he said to Hsiang, "that the general situation is substantially stabilized, Your Majesty can handle it yourself. It is my wish to be permitted to retire and revert to the ranks." This wish was granted, but, before he reached P'engch'eng,[4] Fan died from a skin cancer on his back.

I say that it was a good thing for Fan to leave official life and that, if he had not done so, he would have been put to death by Hsiang Yü. But it is regrettable that he did not leave earlier.

What, then, should have been the occasion for Fan to depart? It will be recalled that he had advised Hsiang Yü to kill the Duke of P'ei[5] but that Hsiang failed to heed this and, because of it, eventually lost his place in the sun. Should Fan have left at that time? No, when Fan expressed the wish to kill the Duke of P'ei, he played the part of a loyal minister, but, when Hsiang Yü refused to take the advice, he showed the magnanimity of a king. Why should Fan have left for this reason?

"Is it not divine," says the *Book of Changes*, "to know the shape of things to come?" "Before snow," said the *Book of Songs*, "sleet first collects." Fan's departure should have been at the time when Hsiang Yü put his Lordship, the Supreme Commander,[6] to death. Just as Ch'en Sheh[7] succeeded in winning the confidence of the people by using the names of Hsiang Yen and Fu-su,[8] so the rise of Hsiang Yü was due to his preferment of Prince Hsin, grandson of King Huai of Ch'u, as head of state.[9] But the rebellion of the feudal lords was because of Hsiang's murder of Emperor I. It happened that Fan had been the chief architect of that emperor's accession to the throne. Thus, the life and death of Emperor I affected not only the rise and decline of Ch'u, but also the personal fortunes of Fan, who could not have survived the death of the emperor.

241

羽之殺卿子冠軍也，是殺義帝之兆也。其殺義帝，則
疑增之本也。豈必待陳平哉？物必先腐也，而後蟲生之。
人必先疑也，而後讒入之。陳平雖智，安能間無疑之主哉？

吾嘗論義帝，天下之賢主也。獨遣沛公入關，不遣項
羽。識卿子冠軍於稠人之中，而擢爲上將。不賢而能如是
乎？

羽既矯殺卿子冠軍，義帝必不能堪，非羽殺帝，則帝
殺羽。不待智者而後知也。增始勸項梁立義帝，諸侯以此
服從。中道而弑之，非增之意也。夫豈獨非其意，將必力
爭而不聽也。不用其言，而殺其所立，羽之疑增，必自此
始矣。

方羽殺卿子冠軍，增與羽比肩而事義帝，君臣之分未
定也，爲增計者，力能誅羽，則誅之；不能，則去之。豈
不毅然大丈夫也哉？增年已七十，合則留，不合則去。不
以此時明去就之分，而欲依羽以成功，陋矣。

雖然，增，高帝之所畏也。增不去，項羽不亡。嗚呼，
亦人傑也哉？

---

[10] Son of Hsiang Yen and uncle of Hsiang Yü, he joined his Ch'u forces with Ch'en Sheh against the Ch'in dynasty.

On Fan Tseng

Hsiang Yü's slaughter of his Lordship, the Supreme Commander, was the prelude to his murder of Emperor I. This act was the origin of his suspicion of Fan. Did he have to wait till Ch'en P'ing hatched his plot? Something must be rotten before worms multiply, and a man must first have some suspicion before slander takes effect. Wise as Ch'en P'ing was, how could he have estranged an unsuspecting ruler from his ministers?

I have once upon a time deduced that Emperor I was a worthy ruler. Had he not been one, how could he have decided to dispatch the Duke of P'ei to face the enemy beyond the pass, without also dispatching Hsiang Yü, and how could he have recognized the merits of his Lordship, the Supreme Commander when he was one of a multitude and promoted him to Supreme Commander?

When Hsiang Yü killed the Supreme Commander by treachery, it was more than what Emperor I could tolerate. It did not take a wise man to know that one would put the other to death eventually. At first, Fan advised Hsiang Liang[10] to place Emperor I on the throne, and it was this act that won the obedience of the feudal lords. The murder of the emperor so shortly after his accession was clearly not Fan's intention. Not only that, but Fan must have stubbornly fought against the murder, though his objection must have been overruled. The refusal of Hsiang Yü to accept Fan's advice and his murder of Fan's candidate for the throne clearly indicated that Hsiang Yü had begun to be suspicious of Fan.

At the time when Hsiang Yü killed his Lordship, the Supreme Commander, Fan and Hsiang owed common allegiance to Emperor I, and their relationship as ruler and subject had not yet been determined. For his own sake, Fan should have killed Hsiang had he had the power, or else he should have retired. Would not either alternative have shown him to be a great and determined man? After all, Fan had reached the advanced age of seventy, and the obvious course for him to adopt was to remain as long as it sutied him and to leave once it ceased to do so. How foolish of him not to have decided at this crucial point whether to continue or to depart, but to have wished to remain with Hsiang in the hope of achieving success and fame!

However, Fan was a man dreaded even by Emperor Kao-tsu of the Han dynasty. If he had remained and survived, Hsiang Yü's cause would not have been lost. Alas, was not Fan after all an outstanding man?

243

留 侯 論

　　古之所謂豪傑之士者必有過人之節。人情有所不能
忍者，匹夫見辱，拔劍而起，挺身而鬪，此不足爲勇也。
天下有大勇者，卒然臨之而不驚，無故加之而不怒，此其
所挾持者甚大，而其志甚遠也。

　　夫子房授書於圯上之老人也，其事甚怪。然亦安知其
非秦之世，有隱君子者，出而試之。觀其所以微見其意者，
皆聖賢相與警戒之義，而世不察，以爲鬼物，亦已過矣。
且其意不在書。

　　當韓之亡，秦之方盛也，以刀鋸鼎鑊待天下之士，
其平居無罪夷滅者，不可勝數。雖有賁育，無所復施。夫
持法太急者，其鋒不可犯，而其勢未可乘。子房不忍忿忿
之心，以匹夫之力，而逞於一擊之間。當此之時，子房之
不死者，其間不能容髮，蓋亦已危矣。千金之子，不死於
盜賊。何者？其身之可愛，而盜賊之不足以死也。子房以
蓋世之材，不爲伊尹太公之謀，而特出於荆軻聶政之計，

---

[1]Chang Liang 張良 helped Emperor Kao-tsu of the Han dynasty 漢高祖 win his
empire. Later, he was invested with the title of Liu 留侯, by which he has been
known in history. His courtesy name was Tzu-fang 子房.

[2]Brave men in ancient times.

[3]Well-known assassins in history.

[4]Prime Minister under Emperor T'ang of the Shang dynasty.

[5]Prime Minister under King Wen of the Chou dynasty.

On Chang Liang[1]

Those who were known as outstanding men in ancient times always had a kind of self-control that was unsurpassed in others. When something happened that could not be borne by human sentiment and when an ordinary man, faced with an insult, unsheathed his sword and girded himself for a fight, this was not enough to indicate bravery. Men of great valor were not overcome with surprise even when suddenly confronted, nor angered when provoked without justification. The reason was that the cause which they upheld was lofty and the goal they sought far-reaching.

The incident in which Chiang Liang received a book from the old man on the bridge was very strange. But how do we know that it was not really some wise hermit in the Ch'in dynasty who emerged from obscurity to put him to a test? We can see that all that the old man implied had the same significance as admonitions to each other, proffered by sages and worthy men. Nevertheless, the unthinking world took him for a ghost, which was indeed an error. Moreover, what the old man had in mind had nothing to do with the book.

With the downfall of Han and the rise of Ch'in, punishments administered by means of swords, saws, tripods and cauldrons were meted out to people all over the empire at random. There were innumerable instances where those who lived in peace and did no harm were put to death. Even if there had been men like Meng Pen and Hsia Yü,[2] they could have done nothing. When the law was enforced with such stringency, there was no way of resisting its severity or opposing its power. Chang Liang was unable to contain his anger and sought, with only the strength of an ordinary man, to satisfy his impulse by striking a blow against the tyrant. At the moment his life was hanging by a hair, and he could well have perished in the attempt. It was indeed a great risk that he took. A son worth a thousand pieces of gold should never die at the hands of a robber, because the son is so highly prized that to suffer such a death would not be worthy of him. However, though a peerless genius, Chang Liang resorted to the tactics of Ching K'o and Nieh Cheng[3] instead of emulating the examples of I Yin[4] and T'ai-kung,[5] in hopes of escaping with his life by a sheer stroke of luck. That is why

以僥倖於不死。此圯上老人所爲深惜者也。是故倨傲鮮腆，而深折之。彼其能有所忍也，然後可以就大事，故曰孺子可教也。

楚莊王伐鄭，鄭伯肉袒牽羊以迎。莊王曰：「其君能下人，必能信用其民矣。」遂舍之。勾踐之困於會稽，而歸臣妾於吳者，三年而不倦。

且夫有報人之志，而不能下人者，是匹夫之剛也。夫老人者，以爲子房才有餘，而憂其度量之不足，故深折其少年剛銳之氣，使之忍小忿而就大謀。何則？非有平生之素，卒然相遇於草野之間，而命以僕妾之役，油然而不怪者，此固秦皇之所不能驚，而項籍之所不能怒也。

觀夫高祖之所以勝，而項籍之所以敗者，在能忍與不能忍之間而已矣。項籍唯不能忍，是以百戰百勝，而輕用其鋒。高祖忍之，養其全鋒而待其弊，此子房教之也。當淮陰破齊，而欲自王，高祖發怒，見於詞色。由此觀之，猶有剛强不忍之氣。非子房其誰全之？

太史公疑子房以爲魁梧奇偉，而其狀貌乃如婦人女子，不稱其志氣。嗚呼，此其所以爲子房歟？

---

[6] King of the state of Yüeh 越.

[7] A mountain in Chekiang Province.

[8] Hsiang Yü 項羽, King of the state of Ch'u 楚霸王.

[9] A famous general under Emperor Kao-tsu.

[10] Author of the *Records of History* 史記.

the old man much deplored Chang Liang's conduct and wished to test his forbearance by haughtily and rudely humiliating him. What the old man envisaged was that, if Chang could bear all his insults, the young man would be considered capable of undertaking important tasks. Hence his statement that the "lad" could still be taught wisdom.

When King Chuang of Ch'u led his troops against the state of Cheng, Duke Hsiang of that land appeared half naked in abject humiliation, leading some goats by the hand, and bade his conqueror welcome. King Chuang spared his life. "A lord who can humble himself before others," he said, "must be able to handle his subjects with confidence." When Kou Chien[6] had been besieged on the K'ueichi,[7] he returned to the state of Wu and served as the king's lackey for three years.

A man determined to take revenge on others but unable to humble himself before them is merely stubborn like any ordinary human being. The old man thought that Chang Liang had sufficient ability, but was worried about his lack of forbearance. He therefore endeavored to bend Chang's youthful stubbornness and impetuosity, so that he could learn to contain anger and measure up to important tasks. How do we know that he could succeed in doing so? From the circumstance that, without having even made the old man's acquaintance and immediately after their chance encounter in the wilds, the youth was ordered about like a servant but remained composed and did not take offense. Such forbearance would be the mark of a man who could not be perturbed by the First Emperor of the Ch'in dynasty or angered by Hsiang Chi.[8]

As we see it, Emperor Kao-tsu of Han succeeded and Hsiang Chi suffered defeat, because the former had forbearance and the latter did not. This is why Hsiang abused his prowess after the repeated victories. On the other hand, Emperor Kao-tsu conserved all his power until Hsiang's strength was broken. This he did on Chang Liang's advice. When Han Hsin[9] destroyed the state of Ch'i and sought to make himself king, Emperor Kao-tsu was angered, and his anger could be seen from his speech and expression. It is clear that he was still stubborn and impetuous. But for a man like Chang Liang at his side, who could have saved him?

The Grand Historian[10] thought that Chang Liang had great physical strength and stature. On the contrary, his complexion was like that of a woman, which gave no clue to his capacity and aspiration. Ah, is this not what made Chang Liang the kind of man he was?

247

上梅直講書

軾每讀詩至鴟鴞，讀書至君奭，常竊悲周公之不遇。及觀史，見孔子厄於陳蔡之間，而絃歌之聲不絕，顏淵仲由之徒，相與問答。夫子曰：「匪兕匪虎，率彼曠野。吾道非邪? 吾何爲於此? 」顏淵曰：「夫子之道至大，故天下莫能容。雖然，不容何病? 不容然後見君子。」夫子油然而笑曰：「回，使爾多財，吾爲爾宰。」夫天下雖不能容，而其徒自足以相樂如此。

乃今知周公之富貴， ‧有不如夫子之貧賤。夫以召公之賢，以管蔡之親，而不知其心，則周公誰與樂其富貴? 而夫子之所與貧賤者，皆天下之賢才，則亦足與樂乎此矣。

軾七八歲時始知讀書。聞今天下有歐陽公者，其爲人如古孟軻韓愈之徒，而又有梅公者從之遊，而與之上下其議論。其後益壯，始能讀其文詞，想見其爲人，意其飄然脫去世俗之樂，而自樂其樂也。

---

[1] Mei Yao-ch'eng 梅堯臣, a high official and noted scholar, who was Su Shih's contemporary. Chih-chiang was the title given to an assistant professor at the Imperial University.

[2] The chapter was written by the Duke of Chou and addressed to King Ch'eng 成王, to express his loyalty to the royal household.

[3] This chapter was written by the Duke of Chou to convey his fraternal advice to his half-brother, the Duke of Chao 召公, who was disenchanted with him.

[4] Names of states in the Spring and Autumn period 春秋.

[5] Outstanding disciples of Confucius.

[6] Brothers of the Duke of Chou.

Letter to Chih-chiang Mei[1]

Whenever I read the chapter on "Ch'ih-hsiao"[2] in the *Book of Songs* and the chapter on "Chün-shih"[3] in the *Book of History*, I cannot help feeling sad for the obscure fortune of the Duke of Chou. I have also read in history that, when Confucius was in want in Ch'en and Ts'ai,[4] the sound of stringed instruments and singing was never interrupted; Yen Yüan and Chung Yu[5] and others exchanged questions and answers. "Though unlike a rhinoceros or a tiger," Confucius said, "I have been driven into the wilderness. Is my philosophy all wrong? Why should this happen to me?" "Master," said Yen Yüan, "your philosophy is the greatest, and so it cannot be tolerated by the world. However, what harm is done by this lack of tolerance? It merely shows that you are a gentleman." "Hui," the Master said with a smile, "if you were very wealthy, I would be your steward." Though Confucius was not tolerated by the world, his disciples still had reason to be happy.

Now I know that the wealth and official distinction of the Duke of Chou cannot be compared to the poverty and lowliness of the Master. However worthy the Duke of Chao was and however intimate Kuan and Ts'ai,[6] they were ignorant of the heart of the Duke of Chou. With whom could he enjoy the wealth and official distinction? On the other hand, those who shared the poverty and lowliness of the Master were worthy and talented figures of the world and happy to share his lot.

Only when I was seven or eight did I begin to know how to study. I heard then that the Honorable Ou-yang was prominent in the world. He was a man like Mencius and Han Yü of earlier times. I also learned that there was the Honorable Mei, who associated with him and engaged in many-sided discussions with him. When I grew older, I began to be able to read their writings; and, thinking of the kind of men that they were, I could see that they had turned away from the pleasures of the vulgar world and found what they themselves regarded as pleasures.

249

方學爲對偶聲律之文，求斗升之祿，自度無以進見於
諸公之間，來京師逾年，未嘗窺其門。今年春，天下之士，
羣至于禮部，執事與歐陽公實親試之。誠不自意，獲在第
二。既而聞之人，執事愛其文，以爲有孟軻之風，而歐陽
公亦以其能不爲世俗之文也而取焉。是以在此，非左右爲
之先容，非親舊爲之請屬。而嚮之十餘年間，聞其名而不
得見者，一朝爲知己。

退而思之，人不可以苟富貴，亦不可以徒貧賤。有大
賢焉而爲其徒，則亦足恃矣。苟其僥一時之幸，從車騎數
十人，使閭巷小民聚觀而贊嘆之，亦何以易此樂也？

傳曰：「不怨天，不尤人。」蓋優哉游哉可以卒歲。執
事名滿天下，而位不過五品。其容色溫然而不怒。其文章
寬厚敦樸而無怨言。此必有所樂乎斯道也。軾願與聞焉。

---

[7]Measures of capacity, equivalent respectively to roughly a pint and a peck.

When I first learned to write rhymed essays with matched couplets and thereby sought a *sheng* or *tou*[7] of official emoluments, I conjectured that I had no way of being introduced to these gentlemen, so I never entered their doors even after being in the capital for more than a year. Last spring, when the country's scholars gathered at the Ministry of Rites, you and the Honorable Ou-yang personally examined them. I unexpectedly won the second place. Subsequently I heard that you had liked my writing, thinking that I showed the refinement of Mencius, and that the Honorable Ou-yang had also felt that I avoided the vulgar style of writing. This was the reason for my success in the examination, and it was due neither to any intercession on the part of those around the examiners nor to requests of any of my relatives and friends. As a result, you two whose names I had heard for more than a decade, but whom I had never been able to see, have since become my close friends.

As I sit back and think, I feel that a man should not lightly seek wealth and official distinction, nor should he merely put up with poverty and lowliness. If he can become the pupil of men of great worth, that is something on which he can sufficiently depend. If, by a stroke of sheer luck, he became a high official, with an entourage of scores of men riding in carriages and on horseback, thus causing the assembled small fry of the neighborhood to utter cries of admiration, would he exchange all this for the pleasure I have just described?

"Do not complain of Heaven," say the *Analects*, "nor lay the blame on men." This is because one can live one's life and end one's years without care. Your name is known all over the country, but you have not yet risen above the fifth rank. However, your deportment is always gentle and you are never angry. Your writing is characterized by tolerance and simplicity, and in it there are no words of recrimination. This must be due to the pleasure you derive from the Way. I should like to associate myself with you in this.

喜 雨 亭 記

亭以雨名，志喜也。古者有喜，則以名物，示不忘也。
周公得禾，以名其書。漢武得鼎，以名其年。叔孫勝狄，
以名其子。其喜之大小不齊，其示不忘一也。

　　余至扶風之明年，始治官舍。爲亭於堂之北，而鑿池
其南，引流種木，以爲休息之所。

　　是歲之春，雨麥於岐山之陽，其占爲有年。既而彌月
不雨，民方以爲憂。越三月，乙卯乃雨，甲子又雨，
民以爲未足。丁卯大雨，三日乃止。官吏相與慶於庭，
商賈相與歌於市，農夫相與忭於野。憂者以樂，病者以愈。
而吾亭適成。

　　於是舉酒於亭上，以屬客而告之，曰：「五日不雨，
可乎？」曰：「五日不雨，則無麥。」「十日不雨，可乎？」
曰：「十日不雨，則無禾。」無麥無禾，歲且荐飢，獄訟
繁興，而盜賊滋熾。則吾與二三子，雖欲優游以樂於此亭，
其可得耶？今天不遺斯民，始旱而賜之以雨，使吾與二三

---

[1] The book was entitled Chia-ho 嘉禾 (Good Rice).

[2] The emperor changed the name of his reign to Yüan-ting 元鼎 (the second character signifying the tripod).

[3] Shu-sun Teh-ch'eng 叔孫德成, who served under Duke Wen of the state of Lu 魯文公, took the barbarian Ch'iao-ju 僑如 captive and named his son after him.

[4] Prefecture in modern Shensi Province.

[5] Situated in the northwest of Shenshan 陝山 *Hsien*, Shensi Province.

The Happy Rain Pavilion

The fact that the pavilion is named after rain is indicative of the happiness it brings. In ancient times, whenever there was a happy event, something would be named after it in commemoration. The Duke of Chou named his book after the auspicious rice plant presented to him.[1] Emperor Wu of Han named his reign after the tripod he received.[2] Shusun named his son after the enemy he took captive.[3] Though the extent of the happiness varied in each case, the idea that it should not be forgotten was the same.

One year after my arrival in Fufeng,[4] I commenced the construction of my official residence. A pavilion was built north of the main hall, and a pond dug to the south. A stream was diverted to the neighborhood of the pavilion, and trees were planted around it, to make it a restful retreat.

In the spring of that year, wheat fell from the sky south of the Ch'i Mountains,[5] and a good year was forecast for the wheat crop. Then the rain did not fall for a full month, which worried the people. It was only three months later on the second day of the fourth month that the rain started falling. On the eleventh day, it rained again but the people did not think it was enough. On the fourteenth day came a downpour, which lasted three consecutive days. Officials exchanged congratulations in their offices, merchants sang together in the market place, farmers showed their happy faces in the countryside. Those who were worried rejoiced; those who were sick were cured. It was just then that the construction of my pavilion was completed.

To mark the event, a drinking party was held in the new structure, at which I toasted my guests and asked them: "What would happen if it did not rain for five days?" "If it did not rain for five days, there would be no wheat," was the reply. "What would happen," I asked again, "if it did not rain for ten days?" "If it did not rain for ten days, there would be no rice." Without wheat and without rice there would be repeated famine. Lawsuits would multiply; burglars and robbers would infest the area. In these circumstances, even if I wanted to be carefree with two or three of my friends and enjoy this pavilion, could I do so? Heaven has not forgotten the people and has favored them with rain

子，得相與優游而樂於亭者，皆雨之賜也。其又可忘邪？

旣以名亭，又從而歌之，歌曰：

「使天而雨珠，寒者不得以爲襦。使天而雨玉，飢者不得以爲粟。一雨三日，繄誰之力？民曰太守，太守不有。歸之天子，天子曰不。歸之造物，造物不自以爲功。歸之太空，太空冥冥。不可得而名，吾以名吾亭。」

after drought. That I can now be carefree with two or three of my friends and enjoy this pavilion is a favor granted by the rain. Should we ever forget it?

After naming the pavilion thus, I sang this song:

> If Heaven rained pearls, the cold could not wear them as clothes.
> If Heaven rained jade, the starving could not eat it as rice.
> It rained for three days. To whom goes the credit?
> "The Prefect," said the people, but it was not he, and he knew it.
> They wished to thank the Son of Heaven, but he did not feel
> That he had anything to do with it.
> Then they turned to the Creator, but no claim
> Was made by Him.
> Was it the universe perchance?
> But the universe was dark and unfathomable.
> What other course have I
> But let my pavilion be named after the rain?

醉 白 堂 記

故魏國忠獻韓公作堂於私第之池上，名之曰醉白，取樂天池上之詩，以爲醉白堂之歌，意若有羨於樂天而不及者。天下之士，聞而疑之。以爲公既已無愧於伊周矣，而猶有羨於樂天，何哉？

軾聞而笑曰：「公豈獨有羨於樂天而已乎？方且願爲尋常無聞之人而不可得者。天之生是人也，將使任天下之重，則寒者求衣，飢者求食，凡不獲者求得。苟有以與之，將不勝其求。是以終身處乎憂患之域，而行乎利害之塗。豈其所欲哉？夫忠獻公既已相三帝，安天下矣，浩然將歸老於家，而天下共挽而留之，莫釋也。當是時，其有羨於樂天，無足怪者。

「然以樂天之平生，而求之於公，較其所得之厚薄淺深，孰有孰無，則後世之論，有不可欺者矣。

「文致太平，武定亂略。謀安宗廟，而不自以爲功。急賢才，輕爵祿，而士不知其恩。殺伐果敢，而六軍安之。四夷八蠻，想聞其風采，而天下以其身爲安危。此公之所有而樂天之所無也。

「乞身於強健之時，退居十有五年。日與其朋友賦詩飲

---

[1] Han Ch'i 韓琦, a renowned prime minister in the Sung dynasty.
[2] The poem composed by Po Chü-i after his retirement. Lo-t'ien 樂天 was the famous T'ang poet's courtesy name.

256

The Drunken Po Hall

The late Honorable Han[1] had a hall constructed by the pond of his private residence. It was named the Drunken Po Hall. As a song to commemorate the event, he adopted Po Chü-i's poem "By the Pond."[2] It seemed that Han admired Po and felt that he would not equal him. The scholars of the empire heard this story and doubted it. They did not understand why the Honorable Han, who could without embarrassment be compared to I Yin and the Duke of Chou, should have admired Po.

When I heard this story, I smiled and said: "Not only did the Honorable Han admire Po, but he wished he had been simply an unknown commoner. A man born to heavy responsibilities in the world faces the wants of the shivering for clothes and of the hungry for food. If these needs are all to be met, there is no end to his search for their fulfillment. That is why he remains bowed down with cares and woe and has to weigh benefit against harm to the people at all times. Is this what he wishes? Having served as prime minister under three emperors and brought peace to the realm, the Honorable Han was on the point of retiring, but the whole country sought to retain him and would not let him go. In this situation, it was not surprising that he admired Po.

"However, if we compare the careers of the two men and see wherein each excelled the other and what each had that the other lacked, we arrive at certain conclusions, which must be unequivocal to posterity.

"First, the Honorable Han succeeded in bringing peace to the country, effectively suppressing armed disturbances and securing the state, so that the spirit of the imperial ancestors can be at rest—all this without claiming any credit to himself. He had little regard for his own titles and emoluments and gave priority to the introduction of worthy talents without this even being appreciated by the scholars as a favor. He conducted the punitive campaigns with firmness and valor, which was a source of gratification to the armed forces. The barbarians all around looked upon him with respect, and the whole country looked to him as the man on whom peace and security depended. This was what he had and Po lacked.

"Secondly, Po asked for his retirement when he was still strong and

257

酒，盡山水園池之樂。府有餘帛，廩有餘粟，而家有聲妓
之奉。此樂天之所有而公之所無也。

「忠言嘉謀，效於當時，而文采表於後世。死生窮達
不易其操，而道德高於古人。此公與樂天之所同也。

「公既不以其所有自多，亦不以其所無自少，將推其同
者而自託焉。方其寓形於一醉也，齊得喪，忘禍福，混貴賤，
等賢愚，同乎萬物，而與造物者遊，非獨自比於樂天而已。

「古之君子，其處己也厚，其取名也廉，是以實浮於名，
而世誦其美不厭。以孔子之聖，而自比於老彭，自同於丘
明，自以爲不如顏淵。

「後之君子，實則不至，而皆有侈心焉。臧武仲自以爲
聖，白圭自以爲禹，司馬長卿自以爲相如，揚雄自以爲孟
軻，崔浩自以爲子房，然世終莫之許也。由此觀之，忠獻
公之賢於人也遠矣。」

昔公嘗告其子忠彥，將求文於軾以爲記而未果。既葬，
忠彥以告。軾以爲義不得辭也，乃泣而書之。

---

[3] A worthy minister in the Shang dynasty.
[4] A commentator on the *Spring and Autumn Annals*.
[5] A great disciple of Confucius.
[6] An official of the state of Lu 魯.
[7] A man of the state of Wei 魏 in the Warring States period 戰國.
[8] First emperor of the Hsia dynasty.
[9] A scholar in the Han dynasty.
[10] A State Minister of Chao 趙 in the Warring States period.
[11] A philosopher in the Han dynasty.
[12] A high official of the Northern Wei 北魏 dynasty.
[13] A famous strategist who helped Emperor Kao-tsu of Han win his empire.

healthy. He then lived away from it all for fifteen years, and spent his time composing poetry, drinking with his friends and enjoying to the hilt the pleasures of the mountain, river, garden and pond. He had an over-abundance of silks in his house and grain to spare in his granary, and at home he was entertained by a company of female musicians. This was what Po had and the Honorable Han lacked.

"Thirdly, both of them gave loyal advice and presented auspicious plans to their sovereigns. They served their own age and left their graceful writings to posterity. Neither life nor death, success nor adversity, could alter their integrity, and their morality was such as to transcend that of the ancients. This was what both of them shared.

"The Honorable Han did not pride himself on what he alone had, nor did he regret what he lacked. He merely wished to be on an equal footing with Po in those things which they both shared. When he whiled away his time in drinking now and then, he viewed gain and loss, weal and woe, the noble and humble, the wise and foolish in the same light; and felt that he was no different from all other living beings, traveling in the company of the Creator and not merely comparing himself to Po.

"The gentlemen of old demanded much of themselves but were modest in seeking fame. As a result, they were greater in fact than in name, and the world is not tired of praising their virtue. For example, a sage like Confucius compared himself to Lao-p'eng,[3] gave himself the same rating as Tso Ch'iu-ming,[4] and regarded himself as inferior to Yen Yüan.[5]

"The gentlemen of later ages, however, entertained extravagent hopes, although in fact they were not equal to them. For example, Tsang Wu-chung[6] compared himself to a sage, Po Kuei[7] to Emperor Yü,[8] Ssu-ma Hsiang-ju[9] to Lin Hsiang-ju,[10] Yang Hsiung[11] to Mencius, and Ts'ui Hao[12] to Chang Liang.[13] But none of these claims has met with the world's approval. It can thus be seen that the Honorable Han was far wiser than others."

The Honorable Han told his son, Chung-yen, that he had meant to ask me to write this account for him, but that he had failed to do so. After his father's burial, Chung-yen informed me of this omission. As I felt that I am duty-bound to comply with the request, I have now penned this record with grievous tears.

前 赤 壁 賦

　　壬戌之秋，七月既望，蘇子與客泛舟遊於赤壁之下。清風徐來，水波不興。舉酒屬客，誦明月之詩，歌窈窕之章。少焉，月出於東山之上，徘徊於斗牛之間。白露橫江，水光接天。縱一葦之所如，凌萬頃之茫然。浩浩乎如馮虛御風而不知其所止。飄飄乎如遺世獨立羽化而登仙。

　　於是飲酒樂甚，扣舷而歌之，歌曰：「桂櫂兮蘭槳，擊空明兮泝流光。渺渺兮予懷，望美人兮天一方。」

　　客有吹洞簫者，倚歌而和之，其聲嗚嗚然，如怨如慕，如泣如訴，餘音嫋嫋，不絕如縷。舞幽壑之潛蛟，泣孤舟之嫠婦。

　　蘇子愀然正襟危坐而問客曰：「何爲其然也?」客曰：「『月明星稀，烏鵲南飛。』此非曹孟德之詩乎？西望夏口，東望武昌，山川相繆，鬱乎蒼蒼。此非孟德之困於周郎者乎？

---

[1] Rhymed or partly rhymed prose.

[2] A mountain in Huangkang 黃岡 Hsien, Hupeh, intentionally or unintentionally confused with another of the same name, situated in Chiayü 嘉魚 Hsien, where Ts'ao Ts'ao was disastrously defeated by the combined forces of Shu 蜀 and Wu 吳 during the Three Kingdoms 三國 period.

[3] Reign of Emperor Shen-tsung of the Sung dynasty 宋神宗, 1068-1085, the fifth year of Yüan-feng (1078-1085) being 1082.

[4] The allusion was to high officials in the capital.

[5] Courtesy name of Ts'ao Ts'ao, the emperor of Wei 魏, another one of the Three Kingdoms, who was one of the most active political figures in his time.

[6] Modern Hankow 漢口, a city in Hupeh Province.

[7] Wuch'ang Hsien, Hupeh.

First *Fu*[1] on the Ch'ih-pi (Red Cliff)[2]

On the sixteenth of the seventh month, in the fifth year of Yüan-feng,[3] I took a trip by boat with some friends to the Ch'ih-pi. The wind was blowing gently; there was not a ripple on the water. I raised my cup and toasted my friends. We recited the poem from the *Book of Songs* on the "Bright Moonlight," containing the line on the sedate lady. Shortly after, the moon rose over the eastern mountain and hovered between the Dipper and Aquila. The white dew lay all over the river, and the light reflected in the water reached up to the sky. We let our small boat drift along over the vast expanse ahead of us. Now we seemed to be borne aloft by the wind, not knowing where to stop; now we seemed to float away, and, freed from this world, to take wing and become immortal.

In this mood, we drank happily and sang, beating out the rhythm with our fingers on the side of the boat:

> On a cassia boat, with orchid oars
> We struck the water, rowing up the river,
> As the moon shone over the waves. I long
> For the beauties on the other side of Heaven![4]

Among my friends there was one who played the flute and who accompanied my song. The sound of the music was melancholy. Now it seemed complaining and yearning; now it seemed weeping and pleading. Even when the song was finished, its reverberations seemed not to die away but lingered on like an unbroken thread. Dragons hiding in the dark ravines would have been roused to dance, and widows languishing in their solitary boats would have been moved to tears.

Overcome by sadness, I adjusted my garment, sat up solemnly and asked my friends: "Why is it that things are what they are?" They replied as follows: " 'The moon is bright and the stars are few. Crows and magpies fly southward.' Was this not the poetry of Ts'ao Meng-teh?[5] Between Hsiak'ou[6] in the west and Wuch'ang[7] in the east intertwined a host of gray mountains and rivers. Was this not the scene of

261

方其破荊州，下江陵，順流而東也，舳艫千里，旌旗蔽空，釃酒臨江，橫槊賦詩，固一世之雄也。而今安在哉？況吾與子，漁樵於江渚之上，侶魚蝦而友麋鹿。駕一葉之扁舟，舉匏樽以相屬。寄蜉蝣於天地，渺滄海之一粟。哀吾生之須臾，羨長江之無窮。挾飛仙以遨遊，抱明月而長終。知不可乎驟得，託遺響於悲風。」

蘇子曰：「客亦知夫水與月乎？逝者如斯，而未嘗往也。盈虛者如彼，而卒莫消長也。蓋將自其變者而觀之，則天地曾不能以一瞬。自其不變者而觀之，則物與我皆無盡也。而又何羨乎？

「且夫天地之間，物各有主。苟非吾之所有，雖一毫而莫取。惟江上之清風，與山間之明月，耳得之而爲聲，目遇之而成色，取之無禁，用之不竭，是造物者之無盡藏也，而吾與子之所共適。」

客喜而笑。洗盞更酌，肴核既盡，杯盤狼籍。相與枕藉乎舟中，不知東方之既白。

---

[8] A famous general of the state of Wu.
[9] Chiangling *Hsien*, Hupeh.
[10] Prefecture in Hupeh.
[11] Each equivalent to one-third of a mile.

his siege by Chou Yü?[8] When Ts'ao Ts'ao sailed down to Chiangling[9] after overrunning Chingchow[10] and followed the waters of the river eastward, his ships lined up the river for one thousand *li*,[11] and his flags covered the sky. Looking out on the river, he drank copious draughts, and, as he grasped his spear, he composed poetry. He was a great hero in his time, but where is he now? Moreover, now that you and I are fishing and cutting wood on the brink of the river, fish and prawns are our companions, stags and deer our friends. We row a flat leaf-like boat and drink with one another. We are like tiny insects in a vast world and mere specks in the deep, deep sea. We lament our ephemeral lives and admire the eternal Yangtze. To travel far and wide with roving immortals and embrace the moon till the end of time is something that cannot be achieved. In this certainty, we have left the reverberations of our music to mingle with the sobbing wind."

"My friends," said I, "do you know about the water and the moon? The former goes on and on, but it never comes to an end. The latter waxes and wanes, but it never decreases or increases. If we see everything from its changing aspect, even heaven and earth cannot last for a twinkling of an eye. If we look at everything from its unchanging aspect, it and we can never end. What is there, then, to be admired?

"Furthermore, everything on earth has its owner. If a thing is not owned by us, we cannot lay hands on the tiniest part of it. Only the gentle breeze on the river and the bright moon over the mountains feast the ear with sound and the eye with color, and these we can take at perfect liberty and use without exhausting them. These are the unlimited reserves of the Creator, which you and I can enjoy together."

My friends were gratified and smiled. We washed our cups and resumed our drinking. When all the food was consumed and the cups and dishes were scattered around, we lay in complete disorder till dawn came up the east and took us unawares.

後 赤 壁 賦

是歲十月之望，步自雪堂，將歸于臨皋。二客從予，過黃泥之坂。霜露既降，木葉盡脫。人影在地，仰見明月。顧而樂之，行歌相答。

已而歎曰：「有客無酒，有酒無肴。月白風清，如此良夜何？」

客曰：「今者薄暮，舉網得魚，巨口細鱗，狀似松江之鱸。顧安所得酒乎？」

歸而謀諸婦，婦曰：「我有斗酒，藏之久矣，以待子不時之須。」

於是攜酒與魚，復游於赤壁之下。江流有聲，斷岸千尺。山高月小，水落石出。曾日月之幾何，而江山不可復識矣。

予乃攝衣而上，履巉巖，披蒙茸，踞虎豹，登虬龍，攀棲鶻之危巢，俯馮夷之幽宮。蓋二客不能從焉。

劃然長嘯，草木震動。山鳴谷應，風起水涌。予亦悄然而悲，肅然而恐，凜乎其不可留也。反而登舟，放乎中流，聽其所止而休焉。

---

[1] A hall built by Su Shih after he was demoted to Huangchow 黃州, a prefecture in modern Hupeh Province.

[2] Sungchiang *Hsien*, Kiangsu Province.

[3] A measure of capacity often translated as "peck."

[4] A measure of length roughly equivalent to a foot.

Second *Fu* on the Ch'ih-pi (Red Cliff)

On the fifteenth of the tenth month in the same year, I left the Hall of Snow[1] and set out on my way back to the Linkao Pavilion. Two friends accompanied me, and all three of us passed the Slope of Huangni. There had been dew and frost, and leaves had all fallen. With the bright moonlight above us, we could see our shadows on the ground. We felt happy as we looked around, and we sang together.

Then a sigh was heard. "We have friends but no wine. Even if we had wine, we would have no food to go with it. While the moon is bright and the wind cool, what shall we do to while away this beautiful night?"

"Toward evening," one of my friends said, "I caught some fish with my net. They have large mouths and small scales; they look like perches from Sungchiang.[2] But where can we get wine?"

I went home to consult my wife. "I have a *tou*[3] of wine," she said, "which I have stored for a long time just for emergencies such as this."

Thereupon we took the wine and fish to our boat and resumed our trip below the Ch'ih-pi. Then the current of the river became audible, as it broke through a thousand *ch'ih*[4] of the bank. The mountains were high; the moon seemed small. The water was low, and we could see the pebbles. Only a short time had elapsed, but we could no longer make out the river and mountains!

I hitched up my gown and stepped ashore. I climbed high cliffs, made my way through luxurious foliage, sat on rocks shaped like tigers and panthers, and mounted trees that looked like dragons. I clambered toward the hawks' nests, perilously perched, and looked down on the dark abode of the River God below. I was alone, because my friends could not follow me.

Suddenly a sharp cry was heard which seemed to make the plants tremble. The mountains and valleys echoed it, the wind arose and the water rushed on. I was so saddened and frightened that I could no longer remain ashore. So I went back to the boat, which was sent drifting to the middle of the stream. I let it drift till it stopped of its own accord.

時夜將半，四顧寂寥。適有孤鶴，橫江東來，翅如車輪，元裳縞衣，戛然長鳴，掠予舟而西也。

須臾客去，予亦就睡。夢一道士，羽衣翩躚，過臨皐之下，揖予而言曰：「赤壁之遊樂乎？」問其姓名，俛而不答。「嗚呼噫嘻，我知之矣。疇昔之夜，飛鳴而過我者，非子也耶？」道士顧笑，予亦驚寤。開戶視之，不見其處。

Second *Fu* on the Ch'ih-pi (Red Cliff).

It was almost midnight, quiet and deserted all around. Then a lone crane came out of the east and flew across the river. With wings like cartwheels and a coat of white and black feathers, the bird uttered a shrill and long drawn out cry, passing my boat and heading westward.

Shortly after, my friends left, and I went to bed. I dreamed of a Taoist priest, who was wearing a garment of feathers and who passed below the Linkao Pavilion. He bowed and asked: "Was the trip to the Ch'ih-pi an enjoyable one?" When I asked him his name, he lowered his head, but did not reply. "Oh," said I, "I know now! Was it not you who flew past me and uttered the cry last night?" The priest looked at me and smiled. Then I awoke. When I opened the door on board to see where we were, I could no longer find him.

方 山 子 傳

方山子，光黄間隱人也。少時，慕朱家，郭解爲人。閭里之俠皆宗之。稍壯，折節讀書，欲以此馳騁當世，然終不遇。晚乃遯於光黄間，曰岐亭。

庵居蔬食，不與世相聞。棄車馬，毁冠服，徒步往來，山中人莫識也。見其所著帽，方屋而高，曰：「此豈古方山冠之遺像乎？」因謂之方山子。

余謫居于黄，過岐亭，適見焉。曰：「鳴呼，此吾故人陳慥季常也。何爲而在此？」方山子亦矍然，問余所以至此者。余告之故，俯而不答，仰而笑。呼余宿其家。環堵蕭然，而妻子奴婢，皆有自得之意。

余既聳然異之，獨念方山子少時，使酒好劍，用財如糞土。前十九年，余在岐山，見方山子，從兩騎，挾二矢，游西山。鵲起于前，使騎逐而射之，不獲。方山子怒馬獨出，一發得之。

因與余馬上論用兵，及古今成敗。自謂一世豪士。今幾日耳，精悍之色，猶見於眉間，而豈山中之人哉？

---

[1] Prefecture in modern Honan Province.

[2] Prefecture in modern Hupeh Province.

[3] A knight-errant of early Han times in modern Shantung Province.

[4] A knight-errant of the Han dynasty in modern Honan Province.

[5] A style of hats worn during sacrificial rites at the imperial ancestral shrine in the Han dynasty, the characters 方 and 山 meaning respectively "square" and "mountain."

Biography of Master Fang-shan (Square Hat)

Master Fang-shan is a recluse living in the vicinity of Kuangchow[1] and Huangchow.[2] In his youth, he was an admirer of Chu Chia[3] and Kuo Chieh,[4] and his example was followed by knights-errant all over the countryside. As he grew older, he turned over a new leaf and began to study. By so doing he had hoped to distinguish himself in contemporary society, but he never succeeded. In his old age, he became a recluse in Ch'it'ing, a place situated between Kuangchow and Huangchow.

He lives in a thatched hut and has become a vegetarian, ceasing to have anything to do with the world. He abandoned his carriage and horses and destroyed his formal headgear and garments. He comes and goes on foot. Unknown to any of the mountaineers, he wears a tall square hat, which is regarded as a relic of the Fang-shan style.[5] Hence the nickname "Master Fang-shan."

When I was demoted to Huangchow, I passed through Ch'it'ing and chanced on Master Fang-shan. "Ah," I said, "this is my old friend, Ch'en Ts'ao, whose courtesy name is Chi-ch'ang. How did he get here?" Master Fang-shan was equally surprised and asked me why I was there. I told him the reason, and he lowered his head without making a reply. Then, looking up again and smiling, he invited me to stay at his home. It is a house with bare walls, but his wife, children, and men and women servants all seemed quite happy.

Being greatly astonished, I recalled how, when he was young, Master Fang-shan had taken to drinking, been fond of fencing and spent money like trash. Nineteen years ago, too, I was in the Ch'i Mountains and saw Master Fang-shan followed by two men on horseback each with a bow and arrow, hunting in the Western Hills. When a magpie took flight in front of us, he ordered the two men to shoot it, but they missed. Thereupon, Master Fang-shan, seated on a robust and agile horse, rushed forth and shot it with one single dart.

At our meeting, he discussed with me on horseback the art of strategy and the secrets of success and failure in ancient and modern times. He regarded himself as a heroic figure in his age. Only a short time has elapsed since then, and I can still see in his eyes the look of distinction and valor. How can I believe that he is now a man of the mountains?

269

然方山子世有勳閥，當得官。使從事於其間，今已顯聞。而其家在洛陽，園宅壯麗，與公侯等。河北有田，歲得帛千匹，亦足以富樂。皆棄不取，獨來窮山中。此豈無得而然哉？

余聞光黃間多異人，往往佯狂垢汙，不可得而見。方山子儻見之與？

---

[6] A main geographical division covering parts of modern Hopei, Honan and Shantung Provinces.
[7] A measure of length for clothing materials.

Master Fang-shan's distinguished family has for generations rendered meritorious service to the state, and because of this he is entitled to an official appointment. If he had taken up this calling, he would have gone very far by now. His family residence in Loyang, with its magnificent gardens, is like that of a duke or marquis. He also owns landed property in Hopei[6] and receives one thousand $p'i$[7] of silk fabric annually. Thus, there is enough to make him rich and happy, but he has abandoned it all and gone into the barren mountains alone. Has he done this for nothing?

I hear that there is a host of extraordinary men settled in the region of Kuangchow and Huangchow. They pretend to be lunatics and look bedraggled, and they are rarely seen in public. Has Master Fang-shan perchance met any of them?

書狄武襄事

狄武襄公者，本農家子。年十六時，其兄素，與里人失其姓名，號鐵羅漢者。鬭於水濱。至溺，救之。保伍方縛素，公適餉田，見之，曰：「殺羅漢者，我也。」人皆釋素而縛公。

公曰：「我不逃死，然待我救羅漢，庶幾復活。若決死者，縛我未晚也。」衆從之。公默祝曰：「我若貴，羅漢當蘇。」乃舉其尸，出水數斗而活。其後人無知者。

公薨，其子諮，詠護喪歸葬西河，父老爲言此。元祐元年十二月五日與詠同館北客，夜話及之。眉山蘇軾記。

---

[1] One of the prime ministers of the Sung dynasty.
[2] A peck.
[3] A district in modern Shansi Province.
[4] 1086, reign of Emperor Cheh-tsung 哲宗.

An Anecdote about Ti Ch'ing[1]

His Excellency Ti Ch'ing was the son of a farmer. When he was sixteen, his elder brother Su wrestled on the bank of a river with a neighborhood man whose name had been lost to records but who was nicknamed the "Iron Arhat." When the latter was drowned and an attempt was made to save him, the local police arrested Su and had him bound. His younger brother, who happened to be in the fields, saw what had taken place. "I was the one that killed the arhat," he said. Su was thereupon released, and his brother Ch'ing was arrested instead.

When he was being bound, Ch'ing said: "I will not escape from even the death sentence. But please wait till I try and revive the arhat, so that his life may be saved. If he is certain to die, it will not be too late to arrest me." The request was granted. Ch'ing prayed silently: "If I am destined to be great, the arhat must revive." As the body was lifted and several *tou*[2] of water forced out of it, the man recovered. None of his descendents heard anything about the incident.

After His Excellency's death, his sons, Tzu and Yung, escorted his remains to be buried in his native town, Hsiho,[3] whose elders told them this story. On the fifth day of the twelfth month of the first year of Yüan-yu,[4] Yung, with whom I stayed in an inn in the north, passed the information on to me in the course of an evening's talk.

Recorded by Su Shih of Meishan.

范文正公文集叙

慶曆三年，軾始總角入鄉校。士有自京師來者，以魯人石守道所作慶曆聖德詩示鄉先生。軾從旁竊觀，則能誦習其詞。問先生以所頌十一人者，何人也。先生曰：「童子何用知之？」軾曰：「此天人也耶？則不敢知。若亦人耳，何爲其不可？」

先生奇軾言，盡以告之，且曰：「韓，范，富，歐陽，此四人者，人傑也。」時雖未盡了，則已私識之矣。

嘉祐二年，始舉進士。至京師，則范公沒。既葬，而墓碑出，讀之至流涕，曰：「吾得其爲人，蓋十有五年，而不一見其面。豈非命也歟？」

是歲登第，始見知于歐陽公，因公以識韓富，皆以國士待軾，曰：「恨子不識范文正公。」其後三年過許，始識公之仲子今丞相堯夫。又六年，始見其叔彝叟於京師。又十一年，遂與其季德孺同僚于徐。皆一見如舊，且以公遺藁見屬爲叙。又十三年，乃克爲之。

---

[1] A famous prime minister in the Sung dynasty.

[2] 1043, reign of Emperor Jen-tsung 仁宗.

[3] Shou-tao was the courtesy name of Shih Chieh 石介, a well-known scholar. Lu was the ancient name for Shantung Province.

[4] Han Ch'i, another famous prime minister.

[5] Fu P'i, another distinguished premier.

[6] Ou-yang Hsiu, see above, pp. 133-138.

[7] 1057, reign of Emperor Jen-tsung.

Preface to the *Collected Works of Fan Chung-yen*[1]

In the third year of Ch'ing-li,[2] when I was a mere child attending a village school, a scholar came from the capital and showed our teacher a poem by Shih Shou-tao of Lu[3] on the "Imperial Virtues of Ch'ing-li." Stealing a look from the side, I could read the lines easily. I asked my teacher who were the eleven persons eulogized in the poem. "What need is there for a child to know?" he said. "Are these heavenly beings?" I remarked. "If so, I would not dare to ask about them. But if they are human beings, why can I not inquire?"

This surprised my teacher, who told me everything about the men in question. "Han,[4] Fan, Fu[5] and Ou-yang[6]—these four," he said, "are outstanding personages." Though I could not understand him fully, I undertook to remember these names.

In the second year of Chia-yu[7] I attained my *chin-shih* degree. But before I arrived in the capital, His Excellency Fan had already died. After his burial, the inscription on his tomb tablet was made public. On reading it, I was so moved that tears came to my eyes. "I have known of the man for fifteen years," I said, "but never had the pleasure of meeting him. Is it not fate?"

On passing the imperial examination in that year, I came to be appreciated by the Honorable Ou-yang, through whom I became acquainted with Han and Fu. All of them have treated me as a scholar held in national esteem. "It is regrettable," they said, "that you did not know His Excellency Fan." Three years later, when passing through Hsüchow, I made the acquaintance of His Excellency's second son, Yao-fu, who is today Prime Minister. Six years later, I met his third son, I-sou, in the capital. Eleven more years after that, I became a colleague of his fourth son, Teh-ju, in Hsüchow. All these gentlemen regarded me as their old friend, and they entrusted me with the writing of a preface to a collection of manuscripts left by His Excellency. This I have been able to do only after the lapse of thirteen more years.

嗚呼，公之功德，蓋不待文而顯，其文亦不待敘而傳。
然不敢辭者，自以八歲知敬愛公，今四十七年矣。彼三傑
者，皆得從之游，而公獨不識，以爲平生之恨。若獲掛名
其文字中，以自托於門下士之末，豈非疇昔之願也哉？

古之君子，如伊尹，太公，管仲，樂毅之流，其王霸
之略，皆定於畎畝中，非仕而後學者也。淮陰侯見高帝於
漢中，論劉項短長，畫取三秦，如指諸掌。及佐帝定天下，
漢中之言，無一不酬者。諸葛孔明臥草廬中，與先主論曹
操孫權，規取劉璋，因蜀之資，以爭天下，終身不易其言。
此豈口傳耳受，嘗試爲之，而僥倖其或成者哉？

公在天聖中，居太夫人憂，則已有憂天下致太平之意，
故爲萬言書，以遺宰相，天下傳誦。至用爲將，擢爲執政，
考其平生所爲，無出此書者。

今其集二十卷，爲詩賦二百六十八，爲文一百六十五。
其於仁義禮樂忠信孝悌，蓋如飢渴之於飲食，欲須臾忘

---

[8] Prime Minister under Emperor T'ang of the Shang dynasty.

[9] Prime Minister under King Wen of the Chou dynasty 周文王.

[10] Prime Minister under Duke Huan of the state of Ch'i 齊桓公.

[11] Commander-in-Chief in the state of Yen 燕.

[12] A famous general under Emperor Kao-tsu of the Han dynasty.

[13] Prefecture in modern Shensi and Hupeh Provinces.

[14] After the fall of the Ch'in dynasty Hsiang Yü divided its territory into three parts, hence the name "Three Ch'ins."

[15] Prime Minister and strategist under Emperor Chao-lieh 昭烈帝 of Shu.

[16] Emperor Chao-lieh of Shu 蜀.

[17] The King of Wei 魏.

[18] Emperor of Wu 吳. Shu, Wei and Wu were known as the Three Kingdoms.

[19] 1023-1032, reign of Emperor Jen-tsung.

Alas, the deeds and virtues of His Excellency do not have to wait to be manifested by his writings, nor would his writings have to depend on a preface for their transmission. But I do not venture to decline the request, because I have learned to respect and love His Excellency since I was eight years old, which was forty-seven years ago. Though I have had the good fortune of being in the company of the other three outstanding men, His Excellency alone was unknown to me personally, and this has been a life-long regret. If I can attach my name to his writings as one of his pupils, is it not what I have always yearned for?

Here are some examples of the great men of old. Men like I Yin,[8] T'ai-kung,[9] Kuan Chung[10] and Yüeh I,[11] even while they were still tilling the fields, had had settled in their minds the strategies with which they were to aid their sovereigns in securing and wielding power; none of them had anything further to learn after becoming officials. Another example is that of Han Hsin.[12] When he met Liu Pang [who later became Emperor Kao-tsu of the Han dynasty] in Hanchung[13] and discussed the respective merits and shortcomings of the future emperor and Hsiang Yü, his opponent, as well as the plan for taking the Three Ch'ins,[14] he already had everything at his fingertips. Later, when he helped Liu Pang take the empire, what had been said at Hanchung all came true. Then there was Chu-ko Liang,[15] who, sleeping in his thatched hut, plotted with Liu Pei[16] against Ts'ao Ts'ao[17] and Sun Ch'üan,[18] to wrest the state of Shu from Liu Chang as the base for winning an empire. He had laid down a policy from which he did not in the least depart for the rest of his life. Were these heroic plans just so much talk put into effect merely as experiments, and did they owe their success to strokes of luck?

During the reign of T'ien-sheng,[19] when His Excellency was in mourning for the death of his mother, he was already keenly concerned with the state of the empire and anxious to bring about peace. To this end, he addressed a letter of ten-thousand words to the then prime minister, which was widely read throughout the country. In all his later life, during which he was promoted to commander-in-chief and prime minister, he never once deviated from the course charted in the letter.

The collection of his works now consists of twenty *chüan*, including two hundred and sixty-eight poems and *fu* and one hundred and sixty-five essays. These writings show that to him benevolence, righteousness, propriety, music, loyalty, sincerity, filial piety and fraternal love were

而不可得，如火之熱，如水之濕，蓋其天性有不得不然者。

雖弄翰戲語，率然而作，必歸於此。故天下信其誠，爭師

尊之。

孔子曰：「有德者必有言。」非有言也，德之發於口

者也。又曰：「我戰則克，祭則受福。」非能戰也，德之

見於怒者也。

元祐四年四月二十一日。

---

[20] 1089, reign of Emperor Cheh-tsung.

as important as food and drink to the hungry and the thirsty and could not be forgotten by him even for an instant. They were as hot as fire and as wet as water—in other words, part of his nature, from which he could not depart. Even in his wit and humor and in his writings of a casual nature, he kept to these consistently. The whole empire therefore trusted his sincerity and was eager to have him as its teacher.

Said Confucius: "He who has virtue must also have words." These are not mere words, but virtues expressed by word of mouth. "When we fight," he also said, "we can win. We are blessed when we make sacrifices." Not that we can fight, but it is the expression of virtue in wrath.

21st day of the 4th month, 4th year of Yüan-yu.[20]

居 士 集 叙

　夫言有大而非誇，達者信之，眾人疑焉。孔子曰：「天之將喪斯文也，後死者不得與於斯文也。」孟子曰：「禹抑洪水，孔子作春秋，而予距楊墨。」蓋以是配禹也。文章之得喪，何與於天？而禹之功與天地並，孔子孟子以空言配之，不已誇乎？

　自春秋作而亂臣賊子懼，孟子之言行而楊墨之道廢。天下以為是固然，而不知其功。孟子既沒，有申商韓非之學，違道而趨利，殘民以厚主，其說至陋也。而士以是罔其上，上之人僥倖一切之功，靡然從之。而世無大人先生如孔子孟子者，推其本末，權其禍福之輕重，以救其惑，故其學遂行。

　秦以是喪天下，陵夷至於勝，廣，劉，項之禍。死者十八九，天下蕭然。洪水之患，蓋不至此也。方秦之未得志也，使復有一孟子，則申韓為空言，作於其心，害於其

---

[1] Philosophers of the Chou dynasty.

[2] All these were philosophers of the legalist school in the Chou dynasty.

[3] Ch'en and Wu were rebel leaders who started the campaign which led to the downfall of the Ch'in dynasty.

[4] The man who eventually established the Han dynasty and became its first emperor, Kao-tsu.

[5] King of the state of Ch'u.

Preface to the Collected Works of the Retired Scholar

There are strong statements which are not exaggerations. The enlightened believe them, while the multitude doubts them. "If it were the will of Heaven," said Confucius, "to let our writings be lost, those who die late would not be able to have any part in them." "Emperor Yü stopped the great flood," said Mencius, "Confucius wrote the *Spring and Autumn Annals* and I refuted Yang Chu and Mo Ti,"[1] implying that his contribution could match that of Yü. What has Heaven had to do with the preservation or loss of writings? The meritorious service of Yü could indeed be regarded as rivaling the work of Heaven and Earth, and was it not an exaggeration to place beside it the empty words of Confucius and Mencius?

However, after the compilation of the *Spring and Autumn Annals*, rebellious ministers and villainous sons were frightened, and after Mencius' statements were put into effect the ways of Yang and Mo were done away with. The world took this achievement for granted and did not realize the extent of the service performed. After the death of Mencius, the theories of Shen Pu-hai, Shang Yang and Han Fei[2] gained currency. They were fallacious views, and ran counter to the principles of nature, by advocating the primacy of profit and the enrichment of the ruler at the expense of the people. Scholars deceived their superiors with these ideas, and the rulers, believing that these are the expedient way to all success, followed them without scruple. Unfortunately, there were not then in the world such great men and teachers as Confucius and Mencius, who could have exposed their falsehoods by examining the essentials and non-essentials and assessing the relative degrees of benefit or harm flowing from these theories. As a result of this omission their ideas gained wide acceptance.

The Ch'in dynasty was in consequence brought to an end after the disasters caused by Ch'en Sheng, Wu Kuang,[3] Liu Pang[4] and Hsiang Yü.[5] In the midst of these disturbances, eight or nine out of every ten lost their lives, and the country became devastated. Even the great flood could not have done so much damage. Had there been a Mencius before the Ch'in dynasty attained its hegemony, the theories of Shen and Han would have been empty words, "For what arises in the mind will

281

事，作於其事，害於其政者，必不至若是烈也。使楊墨得志於天下，其禍豈減於申韓哉？由此言之，雖以孟子配禹，可也。

太史公曰：「蓋公言黃老。賈誼晁錯明申韓。」錯不足道也，而誼亦爲之。余以是知邪說之移人，雖豪傑之士，有不免者。況餘人乎？

自漢以來，道術不出於孔氏而亂天下者，多矣。晉以老莊亡，梁以佛亡，莫或正之。五百餘年而後得韓愈，學者以愈配孟子，蓋庶幾焉。愈之後三百餘年而後得歐陽子，其學推韓愈孟子以達於孔氏，著禮樂仁義之實，以合於大道，其言簡而明，信而通，引物連類，折之於至理，以服人心。故天下翕然師尊之。自歐陽子之存，世之不說者，譁而攻之，能折困其身，而不能屈其言。士無賢不肖，不謀而同曰：「歐陽子，今之韓愈也。」

宋興七十餘年，民不知兵，富而敎之，至天聖景祐極矣。而斯文終有愧於古，士亦因陋守舊，論卑而氣弱。自

[6] A quotation from *Mencius*, Book III, Part B, translation by D. C. Lau.
[7] A scholar of the Han dynasty.
[8] Founder of the school of Taoism.
[9] Philosopher-statesmen of the early Han dynasty.
[10] A philosopher of the Taoist school in the Chou dynasty.
[11] 1023-1032, reign of Emperor Jen-tsung.
[12] 1034-1038, reign of the same emperor.

interfere with policy, and what shows itself in policy will interfere with practice,"[6] and would not have caused such serious trouble. As against this, had Yang and Mo had their way, would the catastrophe have been less than that caused by Shen and Han? It was therefore right to put Mencius in the same category as Emperor Yü.

"Kai Kung[7] commented on the Yellow Emperor and Lao-tzu,"[8] wrote the Grand Historian, "and Chia I and Ch'ao Ts'o[9] were well-read in Shen and Han." While Ch'ao Ts'o is not worth mentioning, it is surprising that even Chia I engaged in that kind of work. This shows to what extent heterodoxy tends to influence all men, not even excluding outstanding scholars, let alone the multitude.

Since the Han dynasty, philosophical and moral principles which did not emanate from Confucius have in numerous instances caused disturbances to the world. The Tsin dynasty ended because of the philosophy of Lao-tzu and Chuang-tzu,[10] and the Liang dynasty perished because of Buddhism. For a long time there was no one to rectify the situation, and it was only after more than five centuries that Han Yü emerged. Scholars were not far wrong in putting him in the same category as Mencius. It was more than three centuries after Han Yü that we had Master Ou-yang, whose learning reached back from Han Yü and Mencius on to Confucius. Master Ou-yang expounded propriety, music, humaneness and righteousness, and showed their concordance with the Way. His statements were brief but lucid, trustworthy and penetrating. He cited examples to prove the most elevated reasoning, which was so persuasive that the people reverenced him as their teacher. However, after his emergence, those who were disenchanted with him launched furious attacks on him, although they only caused him physical distress but failed to disprove the soundness of his position. For this reason, all scholars, whether worthy or otherwise, declared spontaneously with one voice that Master Ou-yang was the modern Han Yü.

With the lapse of more than seventy years since the establishment of the present dynasty of Sung, the people began to enjoy the blessing of peace and affluence as well as a sound education. It was especially during the reigns of T'ien-sheng[11] and Ching-yu[12] that the climax of good government was reached. But the literary tradition still lagged behind the ancient times; and scholars, sticking to their old and inferior style, could not rise above a low level of discussion and evinced a feeble spirit. After the appearance of Master Ou-yang, scholars vied with

歐陽子出，天下爭自濯磨，以通經學古爲高，以救時行道爲
賢，以犯顏納諫爲忠，長育成就，至嘉祐末，號稱多士。
歐陽子之功爲多。嗚呼，此豈人力也哉？非天其孰能使之？

　　歐陽子沒十有餘年，士始爲新學，以佛老之似，亂周
孔之實，識者憂之。賴天子明聖，詔修取士法，風厲學者，
專治孔氏，黜異端，然後風俗一變。論師友淵源所自，復
知誦習歐陽子之書。

　　予得其詩文七百六十六篇於其子棐，乃次而論之
曰：「歐陽子論大道似韓愈，論事似陸贄，記事似司馬遷，
詩賦似李白。」此非余言也，天下之言也。

　　歐陽子諱脩，字永叔，既老，自謂六一居士云。

---

[13] 1056-1063, reign of the same emperor.
[14] See note 1, p. 260 above.

one another in purifying and cultivating themsleves, and regarded the thorough study of the classics and the emulation of ancient writers as elevating, the salvation of the times and the practice of righteousness as a worthy objective and the presentation of remonstrances, even if it incurred the displeasure of the throne, as a form of loyalty. A period of tremendous growth and achievement set in, until the end of the reign of Chia-yu[13] became known for its abundance of scholars. This was due mainly to the meritorious service of Master Ou-yang. Alas, was this merely the result of human effort? Could it all have happened without the blessing of Heaven?

More than ten years after the death of Master Ou-yang, scholars began to diffuse their new learning, confusing the truth of the philosophy of the Duke of Chou and Confucius with the spurious teachings of Buddhism and Taoism. It was a matter which caused anxiety to men of enlightenment. Fortunately, the Son of Heaven has been wise enough to decree the revision of the examination laws, urging scholars to make an exclusive study of Confucius and wipe out heterodoxy. As a result, there has been a change in our customs. Tracing this education to its source, our scholars have resumed their study of the writings of Master Ou-yang.

I have now obtained from the son of Master Ou-yang, Fei, 766 items of these works, including the great scholar's poetry and essays. From these I have come to the conclusion that Master Ou-yang was like Han Yü in the discussion of the Great Way, like Lu Chih in that of governmental affairs, like Ssu-ma Ch'ien in recording historical events, and like Li Po in the writing of poetry and *fu*.[14] Far from being my own opinion, this is the verdict of the whole country.

Master Ou-yang's name was Hsiu, and his courtesy name Yung-shu. When he had reached an advanced age, he styled himself Retired Scholar Liu-i.

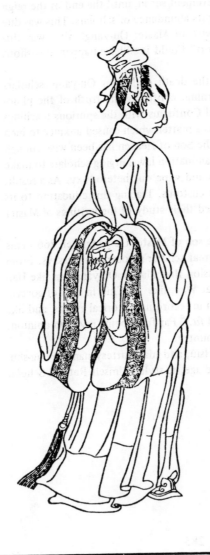

蘇文忠公

東坡先生跋公老子解後謂不意老年見此奇特於栖賢堂記則謂讀之便如在堂中見水石陰森草木膠葛至書趙然堂賦後則以為子由之文詞理精確有不及吾而體氣高妙吾所不及此文精確高妙殆兩得之記其听和八月四日詩則謂子由詩過吾遠甚。

Su Ch'e (1039-1112)

Su Ch'e, whose courtesy name was Tzu-yu 子由, took the imperial examination in the same year as his brother Tung-p'o and received his *chin-shih* degree when he was only nineteen.[1]

Like his brother, he was opposed to Wang An-shih's reforms, and for this reason he also fell into disfavor and could not remain near the court for any length of time. He first served for a while as a subordinate official in Shangchow 商州[2] and Taming 大名.[3] Later, as a result of his brother's poems, which had evoked serious objection, he was demoted to Supervisor of Salt and Wine Taxes in Yünchow 筠州,[4] in which post he remained for five years. Then he was appointed Magistrate of Chich'i 績溪.[5]

Because of his services in the pacification of the King of Hsia's[6] regime in the Northwest, Tzu-yu was promoted to the high office of Private Imperial Secretary and Chung-shu She-jen 中書舍人, a ranking member of the Prime Minister's Office. He was then rewarded for his suggestions regarding the harnessing of the Yellow River by a further promotion to Vice Minister of Finance.

He also acted as Secretary of the Hanlin Academy for his brother and Minister of Personnel. After leading a mission to Khitan 契丹, he became Vice President of the Censorship. Later, he became Vice Minister in the Prime Minister's Office.

In these offices, Tzu-yu had occasion to express his views on important affairs of state. But it was precisely because of

[1] Only eighteen according to the Western custom of reckoning age.
[2] Prefecture in modern Shensi Province.
[3] Prefecture in modern Hopeh Province.
[4] Prefecture in modern Kiangsi Province.
[5] A district (*hsien*) in Anhwei Province.
[6] A rebel in the Northwest.

287

the challenging opportunity .presented to him that things sometimes went wrong and put him in difficulty. In his later years, he had to remain mostly in prefectural posts outside the capital. Finally, he retired and went to live in Hsüchow 許州,[7] and adopted the nickname of "Abandoned Old Man on the Bank of the Ying" 潁濱遺叟. He lived alone for almost ten years without associating with anyone before he died at the age of seventy-four. The posthumous title of Secretary of the Tuan-ming Hall 端明殿學士 was conferred on him, and, during the reign of Emperor Hsiao-tsung 孝宗 (1163-1189), he was canonized as Wen-ting 文定.

The works left by Tzu-yu include the *Exposition of the Book of Songs* 詩傳, the *Exposition of the Spring and Autumn Annals* 春秋傳, *Ancient History* 古史, *Notes on Lao-tzu* 老子解 and his collected works (欒城集). He was a man of serenity and simplicity. His approach to literature was penetrating but dispassionate.

[7]Prefecture in modern Honan Province.

288

六　國　論

　　嘗讀六國世家，竊怪天下之諸侯，以五倍之地，十倍之衆，發憤西向，以攻山西千里之秦，而不免於滅亡。常爲之深思遠慮，以爲必有可以自安之計。蓋未嘗不咎其當時之士，慮患之疎，而見利之淺，且不知天下之勢也。

　　夫秦之所與諸侯爭天下者，不在齊楚燕趙也，而在韓魏之郊。諸侯之所與秦爭天下者，不在齊楚燕趙也，而在韓魏之野。秦之有韓魏，譬如人之有腹心之疾也。韓魏塞秦之衝，而蔽山東之諸侯，故夫天下之所重者，莫如韓魏也。

　　昔者范雎用於秦而收韓，商鞅用於秦而收魏。昭王未得韓魏之心，而出兵以攻齊之剛壽，而范雎以爲憂。然則秦之所忌者，可以見矣。

　　秦之用兵於燕趙，秦之危事也。越韓過魏而攻人之國都，燕趙拒之於前，而韓魏乘之於後，此危道也。而秦之攻燕趙，未嘗有韓魏之憂，則韓魏之附秦故也。夫韓魏，諸侯之障。而使秦人得出入於其間，此豈知天下之勢邪？

---

[1] Ch'i, Ch'u, Yen, Chao, Han and Wei, states in the Warring States period.
[2] Referring to Mount Hsiao 郁山, also known as Hsiao Han 郁函.
[3] Prime Minister under King Chao of Ch'in 秦昭王 .
[4] Prime Minister under Duke Hsiao of Ch'in 秦孝公 .
[5] Localities in modern Shantung Province.

On the Six States[1]

In reading the biographies of the rulers of the six states, I have often wondered why these rulers, with five times as much territory and ten times as many troops as the state of Ch'in, which had only an area of one thousand square *li* west of the mountains,[2] were unsuccessful in their attack on Ch'in and could not escape extinction. I have always given the matter very deep thought and felt certain that those rulers should have had a plan to guard their security. But I have been forced to conclude that the statesmen of the time were not free from blame for their shortsightedness, shallow judgment regarding their interests, and ignorance of the situation in the empire.

In its struggle with the six states, the state of Ch'in focused its attention, not on Ch'i, Ch'u, Yen and Chao, but on the suburbs of Han and Wei. Similarly, in their struggle with Ch'in, the six states should focus their attention, not on Ch'i, Ch'u, Yen and Chao, but on the wilds of Han and Wei. The existence of Han and Wei was to Ch'in like an ailment of the heart and stomach. The two were buffer states between Ch'in and the feudal states east of the mountains. The position of Han and Wei was therefore of crucial importance.

Formerly, when Fan Sui's[3] services were enlisted by Ch'in, he succeeded in conquering Han, and when Shang Yang's[4] services were enlisted by Ch'in, he succeeded in conquering Wei. Without winning the hearts of the people of Han and Wei, King Chao [of Ch'in] sent his troops to invade Kang and Shou[5] of Ch'i, a move that was a source of worry to Fan Sui. It was evidently something that ran counter to Ch'in's interest.

The dispatch of troops to Yen and Chao was equally dangerous. In passing through Han and Wei and attacking the capitals of the other two states, Ch'in would invite the resistance of Yen and Chao in front and enable Han and Wei to pose a threat in the rear. It was therefore a hazardous course to take. And yet when Ch'in attacked Yen and Chao, she did not worry about Han and Wei. This was due to the adherence Ch'in had already won from Han and Wei. Though these states were the shield of the other feudal lands, the men of Ch'in were nevertheless permitted to go in and out of them. Could this have

委區區之韓魏,以當强虎狼之秦, 彼安得不折而入於秦哉?
韓魏折而入於秦, 然後秦人得通其兵於東諸侯, 而使天下
徧受其禍。

　　夫韓魏不能獨當秦, 而天下之諸侯, 藉之以蔽其西,
故莫如厚韓親魏以擯秦。秦人不敢逾韓魏以窺齊楚燕趙之
國, 而齊楚燕趙之國, 因得以自完於其間矣。以四無事之
國, 佐當寇之韓魏, 使韓魏無東顧之憂, 而爲天下出身以
當秦兵。以二國委秦, 而四國休息於內, 以陰助其急。若
此可以應夫無窮, 彼秦者將何爲哉?

　　不知出此, 而乃貪疆場尺寸之利, 背盟敗約, 以自相
屠滅。秦兵未出, 而天下諸侯已自困矣。至使秦人得伺其
隙以取其國。可不悲哉?

happened had there been a real understanding of the situation in the empire? When little Han and Wei were given the task of resisting mighty Ch'in, which was as fierce as a tiger or wolf, how could they have been kept from falling into the hands of Ch'in? After their fall, the men of Ch'in were able to send their troops through to the eastern states and bring catastrophe on the whole empire.

Since Han and Wei could not resist Ch'in by themselves and since the other feudal lords depended on them as a shield against the west, nothing would have served their interests better than to befriend those two states and rely on them to ward off Ch'in. Had they done so, Ch'in would not have dared to pass through Han and Wei to attack the other four states, which could thus have kept themselves intact. The four states, facing no immediate danger, could have helped Han and Wei in their resistance against the common enemy. Thus Han and Wei would have had nothing to fear from the east and could have faced the forces of Ch'in in the interest of the rest of the empire. Only the two states would then have been in direct encounter with Ch'in while the other four would have gained a chance for repose and stood ready to offer secret assistance when necessary. Thus the alliance could have coped with the situation indefinitely. What could a state like Ch'in have done in these circumstances?

Not knowing enough to do this, the states concerned, beguiled by greed for small territorial gains on their borders, violated their treaty of alliance and engaged in mutual massacre and destruction. As a result, even before the forces of Ch'in were deployed, the other feudal lords had placed themselves in distress, and the men of Ch'in took the opportunity to conquer their kingdoms. Was this not a tragedy?

上樞密韓太尉書

太尉執事，轍生好為文，思之至深。以為文者。氣之所形。然文不可以學而能，氣可以養而致。孟子曰：「我善養吾浩然之氣。」今觀其文章，寬厚宏博，充乎天地之間，稱其氣之小大。太史公行天下，周覽四海名山大川，與燕趙間豪俊交游。故其文疏蕩，頗有奇氣。此二子者，豈嘗執筆學為如此之文哉？其氣充乎其中，而溢乎其貌，動乎其言，而見乎其文，而不自知也。

轍生十有九年矣。其居家所與遊者，不過其鄰里鄉黨之人，所見不過數百里之間。無高山大野，可登覽以自廣。百氏之書，雖無所不讀，然皆古人之陳迹，不足以激發其志氣。恐遂汩沒，故決然捨去，求天下奇聞壯觀，以知天地之廣大。

過秦漢之故都，恣觀終南嵩華之高，北顧黃河之奔流，慨然想見古之豪傑。至京師，仰觀天子宮闕之壯，與倉廩府庫城池苑囿之富且大也，而後知天下之巨麗。見翰林歐

---

[1] Han Ch'i 韓琦, one of the best-known prime ministers and commanders-in-chief of the Sung dynasty.

[2] See above, p. 27, Note 15.

[3] Modern Hopei and Shansi Provinces.

[4] A mountain range extending through Kansu, Shensi and Honan Provinces.

[5] A mountain peak in Tengfeng 登封 *Hsien*, Honan Province.

[6] A mountain peak in Huaying 華陰 *Hsien*, Shensi Province.

[7] Ou-yang Hsiu. See above, pp. 133-138.

Letter to Prime Minister Han[1]

Your Excellency:

By nature I am fond of writing, and have pondered on it deeply. In my view, writing is formed by the spirit. While the ability to write is not acquired through study, the spirit can be cultivated. Mencius has said: "I am good at cultivating my great spirit." Today we can see that his writing was broad, substantial, grand and profound, pervading heaven and earth, in direct proportion to his spirit. The Grand Historian[2] toured the world, saw all the famed mountains and great rivers within the four seas and associated with the heroic men of Yen and Chao.[3] His writing was therefore unconventional, and its spirit rather strange. Did Mencius and the Grand Historian ever hold a pen to learn to write as they did? Without their being conscious of it, within themselves these men were filled with a spirit which overflowed and transformed their appearance, moved in the words they spoke, and revealed itself in their writing.

It has been nineteen years since I was born. Those with whom I associate at home are confined to the neighborhood and surrounding country, the range of my vision does not exceed several hundred *li*, and there are no lofty mountains or wild expanses that I can visit to broaden my view. Though I do not leave unread the books of the hundred schools, these are merely the remnants of the ancients and cannot stimulate my ambition. Lest I be totally eclipsed, I have decided to leave home, to listen to the strange tales and see the magnificent sights of the world so as to become acquainted with the vast extent of heaven and earth.

I have passed the erstwhile capitals of the Ch'in and Han dynasties, gazed lavishly at the heights of the Chungnan,[4] Sung[5] and Hua[6] Mountains, turned my eyes northward to the rushing waters of the Yellow River, and pondered with deep feeling over the heroes of old. On reaching the capital, I have looked up toward the grandeur of the palaces and gates of the Son of Heaven and the opulence and magnitude of his granaries, treasuries, walls, moats, parks and gardens. Then I realized the vastness and beauty of the world. I have met the Honorable Hanlin Ou-yang,[7] listened to his eloquent discussions, looked on his handsome

陽公，聽其議論之宏辯，觀其容貌之秀偉，與其門人賢士
大夫游，而後知天下之文章聚乎此也。

　　太尉以才略冠天下，天下之所恃以無憂，四夷之所憚
以不敢發，入則周公召公，出則方叔召虎，而轍也未之見
焉。

　　且夫人之學也，不志其大，雖多而何爲？轍之來也，
於山見終南嵩華之高，於水見黃河之大且深，於人見歐陽
公。而猶以爲未見太尉也。故願得觀賢人之光耀，聞一言
以自壯，然後可以盡天下之大觀，而無憾矣。

　　轍年少，未能通習吏事。嚮之來，非有取於斗升之祿，
偶然得之，非其所樂。然幸得賜歸待選，使得優游數年之
間，將以益治其文，且學爲政。太尉苟以爲可敎而辱敎之，
又幸矣。

---

[8] Regents during the reign of King Ch'eng of the Chou dynasty 周成王.

[9] Worthy ministers under King Hsüan of Chou 周宣王.

[10] *Sheng* = pint; *tou* = peck.

and impressive face, and associated with his pupils who have become distinguished officials. Then I knew that the great writings of the world are concentrated in this circle of people.

Your Excellency's ability and strategy are unequaled. On them the world relies to be free from apprehension, and your qualities so awe the barbarians that they do not dare to start trouble. When you are at court, you are like the Dukes of Chou and Chao,[8] when you are away from it, you are like Fang Shu and Chao Hu.[9] But I have not had the pleasure of meeting you.

Moreover, what does it profit a man to study, if his effort, however intensive, does not aim high? On my way here, I have seen mountains as lofty as the Chungnan, Sung and Hua, a body of water as vast and deep as the Yellow River and a man like the Honorable Ou-yang. Yet I have not seen the Prime Minister. I therefore entertain the wish to bask in the brilliant light shed by the wise and hear a word from you to enrich myself. Then I shall have exhausted the magnificent sights of the world and need have no more regrets.

As I am a young man, I have not yet learned to practice the affairs of government. My previous visit was not aimed at securing a *sheng* or *tou*[10] of official emolument. If perchance I earned it, I would not have been happy about it. But, if I can now have the good fortune to be given leave to return home and wait till I am selected for a post, so that I can have a few years of leisure, I shall devote myself more assiduously to writing and learning the art of government. If Your Excellency feels that I can be taught and does not regard it as beneath you to teach me, it will be my added good fortune.

巢谷傳

巢谷，字元脩。父中，世眉山農家也，少從士大夫讀書，老爲里校師。

谷幼傳父學，雖朴而博。舉進士京師，見舉武藝者，心好之。谷素多力，遂棄其舊學，畜弓箭，習騎射。久之，業成，而不中第。聞西邊多驍勇，騎射擊刺，爲四方冠。去遊秦鳳涇原間，所至友其秀傑。

有韓存寶者，尤與之善。谷敎之兵書，二人相與爲金石交。熙寧中，存寶爲河州將，有功，號熙河名將，朝廷稍奇之。會瀘州蠻乞弟擾邊，諸郡不能制，乃命存寶出兵討之。存寶不習蠻事，邀谷至軍中問焉。

及存寶得罪，將就逮，自料必死。謂谷曰：「我涇原武夫，死非所惜，顧妻子不免寒餓。橐中有銀數百兩，非君莫使遺之者。」谷許諾，即變姓名，懷銀步行，往授其

---

[1] A district in Szechwan Province, also the home of the author.
[2] Parts of Shensi and Kansu Provinces.
[3] 1068-1077, reign of Emperor Shen-tsung.
[4] Prefecture in modern Kansu Province.
[5] Prefecture in modern Szechwan Province.

Biography of Ch'ao Ku

Ch'ao Ku had the courtesy name of Yüan-hsiu. His father, Chung, was from a farming family in Meishan,[1] which traced its history back for some generations. As a young man, he studied under scholars, and as he became older, he served as a teacher in the village school.

Even in his young days Ku had inherited from his father rich scholarship. Though of average intelligence, he was widely read. When he went up to the capital to take the examination for the *chin-shih* degree, he saw the youths seeking to enter the military profession and took a fancy to it. Endowed with physical prowess, he abandoned his old studies, bought himself bows and arrows and practiced archery and riding. But, after completing his long training, he did not succeed in passing the military examination. Hearing that there were innumerable brave men on the western border who excelled all others in the country in archery and swordsmanship, he repaired to the vicinity of Ch'infeng and Chingyüan,[2] where he made friends with the most outstanding of them.

One of these, Han Ts'un-pao, was on especially good terms with him. Ku taught Han military science, and the two became bosom friends. In the reign of Hsi-ning,[3] Ts'un-pao was a general in Hochow.[4] As he had rendered meritorious service, he was known as the "Famous General of Hsiho"; his exploits amazed the court. Later, a barbarian of Luchow,[5] Ch'i-ti, caused disturbances on the border, and there was no one in the prefectures who could stop him. Ts'un-pao was ordered to send his troops to suppress the rebellion. As he was unfamiliar with barbarian customs, Ts'un-pao invoked Ku's assistance.

Ts'un-pao was subsequently charged with a crime. Before he was even arrested, he had expected to be put to death. "Being a soldier from Chingyüan," he said to Ku, "I will not regret my death. But my wife and children are in danger of suffering cold and hunger. In my purse there are several hundred taels. I can trust none but you to remit them." After undertaking to do so for his friend, Ku changed his name and set out on foot, carrying with him the silver which was to be delivered to Ts'un-pao's son. The secret was so well kept that the mission was never known to anyone. After Ts'un-pao's death, Ku

299

子，人無知者。存寶死，谷逃避江淮間，會赦乃出。

予以鄉閭，故幼而識之，知其志節緩急可託者也。予之在朝，谷浮沉里中，未嘗一見。紹聖初，予以罪謫居筠州，自筠徙雷，自雷徙循。予兄子瞻亦自惠再徙昌化。士大夫皆諱與予兄弟遊，平生親友無復相聞者。谷獨慨然自眉山誦言，欲徒步訪吾兄弟，聞者皆笑其狂。

元符二年春正月，自梅州遺予書曰：「我萬里步行見公，不自意全。今至梅矣。不旬日必見。死無恨矣。」予驚喜曰：「此非今世人，古之人也。」既見，握手相泣，已而道平生，逾月不厭。

時谷年七十有三矣。瘦瘠多病，非復昔日元脩也。將復見子瞻於海南。予愍其老且病，止之曰：「君意則善，然自此至儋數千里，復當渡海，非老人事也。」谷曰：「我自視未即死也。公無止我。」

留之，不可。閱其橐中，無數十錢。予方乏困，亦強資遣之。船行至新會，有蠻隸竊其橐裝以逃，獲於新州。

[6] 1094-1098, reign of Emperor Cheh-tsung.
[7] Prefecture in modern Kiangsi Province.
[8] Prefecture in modern Kwangtung Province.
[9] Prefecture in the same Province.
[10] Prefecture in the same Province.
[11] A district in the same Province.
[12] 1099, reign of Emperor Cheh-tsung.
[13] Prefecture in modern Kwangsi Province.
[14] A district in Kwangtung Province.
[15] A district in Kwangtung Province.
[16] Prefecture in modern Kwangtung Province.

escaped to the Yangtze and Huai regions and did not emerge from concealment until he was pardoned.

As a neighbor of his, I knew him from childhood, and had learned of his ambition, integrity and reliability. When I was at court, Ku remained obscure in the countryside, and I never had a chance to see him. At the beginning of Shao-sheng,[6] I was demoted to Yünchow,[7] and then I had to move again to Leichow[8] and Hsünchow.[9] My elder brother, Tzu-chan [Tung-p'o], had also to move from Huichow[10] to Ch'anghua.[11] We were shunned by official circles, and we never heard from relatives and friends. Only Ku was thoughtful enough to declare openly in Meishan that he would make a trip on foot to visit my brother and me. All those who heard him laughed at his madness.

In the first month of the second year of Yüan-fu,[12] Ku sent me a letter from Meichow.[13] "I am walking a long distance," it said, "to see you. Almost beyond my expectations, I have now arrived in Meichow. In less than ten days I am sure to meet you, and then I shall have no regrets, even if I am to die." I was amazed and delighted. "This does not should like a man of today," I said, "but someone from ancient times!" When we met soon afterwards, we shook hands and wept together. Then we talked about our lives, and this occupied us untiringly for more than a month.

At that time, Ku was already seventy-three years of age. He was emaciated and chronically sick, no longer the same man as the Yüan-hsiu I once knew. He planned to see Tzu-chan at Hainan. I pitied him for his age and poor health and tried to stop him. "Though your intention is good," I said, "from here to Tan[14] the distance is several thousand *li*, and you have to cross the sea. It is not a journey for an old man." "I do not think," replied Ku, "that I am in danger of dying immediately. Please do not try to stop me."

Thus, my attempt to dissuade him was unsuccessful. Looking through his purse, however, I could not even find a few scores of cash. Though I was in financial straits myself, I did my best to make his trip possible. When his boat reached Hsinhui,[15] a barbarian slave stole his purse and luggage and escaped. The thief was caught in Hsinchow.[16] Ku

301

谷從之至新，逐病死。予聞哭之失聲。恨其不用吾言，然
亦奇其不用吾言而行其志也。

昔趙襄子厄於晉陽，知伯率韓魏決水圍之。城不沈者
三版，縣釜而爨，易子而食。羣臣皆懈，惟高恭不失人臣
之禮。及襄子用張孟談計，三家之圍解，行賞，羣臣以恭爲
先。談曰：「晉陽之難，惟恭無功。曷爲先之？」襄子曰：「晉
陽之難，羣臣皆懈，惟恭不失人臣之禮，吾是以先之。」

谷於朋友之義，實無愧高恭者。惜其不遇襄子，而前
遇存寶，後遇予兄弟。予方雜居南夷，與之起居出入，蓋
將終焉。雖知其賢，尚何以發之？

聞谷有子蒙，在涇原軍中，故爲作傳，異日以授之。

谷始名穀，及見之循州，改名谷云。

---

[17] A feudal lord of the state of Tsin 晉.
[18] A district in Shansi Province.
[19] A high official of the state of Tsin.
[20] Two other noble families in the same state.
[21] The two names are homophonous.

followed him to that prefecture, and there he died. I was grieved by the news, and cried until I lost my voice. I regretted that he had not taken my advice, but I was equally amazed by his determination to ignore my warning and persist in his resolve.

In ancient times, when Viscount Hsiang of Chao[17] met with disaster at Tsinyang,[18] Chih-po,[19] at the head of the Hans and Weis,[20] laid siege to him by flooding the land round the city. The water was so high that only twenty-four *ch'ih* of the city wall had not been submerged. People had to do their cooking by hanging pots and pans above the flood level, and the practice was adopted of exchanging sons and eating their flesh. All the ministers were loose in their conduct, with the exception of Kao Kung, who never deviated from the respect due from a subject to his lord. When Viscount Hsiang adopted Chang Meng-t'an's plan and raised the siege of the three families, a number of persons were rewarded. Kung headed the list. "Kung is the only one that could not claim any credit for bringing relief to Tsinyang," Meng-t'an said. "Why should he be the first to be rewarded?" "In the Tsinyang crisis," Viscount Hsiang said, "all my ministers were loose in their conduct, with the exception of Kung, who never deviated from the respect due from a subject. That is why I reward him first."

In his loyal friendship, Ku was as unimpeachable as Kao Kung. Unfortunately, he did not have a chance to meet Viscount Hsiang; indeed, he encountered first Ts'un-pao and then my brother and me. As I was living with the Southern barbarians and it seemed that I would spend the remainder of my life with them, I could not secure for Ku the recognition he deserved, though I knew that he was a worthy man.

I hear that Ku has a son named Meng, who is in military service in Chingyüan. Hence I have written this biography, to be handed to him later.

Ku's name was at first Ku 縠, but, when I saw him in Hsünchow, it had been changed to Ku 谷.[21]

曾文定

公性孝友父亡奉繼母益至撫四弟九妹於委廢單弱中官學婚嫁一出其力為

文章上下馳騁太原六經斟酌於司馬遷韓愈時鮮能過也

Tseng Kung (1019-1083)

Tseng Kung's courtesy name was Tzu-ku; his home was in Nanfeng 南豐.[1] When he was a child, he was alert and intelligent, and he started to write at an early age. His name was known far and wide when he was scarcely twenty. He won his *chin-shih* degree in the imperial examination of the second year of Chia-yu 嘉祐.[2] He was first appointed to the Chi-hsien Council 集賢院 as one of its editors and later transferred to the History Compilation Office. Thereafter he was assigned successively to eight prefectures, seven of which he headed.

When he was Prefect of Foochow,[3] his office was not allotted any land as part of his emoluments, as was the practice at the time. Before he arrived, it had been customary for the prefect to sell vegetables annually from certain gardens to supplement his income, which often brought in as much as three or four thousand cash.[4] On his assumption of office, Tzu-ku abolished the system for himself as well as for his successors. "The prefect," he declared, "should not compete with the people for profit."

As he was away from the capital for many years, Tseng was considered by some to be out of favor. At the same time, those junior to him were one after another placed in positions of prominence. But this did not perturb him in the least.

On one occasion he was given an audience by Emperor Shen-tsung 神宗, who showed him extreme courtesy and detained him at court. While there, he memorialized the throne on the importance of economy, which met with the sovereign's approval. At the time, the emperor had the intention of having a general history compiled out of the

---

[1] A district in Kiangsi Province.
[2] 1057, reign of Emperor Jen-tsung.
[3] Prefecture in modern Fukien Province.
[4] The smallest unit of currency at the time.

voluminous dynastic chronicles and of appointing Tseng to the chief editorship. The plan came to nought, however, and he was appointed instead as a ranking official in the Prime Minister's office. In his last post, he served as Secretary to one of the imperial princes.

Tseng Kung died at the age of sixty-five. He was a filial son and loyal brother. After his father died, he was the one who brought up four younger brothers and nine sisters in circumstances of tremendous difficulty. Subsequently, he also assumed the responsibility for their studies and their marriages until the brothers entered public service.

Tzu-ku's literary style was surpassed by few of his contemporaries. It was modeled on the six classics, and showed the influence of Ssu-ma Ch'ien and Han Yü. He was one of the protégés of the great Ou-yang Hsiu, who had presided over the imperial examination in which Tseng won his *chin-shih* degree. He was also a friend of Wang An-shih, another of the eight great masters, who later became Prime Minister. It was through Tseng Kung that Wang was recommended to Ou-yang. But, as soon as Wang An-shih became prominent, Tseng kept aloof from him.

Emperor Shen-tsung had occasion to ask Tseng's opinion of Wang. "An-shih's literary talent and conduct," he said in reply, "are not inferior to those of Yang Hsiung 揚雄, but he falls behind because of his stinginess." "Since An-shih cares little for wealth and distinction," said the emperor, "how can he be said to be stingy?" "Because," Tzu-ku replied, "he is stingy about rectifying his faults, though he is bold in seeking achievement."

墨　池　記

　　臨川之城東，有地隱然而高，以臨于溪，曰新城，新城之上，有池窪然，而方以長，曰王羲之之墨池者，荀伯子臨川記云也。羲之嘗慕張芝臨池學書，池水盡黑。此爲其故跡。豈信然邪？

　　方羲之之不可強以仕，而嘗極東方，出滄海，以娛其意于山水之間，豈有徜徉肆恣，而又嘗自休于此耶？

　　羲之之書，晚乃善，則其所能，蓋亦以精力自致者，非天成也。然後世未有能及者，豈其學不如彼耶？則學固豈可以少哉？況欲深造道德者邪？

　　墨池之上，今爲州學舍。教授王君盛恐其不彰也，書「晉王右軍墨池」之六字于楹間以揭之，又告于鞏曰：「願有記。」

　　推王君之心，豈愛人之善，雖一能不以廢，而因以及乎其跡邪？其亦欲推其事以勉其學者耶？夫人之有一能，而使後人尚之如此。況仁人莊士之遺風餘思，被于來世者，何如哉？慶曆八年九月十二日，曾鞏記。

---

[1] A district in Kiangsi Province.
[2] One of the greatest Chinese calligraphers who lived in the Tsin dynasty.
[3] A well-known calligrapher in the Eastern Han dynasty.
[4] The title of a general.
[5] 1048, reign of Emperor Jen-tsung.

The Ink Pond

There is a terrace concealed from view east of the city of Linch'uan.[1] It juts out onto a brook and is known as Hsinch'eng. On top of Hsinch'eng is a pond, which is deep and rectangular in shape and which, according to the *Chronicles of Linch'uan*, by Hsün Po-tzu, bore the name of "Wang Hsi-chih's[2] Ink Pond." As he admired Chang Chih,[3] Hsi-chih followed his example by practicing calligraphy on the banks of the pond until the water became wholly black. It is said that here is the site of the old pond. Can it be the truth?

Wang Hsi-chih refused to be pressed into the civil service; he journeyed to the east, reaching as far as the Gulf of Pohai, to amuse himself by frequenting mountains and rivers. Could it be that in the midst of his roamings he had some rest near this pond?

The calligraphy of Hsi-chih was not prefected until late in his life. In other words, instead of being a born calligrapher, he acquired his skill through the energetic pursuit of the art. But he has had no equal in subsequent generations. Could it be that they never equaled him in practicing? Indeed, can practice ever be dispensed with, especially by those who are bent on cultivating their morality?

Above the Ink Pond now stands the prefectural school. Teacher Wang, deeply apprehensive that the name might not be known, wrote the words: "Ink Pond of Yu-chün[4] Wang of the Tsin dynasty" and had them displayed over the pillars. "I hope," he also said to me, "that you will put this incident in writing."

From what Mr. Wang had in mind, can it not be inferred that he loves skill in others so much that he does not wish to disregard even a single talent and that he wishes to extend this admiration even to the site of the old pond and apply Hsi-chih's story to the practice of scholars? Since one single talent can arouse the admiration of later ages to this extent, how much more will the heritage left by benevolent and upright men, whose abiding thought is destined to influence rising generations?

> Recorded by Tseng Kung, the 12th day of
> the 9th month, 8th year of Ch'ing-li[5]

撫州顏魯公祠堂記

贈司徒魯郡顏公，諱眞卿，事唐爲太子太師，與其從父兄杲卿，皆有大節以死，至今雖小夫婦人，皆知公之爲烈也。

初，公以忤楊國忠斥爲平原太守，策安祿山必反，爲之備。祿山既舉兵，與常山太守杲卿伐其後。賊之不能直闚潼關，以公與杲卿撓其勢也。

在肅宗時，數正言，宰相不悅，斥去之。又爲御史唐旻所構，連輒斥。李輔國遷太上皇居西宮，公首率百官，請問起居，又輒斥。代宗時，與元載爭論是非，載欲有所壅蔽，公極論之，又輒斥。楊炎、盧杞既相，德宗益惡公所爲，連斥之。猶不滿意，李希烈陷汝州，杞即以公使希烈，希烈初慚其言，後卒縊公以死。是時公年七十有七矣。

天寶之際，久不見兵，祿山既反，天下莫不震動，公

---

[1] Prefecture in modern Kiangsi Province.　[2] Title of one of the highest officials.
[3] When Ch'angshan was captured by An Lu-shan 安祿山 shortly after the outbreak of the An rebellion, Yen Kao-ch'ing was taken prisoner. With angrily glaring eyes, he reviled the rebels loudly. They then cut off his tongue and asked him if he could still curse them. He continued his vain attempts until he died.
[4] Prime Minister under Emperor Hsüan-tsung.
[5] Prefecture in modern Shantung Province.
[6] 755-757.　[7] Prefecture in modern Hopei Province.
[8] A pass in Shensi Province.　[9] He reigned in 756-762.
[10] A eunuch and powerful official under Emperors Su-tsung 肅宗 and Tai-tsung 代宗.
[11] He reigned in 762-779.　[12] Prime Minister under Emperor Hsün-tsung.
[13] 782.　[14] Prefecture in modern Honan Province.
[15] 742-756, reign of Emperor Hsüan-tsung.

The Temple of Yen, Duke of Lu, at Fuchow[1]

Yen Chen-ch'ing, Duke of Lu, on whom the posthumous title of Ssu-t'u[2] was conferred, attained the high position of Teacher of the Imperial Household, and was as great a martyr as his cousin, Kao-ch'ing.[3] To this day, even ordinary men and women are familiar with the heroism with which he laid down his life for the country.

Early in his career, having offended Yang Kuo-chung,[4] Duke Yen was demoted to P'ingyüan[5] as Prefect. He foresaw the revolt of An Lu-shan[6] and made preparations to counter it in advance. When the rebellion broke out, the duke cooperated with his cousin, Kao-ch'ing, who was then Prefect of Ch'angshan,[7] in cutting off Lu-shan's forces in the rear, thus preventing them from threatening T'ungkuan.[8]

During the reign of Emperor Su-tsung,[9] Duke Yen displeased the prime minister by his frankness and was reprimanded. He was also falsely accused by Censor T'ang Min and again reprimanded. When Li Fu-kuo[10] transferred the emperor's father to the western palace, Duke Yen was the first to pay his respects to him at the head of the official hierarchy. For this he was again reprimanded. In the reign of Emperor Tai-tsung,[11] in an argument with Yüan Tsai,[12] who concealed the truth from the emperor, he offended Yüan by carrying the discussion through to the end, and was once more reprimanded. When Yang Yen and Lu Ch'i became prime ministers under Emperor Teh-tsung, he fell into even greater disfavor and was again repeatedly reprimanded. Not content with this, the two men plotted to send him off to placate Li Hsi-lieh, who was in revolt[13] and had taken Juchow.[14] Though the words of Duke Yen put Li to shame, the rebel finally strangled him to death. At that time the duke had reached the age of seventy-seven.

During T'ien-pao[15] the country had not seen fighting for a long time. The revolt of An Lu-shan shook the whole empire. However, Duke Yen, though with only the small area of P'ingyüan under his

311

獨以區區平原，遂折其鋒。四方聞之，爭奮而起。唐卒以振者，公爲之唱也。當公之開土門，同日歸公者，十七都，得兵二十餘萬。繇此觀之，苟順且誠，天下從之矣。

自此至公歿，垂三十年，小人繼續任政，天下日入于弊，大盜繼起，天子輒出避之。唐之在朝臣，多畏怯觀望。能居其間，一忤于世，失所而不自悔者，寡矣。至于再三忤于世，失所而不自悔者，蓋未有也。若至于起且仆，以至于七八，遂死而不自悔者，則天下一人而已，若公是也。

公之學問文章，往往雜於神仙浮圖之說，不皆合于理。及其奮然自立，能至于此者，蓋天性然也。故公之能處其死，不足以觀公之大。何則？及至于勢窮，義有不得不死，雖中人可勉焉，況公之自信也歟？維歷忤大奸，顛跌撼頓，至于七八，而始終不以死生禍福爲秋毫顧慮，非篤于道者，不能如此，此足以觀公之大也。

夫世之治亂不同，而士之去就亦異。若伯夷之清，伊尹之任，孔子之時，彼各有義。夫既自比于古之任者矣，

---

[16] A pass between Hopei and Shansi Provinces.

[17] Eldest son of the ruler of the state of Ku-chu 孤竹, who refused to eat the rice of the Chou dynasty and starved to death with his brother Shu-ch'i 叔齊 after the fall of the Shang dynasty.

[18] Prime Minister under Emperor T'ang of the Shang dynasty.

control, successfully weakened the major thrusts of the rebel forces. This raised the morale of the people all over the country, and it was due to the leadership and inspiration of the duke that the T'ang dynasty was saved. When the duke opened up the pass of T'umen,[16] seventeen units joined him on the same day, and he was assured of more than two hundred thousand men. From this it can be seen that, as long as there is loyalty and sincerity, the whole empire will rally to its cause.

From this time until the duke's death, a period of almost thirty years, political power fell successively into the hands of unworthy men. The country was increasingly on the decline, and brigandage was rampant. Even the emperor himself often had to seek refuge outside of the capital. Officials at the T'ang court were so terrified that they adopted an attitude of watchful waiting. There were few who would risk for once going against the tide and losing their positions without regret. Fewer still could have done so more than once. Duke Yen was the only man in the whole empire who rose and fell seven or eight times until he died without regret.

The duke's scholarship and writings were frequently tainted with the theories of immortality and Buddhism and consequently not always rational. That he could courageously stand up as he did was due to his inborn character. His attitude toward life and death alone does not therefore bring out his greatness. For, when a situation becomes desperate and death cannot justly be avoided, even an average man can make an effort to reach the right decision. Could a man with the duke's faith have done otherwise? However, after offending arch-villains and falling seven or eight times, the duke never gave the slightest thought to life and death, weal and woe. But for his firm moral convictions, he could not have acted thus. Herein indeed one perceives the secret of his greatness.

Every age has its periods of peace and disorder, and a scholar's decision on whether or not to remain in public office differs according to circumstances. The purity of Po-i,[17] the sense of responsibility of I Yin,[18] the timeliness of Confucius all had their own justification. But, since a man compares himself to the ancient gentlemen who had a sense of responsibility, how can he retire and seek his own profit in the market place? That is why Confucius abhorred unworthy men, because of their unfitness for the service of their ruler, and exalted

乃欲睠顧回隱，以市于世其可乎？故孔子惡鄙夫不可以事君，而多殺身以成仁者。若公非孔子所謂仁者歟？

今天子至和三年，尚書都官郎中知撫州聶君厚載，尚書屯田員外郎通判撫州林君慥，相與慕公之烈，以公之嘗爲此邦也，遂爲堂而祠之。既成，二君過予之家而告之曰：「願有述。」

夫公之赫赫不可盡者，固不繫于祠之有無，蓋人之嚮往之不足者，非祠則無以致其至也。聞其烈，足以感人，況拜其祠而親炙之者歟？

今州縣之政，非法令所及者，世不復議。二君獨能追公之節，尊而事之，以風示當世，爲法令之所不及，是可謂有志者也。

---

[19] 1056, reign of Emperor Jen-tsung.
[20-21] Titles of ministerial officials.
[22] Assistant to the prefect.

those who laid down their lives for the sake of benevolence. Was the duke not one of those men whom Confucius would call benevolent?

During the reign of the present Son of Heaven, in the third year of Chih-ho,[19] Nieh Hou-tsai, Lang-chung[20] of the Ministry of Justice and Prefect of Fuchow, and Lin Ts'ao, Yüan-wai-lang[21] of the Ministry of Works and T'ung-p'an[22] of Fuchow, equally admiring the duke for his heroic sacrifice and recalling his former administration of this prefecture, built a temple to his memory. When the temple was completed, the two men came over to my residence and asked me to record this event.

The undying fame of the duke does not rest on the existence of a temple. But, without it, people's admiration for him may not be expressed to the utmost. Since the story of his heroic sacrifice is touching enough, can it not be made more meaningful if one worships and obtains one's personal inspiration at the temple?

Today, the administration of prefectures and districts does not extend beyond the scope of established laws and decrees. The two men, however, have looked back to the duke's integrity and seen fit to bring him as a paragon to the attention of the contemporary world. This is beyond the scope of ordinary laws and decrees, which bears witness to the farsightedness of these men.

醒心亭記

滁州之西南，泉水之涯，歐陽公作州之二年，構亭曰豐樂。自爲記，以見其名之意。

既又直豐樂之東幾百步，得山之高，構亭曰醒心，使鞏記之。

凡公與州之賓客者遊焉，則必即豐樂以飲。或醉且勞矣，則必即醒心而望，以見夫羣山之相環，雲烟之相滋，曠野之無窮，草樹衆而泉石嘉，使目新乎其所覩，耳新乎其所聞，則其心灑然而醒，更欲久而忘歸也。故即其所以然而爲名，取韓子退之「北湖」之詩云。噫，其可謂善取樂于山泉之間，而名之以見其實，又善者矣！

雖然，公之樂，吾能言之。吾君優游而無爲于上；吾民給足而無憾于下；天下學者皆爲才且良；夷狄，鳥獸，草木之生者，皆得其宜，公樂也。一山之隅，一泉之旁，豈公樂哉？乃公所以寄意于此也。

若公之賢，韓子歿數百年而始有之。今同遊之賓客，尚未知公之難遇也。後百千年，有慕公之爲人，而覽公之迹，思欲見之，有不可及之嘆，然後知公之難遇也。則凡

---

[1] Prefecture in modern Anhwei Province.
[2] See pp. 182-185, above.
[3] See pp. 23-27, above.
[4] *Ch'ang-li hsien-sheng shih chi-chu* 昌黎先生詩集註, *chüan* IX, p. 15.

The Sober Mind Pavilion

One year after the Honorable Ou-yang was appointed to Ch'uchow[1] as its Prefect, he had a pavilion constructed on the bank of the spring to the southwest. He named it the Pavilion of Prosperity and Happiness, and explained the meaning of this title in an essay he composed himself.[2]

Later, he had another pavilion built on a mountain peak some one hundred paces east of the first one and named it the Sober Mind Pavilion. For this occasion, I have been asked to record the event.

On his outings with his friends the Honorable Ou-yang invariably visits the Pavilion of Prosperity and Happiness and has his drinks there. After feeling tipsy and tired, he goes to the Sober Mind Pavilion. There, he views the surrounding mountains, the dense clouds and smoke, the boundless wilderness, the rich expanses of grass and trees, and the fair spring and pebbles. New sights greet his eyes and new sounds please his ears. As he becomes wide awake, he lingers longer and wants to forget to return home. Thus he gives the pavilion its name, which has been taken from the poem by Han Yü[3] on the "North Lake."[4] Oh, he is really a man who can derive pleasure from mountains and rivers, and the name he has chosen is not only consistent with the facts, but also most felicitous.

However, so far as I can see, the Honorable Ou-yang's pleasure lies deeper. He is pleased now, because our emperor is carefree and has little cause for concern. Our people have enough and do not hanker after anything; the scholars of the empire are all talented and highly qualified; and the barbarians, the birds and animals, the grasses and trees—all living beings—are content in their proper places. How, then, can he confine his delight to a mountainside or the bank of a spring? These are only the media through which he expresses his delight.

It is several hundred years since the death of Han Yü that we have had a man as worthy as the Honorable Ou-yang. Those guests who are with him today do not realize how rare it is to have the opportunity of meeting such a man. A hundred or thousand years hence, those who look back to him in admiration and are acquainted with his rich spiritual legacy will regret that, despite their eagerness to see him in the flesh, it will be too late, and then they will really see how rare it is to meet a

同遊于此者，其可不喜且幸歟？而鞏也，又得以文詞託名
於公文之次，其又不喜且幸歟？

慶曆七年八月十五日記。

---

man like him. This being so, should we not all feel happy and fortunate to be able to associate with this distinguished person on his visit here? For my part, should I not feel particularly happy and fortunate, since I have the additional honor of placing my humble writing next to his?

Fifteenth day of the eighth month of the
seventh year of Ch'ing-li[5]

徐 復 傳

徐復，字希顏，興化軍莆田人。嘗舉進士，不中，去不復就。博學，於書無所不讀，尤通星曆五行術數之說，世罕有能及者。為人偶儻有大志，內自飭厲，不求當世之譽，樂其所自得。謂富貴不足慕也，貧賤不足憂也。故窮廬漏屋，敝衣糲食，或至於不能自給，未嘗動其意也。遇人無少長貴賤，皆盡恭謹。

其言前世因革興壞是非之理，人少能及。然其家未嘗畜書，蓋其強記如此也。

康定中，李元昊叛，詔求有文武材可用者。參知政事宋綬，天章閣侍讀林瑀，皆薦復。詔賜裝錢，州郡迫趣上道。

既至，仁宗見復於崇政殿，訪以世務，復所以為上言者，世莫得聞也。仁宗因命講易乾坤既濟未濟，又問：「今歲直何卦，西兵欲出，如何。」復對：「歲直小過，而太

---

[1] P'ut'ien, a district in modern Fukien Province, under the prefecture of Hsinghua.

[2] 1040-1041, reign of Emperor Jen-tsung.

[3] A rebel, on whom the imperial surname, Chao 趙, had been conferred and who later became the ruler of Western Hsia 西夏, a state in the Sung dynasty covering parts of modern Suiyuan, Ninghsia and Kansu Provinces.

Biography of Hsü Fu

Hsü Fu, whose courtesy name was Hsi-yen, hailed from P'ut'ien, Hsinghua.[1] He failed the imperial examination, and he never took it again. He was a learned man, and left no book unread. He was especially versed in astrology, the sidereal calendar, the five elements and magical calculations, in which he had few equals. He had no restraint and had great ambition. Inwardly, however, he was prudent and observed strict discipline. He never sought fame in his time and was always contented with his lot. He held that wealth and official distinction were not worth seeking and that poverty and lowliness should cause no distress. Though he lived in a ramshackle and leaky house, wore tattered clothes, ate coarse food and often could not make both ends meet, he was never worried on this account. In dealing with people, young and old, gentle and simple, he was always polite and attentive.

Few people were so accurate as he in explaining the measures adopted and rescinded in former ages, the rise and fall of dynastic regimes, the rights and wrongs of every case. But he never kept any books in the house; his excellent memory enabled him to do without them.

In the reign of K'ang-ting,[2] Li Yüan-hao[3] revolted. An Imperial decree was issued calling for nominations of civilian and military talents. Both Sung Shou, Deputy Prime Minister, and Lin Yü, Reader of the T'ien-chang Hall, recommended Hsü for service in the government. An allocation was made by the court for his clothes and traveling expenses. The local prefecture urged him to set out for the capital.

On his arrival, he was given an audience by Emperor Jen-tsung at the Ch'ung-cheng Hall. Questions were addressed to him on current affairs, and his answers were such as no one else could have furnished. The emperor ordered him to lecture on those parts of the *Book of Changes* which dealt with the trigrams *Ch'ien* and *K'un* and the hexagrams *Chi-chi* and *Wei-chi*. He was also asked what steps should be taken to deal with the Western rebels. He replied that the hexagram *Hsiao-kuo* was operative that year and that the T'ai-i star was on guard at the North Pole, which signified that the empire's military strength should be concentrated in the center, and not in the outlying parts, of the

321

一守中宮。兵宜內不宜外。」仁宗善其言。

復又獻所爲邊防策, 太一主客位成曆,洪範論。上曰:「卿
所獻書, 爲卿留中。」必欲官之, 復固辭, 迺官其子晞。
留復登聞鼓院, 與林瑀同脩周易會元紀。歲餘, 固求東歸。
仁宗高其行, 禮以束帛, 賜號「沖晦處士」。

復久遊吳, 因家杭州。州牧每至, 必先加禮, 然復未
嘗肯至公門。范仲淹知杭州, 數就復訪問, 甚禮重之。仲
淹嘗言:「西兵旣起, 復預言:『罷兵歲月,』又斗牛間, 嘗
有星變, 復言:『吳當大疫, 死者數十萬人。』後皆如其言。」

復平居以周易, 太玄授學者。人或勸復著書, 復曰:「古
聖賢書已具, 顧學者不能求。吾復何爲以徼名後世哉?」
晚取其所爲文章, 盡焚之。今其家有書十餘篇, 皆出於門
人故舊之家。

復卒時, 年七十餘。旣病, 故人王稷居睦州, 欲往省
之, 復報曰:「來以五六月之交, 尚及見子。」稷未及往,
至期, 復果已死。其終事皆預自處。

子晞, 年五十餘, 亦致仕, 官至國子博士。

復贈尚書虞部員外郎。復死十餘年, 而沈遘知杭州,

---

[4] Ancient name of parts of modern Kiangsu, Anhwei and Chekiang Provinces.
[5] A great prime minister in the Sung dynasty.
[6] A work by Yang Hsiung 揚雄, a philosopher of the Han dynasty.
[7] Prefecture in modern Chekiang Province.
[8] Title of an official on ministerial staffs.

country. The emperor agreed.

Hsü then presented to His Majesty his works on *Strategy of Border Defenses*, the *Calendar Based on the Position of the T'ai-i Star* and the *Great Plan*. The emperor ordered that his books be placed in safe-keeping, but insisted on appointing Hsü to an official position. As this honor was firmly declined, Hsü's son, Hsi, was placed in the government instead. The elder Hsü was nevertheless retained in the council in charge of the people's petitions, in order to collaborate with Lin Yü in editing the *Book of Changes*. A year or so later, Hsü insisted on returning to the east. Emperor Jen-tsung, impressed by his lofty character, bestowed on him silk fabrics and the title of "The Humble Recluse."

As a frequent visitor to Wu,[4] Hsü made his home in Hangchow. Before each prefect assumed office, he always paid Hsü his respects. On his part, however, Hsü never entered the prefect's office once. When Fan Chung-yen[5] became prefect, he showed Hsü the special courtesy of calling on him frequently. According to Fan, when the Western rebels rose in revolt, Hsü forecast the date of the cease-fire; and, when a change was observed in the positions of the Dipper and Aquila, he predicted that there would be a serious plague in Wu entailing several hundred thousand deaths. Both prophecies came true.

At home, he used to teach the *Book of Changes* and the *Great Mystery*.[6] Some suggested that he write more books. "There are already plenty of books by ancient sages and worthy men," said Hsü, "but scholars have not been able to read them all. What need is there for me to write except to seek future fame?" Subsequently, he set fire to all his writings. The more than ten works that remained were found in the homes of his pupils and old friends.

When Hsü died, he was over seventy. While he was sick, an old friend, Wang Chi, then at Muchow,[7] wished to visit him. In his reply, Hsü indicated that, if Wang arrived between the fifth and sixth months, he could probably still be in time to see him. But Wang failed to set out in time, and Hsü died as prophesied. All the advance preparations had been made by Hsü for his own funeral.

His son, Hsi, retired when over fifty, after becoming Doctor of the Imperial University.

Hsü was posthumously granted the honorary title of Yüan-wai-lang[8] of the Ministry of Forestry. More than a decade after his death, Shen Kou, who had become Prefect of Hangchow, placed over his dwelling

牓其居曰「高士坊」云。

　　贊曰:

　　「復之文章, 存者有『愼習贊』, 『困蒙養』等篇,歸
於退求諸己, 不矜世取寵。予論次復事, 頗采其意云。
若復自拔汙濁之中, 隱約於閭巷, 久而不改其操, 可謂樂
之者已。」

the inscription: "Abode of a Lofty Scholar."

Here is my eulogy:

"The writings of Hsü which have survived include the *Encomium of Careful Study* and *Drudgery in Elementary Education*. In essence, they stress soul-searching and abstention from competition aimed at currying favor with the world. After reviewing the life of the man, I am inclined to agree with him. Hsü can be said to have been pleased with his lot, though he had to remove himself from impure surroundings and keep himself in obscurity for a long time behind rustic lanes, thus avoiding ever compromising his integrity."

洪渥傳

洪渥，撫州臨川人。爲人和平。與人遊，初不甚歡，久而有味。家貧，以進士從鄉舉，有能賦名。

初進於有司，連三黜。久之，乃得官。官不自馳騁，又久不進。卒監黄州蘄城之茶場以死。死不能歸葬，亦不能返其孥。里中人聞渥死，無賢愚，皆恨失之。

予少與渥相識，而不深知其爲人。渥死，迺聞有兄，年七十餘。渥得官，而兄已老，不可與俱行。渥至官，量口用俸，掇其餘以歸，買田百畝，居其兄，復去而之官，則心安焉。

渥既死，兄無子，數使人至蘄城撫其孥。欲返之而居以其田，其孥蓋弱，力不能自致，其兄益已老矣。無可奈何，則念輒悲之。其經營之猶不已，忘其老也。渥兄弟如此，無愧矣。

渥平居若不可任以事，及至赴人之急，早夜不少懈，

[1] Prefecture in modern Kiangsi Province.
[2] Rhymed or partly rhymed prose.
[3] A district in Hupeh Province.
[4] Equivalent roughly to one-sixth of an acre.

Biography of Hung Wo

Hung Wo was from Linch'uan, Fuchow.[1] He was goodnatured, and though, on first acquaintance, lacking great warmth, his cordiality was appreciated when people came to know him. He came from a poor family. He was recommended by his home district and succeeded in securing his *chin-shih* degree. He was noted for his *fu*[2] compositions.

After receiving his first official appointment, he was dismissed three times in succession. It was only after a long wait that he was reappointed, but as he was unsuccessful in making himself known, he made no progress for a considerable period of time. Finally, he was appointed to the tea farm of Mach'eng, Huangchow[3] as supervisor. He died in office without the means for burial in his native town and for returning his wife and children to their home. All the residents of the town, worthy or otherwise, were grieved by the news of his death and regretted his loss.

In my youth, I was acquainted with Wo but did not know much about him. After his death, I heard that he had an elder brother, who was over seventy years of age. When Wo was in office, his brother was already aged and could not accompany him. On assuming his official functions, Wo made sparing use of the available funds, which he doled out according to the number of mouths to be fed. He took home the surplus and devoted it to the purchase of one hundred *mou*[4] of land, on which his brother could live, so that Wo did not have to worry about him after returning to office.

At the time of Wo's death, his brother had no children, and sent to Mach'eng several times for Wo's wife and children to live on the farm. Unfortunately, the children were too weak to devote themselves to the work. What was worse, their uncle, having aged even more, was unable to do anything under the circumstances, and grieved whenever he pondered over it. He now forgets his age and works harder even than before. The fraternal love of the two brothers is something of which no one can ever feel ashamed.

Ordinarily, Wo did not appear to be conscientious. But, when he had to attend to some urgent matter for others, he never stopped working day and night and showed that he had truly been a bene-

其與人，眞有恩者也。

予觀古今豪傑士，傳論人行義不列於史者，往往務摭奇以動俗，亦或事高而不可爲繼；或伸一人之善，而誣天下以不及。雖歸之輔教警世，然考之中庸，或過矣。如渥所存，蓋人人所易到，故載之云。

factor to many.

In my observation, outstanding men of ancient and modern times hand down their discussions of those whose good deeds have not been recorded in history. Frequently, unusual acts have been exalted in order to inspire the public, albeit they are so lofty that they are hardly feasible. Then the whole world may be unjustifiably condemned for failing to emulate a single man's good deeds. This may be due to the keen desire to edify and admonish the world, but it is perhaps excessive in the light of the Golden Mean. As the example Wo has set is within easy reach of all, I have noted it down.

范貫之奏議集序

尚書戶部郎中直龍圖閣范公貫之之奏議，凡若干篇，
其子世京，集爲十卷，而屬予序之。

蓋自至和以後，十餘年間，公常以言事任職。自天子
大臣至於羣下，自掖庭至於四方幽隱，一有得失善惡，關
於政理，公無不極意反復，爲上力言，或矯拂情欲，或切
劘計慮，或辨別忠佞，而處其進退。章有一再，或至於十
餘上。事有陰爭獨陳，或悉引諫官御史合議肆言。

仁宗常虛心采納，爲之變命令，更廢舉。近或立從，
遠或越月踰時，或至於其後，卒從聽用。蓋當是時，仁宗
在位歲久，熟於人事之情僞，與羣臣之能否，方以仁厚清
靜，休養元元。至於是非與奪，則一歸之公議，而不自用
也。其所引拔以言爲職者，如公皆一時之選，而公與同時
之士，亦皆樂得其言，不曲從苟止。

故天下之情，因得畢聞於上，而事之害理者，常不果

---

[1] Title of a ministerial official.
[2] Name of an imperial library.
[3] 1054-1056, reign of Emperor Jen-tsung.

Preface to the Collected Memorials of Fan Kuan-chih

The memorials of the Honorable Fan Kuan-chih, Lang-chung[1] of the Ministry of Finance and Assistant Councillor of the Lung-t'u Library,[2] have been collected by his son, Shih-ching, into ten *chüan*. I have been asked to write a preface to the collection.

For more than a decade after Chih-ho,[3] the Honorable Fan made it a point at all times to present strong views to the throne, even at the risk of repetition, on questions of gain and loss, good and evil, affecting the political administration and involving all from the Son of Heaven and his high officials on down to the multitude of their subordinates, from the imperial household on down to recluses in all parts of the country. In making his propositions, Fan admonished against indulgence in all kinds of excesses, made careful analysis of various plans, or distinguished between loyalty and mere flattery as the basis of promotion or demotion. His memorials were submitted once, twice or even over ten times. They were in the form of secret remonstrances of his own or joint statements submitted in the company of other remonstrators and censors.

His late Majesty accepted Fan's views with humility; in accordance with them, he often went so far as to change his imperial mandates and rescind his decisions. His Majesty's concurrence was either given immediately or postponed for a month, a quarter of a year, or even longer. For by then the emperor had been on the throne for a long time and familiarized himself with the truth and falsehood of all situations and the ability and inability of all officials. With benevolence, good grace and serenity, he was giving the people the opportunity to enjoy their repose. He left to public discussion all questions of right and wrong. reward and penalty, without overweening pride. Those whom he had chosen for censorial functions, like the Honorable Fan, were the elite of the time. The Honorable Fan and his colleagues were eager to submit their suggestions and were unwilling to compromise their own convictions by outward conformity.

Accordingly, the people of the country could all have the benefit of an imperial hearing for their wishes, and whatever was unreasonable was never carried out. Those who committed strange, evil and licentious

331

行。至於奇衺恣睢，有爲之者，亦輒敗悔。故當此之時，
常委事七八大臣，而朝政無大闕失，羣臣奉法遵職，海內
乂安。

夫因人而不自用者，天也。仁宗之所以其仁如天，至
於享國四十餘年，能承太平之業者，繇是而已。後世得公
之遺文，而論其世，見其上下之際，相成如此，必將低回
感慕，有不可及之嘆，然後知其時之難得，則公言之不沒，
豈獨見其志，所以明先帝之盛德於無窮也。

公爲人溫良慈恕，其從政寬易愛人，及在朝廷，危言
正色，人有所不能及也。凡同時與公有言責者，後多至大
官，而公獨早卒。

公諱師道，其世次州里，歷官行事，有今資政殿學士
趙公抃爲公之墓誌銘云。

---

acts defeated their own ends and were made to regret them. In consequence, while the affairs of state were entrusted to seven or eight high officials, there was no serious flaw in the administration. The multitude of officials obeyed the law and faithfully discharged their functions, and the country enjoyed peace.

Only Heaven can rely on others without overweening pride. Emperor Jen-tsung was as benevolent as Heaven, and because of this he enjoyed more than forty years of peaceful reign. When future generations read the writings handed down by the Honorable Fan and review the times in which he lived, they will see how the throne and its subjects acted in unison and, looking back with appreciation and admiration and expressing wonderment for those incomparable times, will doubtless realize what a rare occurrence they were. Hence, the preservation of the Honorable Fan's words will not only illustrate his elevated ideals, but shed inexhaustible light on the magnificent virtue of His late Majesty.

The Honorable Fan was a man gentle, good, merciful and forgiving. In his official life, he was liberal and fond of the people. But at court, he spoke with austerity and gravity, and he was unequaled in the practice of these virtues. Most of his colleagues, who shared censorial functions with him at the time, were subsequently promoted to high positions. He alone died early.

The Honorable Fan's first name was Shih-tao.[4] His family and local background, official career and the record of his deeds have been set down in the inscription for his tomb tablet, which was written by the Honorable Chao Pien, now Secretary of the Tzu-cheng Hall.

王平甫文集序

王平甫既没，其家集其遺文爲百卷，屬予序。

平甫自少已傑然以材高見於世。爲文思若決河，語出驚人，一時爭傳誦之。其學問尤敏，而資之以不倦，至晚愈篤。博覽強記，於書無所不通，其明於是非得失之理爲尤詳。其文閎富典重，其詩博而深矣。

自周衰，先王之遺文既喪，漢興，文學猶爲近古，及其衰，而陵夷盡矣。至唐，久之而能言之士，始幾於漢，及其衰，而遂泯泯矣。宋受命百有餘年，天下文章，復侔於漢唐之盛。

蓋自周衰，至今千有餘歲，斯文濱於泯滅，能自拔起，以追於古者，此三世而已。各於其盛時，士之能以特見於世者，率常不過三數人。其世之不數，其人之難得如此。

平甫之文，能特見于世者也。世皆謂平甫之詩，宜爲樂謌，薦之郊廟，其文宜爲典册，施諸朝廷，而不得用於世。

而推其實，千歲之日，不爲不多，焦心思於翰墨之間

---

[1] Younger brother of Wang An-shih.
[2] The Han, T'ang and Sung dynasties.

Preface to the Collected Works of Wang P'ing-fu[1]

On his death, Wang P'ing-fu's family collected his writings into one hundred *chüan* and asked me to write a preface.

From his youth, P'ing-fu was known to the world for his outstanding talent. When he wrote, his thinking was as rapid as a river that had overflowed and his choice of words was so striking that he was soon read all over the country. His scholarship was especially profound, and with his tirelessness he attained greater depths in his later life. He was extremely well-read and had a remarkable memory. There was no book that he did not know intimately; and he had a particularly detailed grasp of the principles of right and wrong and of success and failure in history. His prose writings were rich and classical; and his poetry was profound and covered an extensive range of subjects.

After the decline of the Chou dynasty and the loss of the writings handed down from the ancient kings, the literature of the Han dynasty was nevertheless still close to the classical style. However, the decadence was complete when the Han dynasty declined. Long after the establishment of the T'ang dynasty, those who were gifted with literary ability could barely keep up the Han tradition. But another decline set in as the T'ang administration faded. It was more than a century after the inauguration of the Sung dynasty that the writings of the empire caught up with the golden ages of Han and T'ang.

It is more than a thousand years since the decline of the Chou dynasty. During only three intervals[2] has our literature been lifted from the brink of disaster and restored to the glory of ancient writings. Even then there were only a handful of scholars who achieved particular distinction in the world in each of the flourishing periods. So seldom are such ages and so rare the men who have adorned them!

With his writings P'ing-fu was capable of achieving particular distinction in the world. His poetry, it is often said, should be set to music and sung at temples and shrines, and his prose should be incorporated into official records and serve the purposes of the imperial court. However, both his poetry and prose have somehow been neglected by the world.

When we consider the facts, a millenium is not a short period. Those

335

者，不爲不衆，在富貴之位者，未嘗一日而無其人。彼皆
湮滅而無傳，或播其醜於後。平甫乃躬難得之姿，負特見
之能，自立于不朽，雖不得其志，然其文之可貴，人亦莫
得而掩也。則平甫之求於內，亦奚憾乎？

古今作者，或能文，不必工於詩，或長於詩，不必有
文。平甫獨兼得之，其於詩，尤自喜其憂喜哀樂，感激
怨懟之情，一於詩見之，古詩尤多也。

平甫居家孝友，爲人質直簡易，遇人豁然推腹心，不
爲毫髮疑礙，與人交，於恩意尤篤也。其死之日，天下識
與不識，皆聞而哀之。其州里世次，歷官行事，將有待于
識平甫之葬者，故不著於此云。元豐元年。

---

[3] 1078, reign of Emperor Shen-tsung.

who have diligently applied themselves to writing have been far from few, and not a day has passed but men have attained wealth and occupied positions of distinction. All of them have died without leaving behind anything of value. Perhaps they have even brought on themselves lasting infamy. By contrast, with his rare intelligence and extraordinary ability, P'ing-fu has alone achieved immortality with his invaluable contributions to literature, which cannot be concealed, though he failed to fulfill his ambition in the world of affairs. Thus, in his inner self, could P'ing-fu have any regrets?

Writers of ancient and modern times, noted for their prose, need not have been skilled in poetry, and those outstanding in poetry need not have written good prose. P'ing-fu alone was accomplished in both. He was especially pleased that he was able to express his feelings of sadness and joy, grief and pleasure, appreciation and discontent in his poetry. In particular, he wrote a great many poems in the ancient style.

In his domestic life, P'ing-fu was filial and fraternal. He was a straightforward, simple man. He opened his heart to others, and no cause for suspicion whatsoever could keep him from doing so. He was especially generous in doing favors to his friends. When he died, the whole country, including those who had not even been acquainted with him, mourned his loss. His local and family background, his official career and the record of his deeds are omitted here, but will be supplied by those who knew him well and who will supervise his funeral. The first year of Yüan-feng.[3]

寄歐陽舍人書

去秋人還，蒙賜書，及所譔先大父墓碑銘。反覆觀誦，感與慚幷。

夫銘誌之著於世，義近於史，而亦有與史異者。蓋史之於善惡，無所不書。而銘者，蓋古之人有功德材行，志義之美者，懼後世之不知，則必銘而見之，或納於廟，或存於墓，一也。苟其人之惡，則於銘乎何有？此其所以與史異也。

其辭之作，所以使死者無有所憾，生者得致其嚴。而善人喜於見傳，則勇於自立。惡人無有所紀，則以媿而懼。至於通材達識，義烈節士，嘉言善狀，皆見於篇，則足為後法。警勸之道，非近乎史，其將安近？

及世之衰，人之子孫者，一欲襃揚其親，而不本乎理。故雖惡人，皆務勒銘，以誇後世。立言者，既莫之拒而不為，又以其子孫之所請也。書其惡焉，則人情之所不得，於是乎銘始不實。

後之作銘者，當觀其人。苟託之非人，則書之非公與是，則不足以行世而傳後。故千百年來，公卿大夫，至於

---

[1]Ou-yang Hsiu. See pp. 133-138, above.

Letter to the Honorable Ou-yang[1]

With the return of my messenger last autumn, I received the favor of Your Excellency's letter, together with the epigraph you were good enough to write for my deceased grandfather's tomb tablet. After perusing them repeatedly, I have felt both gratified and abashed.

A message of this kind is noted by the world, because it has nearly the same significance as history. But is is also different from history, in that history records everything, good or bad, while an epigraph gives only an account of the merits, virtues, talents and good deeds of the ancients, whose example it was feared might be lost to posterity. Such an inscription was either placed in a temple or deposited in a grave, which had the selfsame meaning. As to their bad deeds, if there were any, there was no need to record them in an epigraph. In this respect, an epigraph, therefore, differs from history.

The epigraph is so worded that the deceased should not have felt any regrets and the living could have something to look up to. A good man is glad to see the memory of his deeds handed down, and so would always endeavor to stand upright. On the other hand, a bad man, lest others say nothing about him, turns from embarrassment to fear. As to men of all-round talent, mature judgment, righteousness, heroism and integrity, their examples can more readily be emulated by posterity if their good words and deeds are put in writing. If the admonition and exhortation thus implied did not come close to forming part of history, how could they be better described?

With the moral degeneration of these times, children and grand-children of the deceased, animated by a single-minded desire to glorify their forbears, no longer act on the basis of reason. Even bad men have epigraphs engraved for them, which enable their offspring to take pride in them. In such cases, since writers do not refuse to render the service when the request is made by the children and grandchildren of the deceased, to write about the evil that is done would be contrary to human sentiment. As a result, epigraphs have begun to be untrue.

The nature of later inscriptions of this kind depends on that of the man writing them. If he were the wrong person, the inscriptions would not be fair and right, nor would it be circulated in the world and

里巷之士，莫不有銘，而傳者蓋少，其故非他，託之非人，書之非公與是故也。

然則孰爲其人，而能盡公與是歟？非畜道德而能文章者，無以爲也。蓋有道德者之於惡人，則不受而銘之，於衆人則能辨焉。而人之行，有情善而迹非，有意奸而外淑，有善惡相懸而不可以實指，有實大於名，有名侈於實。猶之用人，非畜道德者，惡能辨之不惑，議之不徇？不惑不徇，則公且是矣。而其辭之不工，則世猶不傳，於是又在其文章兼勝焉。故曰，非畜道德而能文章者，無以爲也。豈非然哉？

然畜道德而能文章者，雖或並世而有，亦或數十年或一二百年而有之，其傳之難如此，其遇之難又如此。若先生之道德文章，固所謂數百年而有者也。先祖之言行卓卓，幸遇而得銘其公與是，其傳世行後無疑也。而世之學者，每觀傳記所書古人之事，至其所可感，則往往盡然不知涕之流落也，況其子孫也哉？況鞏也哉？其追晞祖德，而思所以傳之之由，則知先生推一賜於鞏，而及其三世。其感與報，宜若何而圖之？

340

handed down to posterity. Though for hundreds of years officials, high and low, and even men in the street and in the countryside have had their epigraphs written for them, very few of these have therefore been handed down. This is simply because the writer was the wrong person and epigraphs written by him were neither fair nor true.

Who then can be entirely fair and true? None but those who possess a fund of virtues and who excel in the art of writing. This is because those who are virtuous do not undertake to write about a bad man. Though ordinary men are easily distinguishable, some men with good sentiments do not show them; some with evil intentions are outwardly virtuous; in some, good and evil exist side by side and it is impossible to separate them; some are greater in fact than they are in name, others greater in name than they are in fact. As in the employment of men, who but those with a fund of virtues can distinguish them discriminately and comment on them without partiality? Discrimination and impartiality make up what is fair and true. However, if the language is not skillful, transmission to posterity is not assured. Hence the necessity for surpassing ability on the part of the writer. I therefore say that none but those who have a fund of virtues and who are good at writing can undertake the work. Is this not incontestable?

Nevertheless, while there may now and then be somone who has both a fund of virtues and the ability to write, it is also possible that such a person will not appear in several decades or even in one or two centuries. Thus, it is difficult to find examples of such men in history and even more so to encounter them in person. A man of Your Excellency's virtue and literary ability can indeed be found only once in several hundred years. Having had the good fortune of meeting you and securing for my deceased grandfather's distinguished words and deeds a record which is fair and true, I have no doubt that it will be circulated in the world and transmitted to posterity. When a student is touched by accounts of the ancients recorded in history, he is frequently moved unconsciously to a flood of tears. Is this not all the more true of the descendants of the man written about? Is it not especially true of me? Being an admirer of my grandfather's virtues and thinking of the cause of their transmission to posterity, I realize that the favor Your Excellency has done to me has been done to three generations of my family. I am at a loss to know how to express my gratitude and repay my debt.

抑又思若鞏之淺薄滯拙，而先生進之，先祖之屯蹶否塞，以死而先生顯之。則世之魁閎豪傑不世出之士，其誰不願進於門？潛遁幽抑之士，其誰不有望於世？善誰不為，而惡誰不愧以懼？為人之父祖者，孰不欲敎其子孫？為人之子孫者，孰不欲寵榮其父祖？

此數美者，一歸於先生。既拜賜之辱，且敢進其所以然。所論世族之次，敢不承敎而加詳焉。愧甚不宣。

---

[2]The author was a successful candidate and received his *chin-shih* degree in the imperial examination of 1057, over which Ou-yang Hsiu presided.

Furthermore, I am mindful of the fact that a man as shallow and stupid as myself has owed his advancement to you,[2] and that my grandfather, who died from misfortune, has been exalted by you. In consequence, among the great and heroic personages rarely born to the world, who would not be eager to come under your tutorship? Of those who are disappointed and would escape from the world, who would not still have hope for recognition? Who would not do good and, of those who committed evil, who would not turn from embarrassment to fear? Of those who are fathers and grandfathers, who would not teach and improve their children and children's children? Of those who are descendants, who would not glorify their fathers and grandfathers?

We owe to you all these things. I am grateful for what you have given me, and I have ventured to set down my reasons for gratitude. As to the genealogical sequence to which you have alluded, I shall of course take your advice and supply the details. With great diffidence, I am unable to do full justice to my thoughts on this matter.

王文公

公作字說時。用意良苦。置石蓮百許枚几案上。咀嚼以運其思。遇盡未及益。即嚼其
指至流血不覺。世傳公初生。家人見有獾入其產室。有頃公生。故小字獾郎。又傳公
在金陵。有僧清曉于鐘山道上見有童子數人持幡幢羽蓋之僧問之曰往迎王相公
幡上書云中含法性外智塵氛到寺未久聞公薨。

Wang An-shih (1021-1086)

Wang An-shih, whose courtesy name was Chieh-fu 介甫, was a native of Linch'uan.[1] When he was young, he was fond of studying. He had such a remarkable memory that he could remember everything for life after only one reading. He could write so fast that his pen seemed to fly over the paper. Those who had seen him write were amazed by the elegance of his style.

One of his greatest admirers in those days was his friend, Tseng Kung,[2] who submitted his writings to Ou-yang Hsiu. Ou-yang praised them very highly, and was in the forefront in extolling Wang and making him known.

After receiving his *chin-shih* degree, he was appointed to Huainan 淮南[3] as a subordinate official. On the expiration of his term of office, he could have applied for an examination qualifying him for service at court, but he refrained from doing so. He was then transferred to Yin *Hsien* 鄞縣[4] as Magistrate. In that office, he did outstanding work in connection with water conservancy and grain loans, which proved of great benefit to the people. Later, he was appointed to Shuchow 舒州[5] as a subordinate official.

When Wen Yen-po 文彥博 was Prime Minister, he recommended Wang An-shih for a higher post and summoned him to take the special examination for a position at court, but he declined. At Ou-yang Hsiu's instance, he was appointed to the Censorship, but, because of the advanced age of his grandmother, he resigned. After holding some more local offices,

---

[1] A district in Kiangsi Province.
[2] See pp. 305-306, above.
[3] An administrative division equivalent to a province, including parts of Hupeh, Kiangsu and Anhwei Provinces.
[4] A district in Chekiang Province.
[5] Prefecture in modern Anhwei Province.

he was appointed to the Ministry of Finance.

Wang An-shih was not lacking in self-confidence, and had the ambition of transforming society and enhancing the welfare of his country. He took upon himself to make suggestions to that end which were embodied in a memorial, his famous message of ten thousand words. This he saw fit to submit to the throne. It was the document to which he adhered steadfastly in principle in later life and on which he based all his subsequent policies as an influential statesman.

In the meantime, Wang gradually won greater distinction at court, and held higher positions, including those of Private Imperial Secretary and Draftsman of Imperial Orders and Decrees.

Before he became a national figure, Wang had close contacts with members of two prominent families, the Han 韓 and Lü 呂, especially Han Chiang 韓絳 and his brother Wei 維, and Lü Kung-chu 呂公著,[6] who later served as Prime Minister. Through their influence, An-shih's name became better known. For one thing, before Emperor Shen-tsung ascended the throne, he had already heard Wang's name from Han Wei, his secretary. Whenever Wei was praised by the future emperor for anything he said, he attributed it to Wang An-shih. At one time, he even recommended Wang as his successor, thus making a strong impression on the young prince.

Upon Emperor Shen-tsung's accession, one of his first acts was to appoint Wang to Chiangning 江寧[7] as Prefect. A few months later, he was called to the palace as Secretary of the Hanlin Academy. As a result of several imperial audiences at which he exhibited unusual superiority of judgment and the highest sagacity, the emperor made him Prime Minister.

The stage was then set for the introduction of Wang An-shih's reforms. These were extensive and included such measures as the planning of state finance, farm loans, raising

[6]Prime Minister under Emperor Shen-tsung.
[7]Prefecture in modern Kiangsu Province.

of revenue from tributes, land survey and taxes, local police, military defense, replanning the trade system and the imperial examination. The result was a general increase in taxation, which added to the discontent of the people. Five years later, the emperor began to doubt the feasibility of Wang's program of reforms and removed him from the Premiership, naming him Grand Secretary of the Kuan-wen Hall 觀文殿大學士 and Prefect of Chiangling 江陵.[8] After the lapse of another year, however, he was reappointed Prime Minister, but because of his frequently expressed wish to be relieved, especially after the death of his son, the emperor was forced to accept his resignation shortly afterward. Wang retained the title of Prime Minister and was once more appointed as Prefect of Chiangning. Subsequently, he was granted the titles of Commissioner for Public Works 司空, Duke of Shu 舒國公 and Duke of Ching 荊國公.

Wang An-shih died at the age of sixty-eight. The posthumous title of Grand Tutor of the Imperial Household 太傅 was conferred on him, and he was canonized as Wen 文. His tablet was placed in the Imperial Ancestral Shrine by order of Emperor Cheh-tsung, and in the Temple of Confucius by order of Emperor Hui-tsung 徽宗, who also named him Prince of Shu 舒王—honors which were all rescinded by later rulers of the Sung dynasty.

[8] Prefecture in modern Hupeh Province.

讀孟嘗君傳

世皆稱孟嘗君能得士，士以故歸之，而卒賴其力，以
脫於虎豹之秦。

嗟乎! 孟嘗君特雞鳴狗盜之雄耳。豈足以言得士?

不然，擅齊之强，得一士焉，宜可以南面而制秦，尚
何取雞鳴狗盜之力哉?

夫雞鳴狗盜之出其門，此士之所以不至也。

---

[1] A prince of the feudal state of Ch'i 齊, situated in modern Shantung Province.

[2] The feudal state, situated in modern Shensi Province, which later unified China under the First Emperor 秦始皇.

[3] When Prince Meng-ch'ang was imprisoned in Ch'in, he besought Hsing 幸姬, a concubine of King Chao 昭王, to intercede for him. A certain white-fox furcoat was named by her as the price. It happened that the coat had already been delivered to the king. One of the prince's retainers, being able to steal like a dog, succeeded in abstracting it by stealth and presenting it to Hsing. Thus the prince was released. However, after leaving the capital and reaching Hanku Kuan 函谷關, he could not escape through the gate, which was not opened until cock-crow. Another of the retainers could crow like a cock, which he did, and all the cocks followed suit. As a result, the gate was opened and the prince was permitted to leave.

348

After Reading the Biography of Prince Meng-ch'ang [1]

All over the empire, Prince Meng-ch'ang was known for his ability to attract scholars by his patronage. It was said that for this reason they flocked to him and that through their effort, he was ultimately freed from the fierce domination of the state of Ch'in. [2]

Alas, Prince Meng-ch'ang was merely the chieftain of those who crowed like cocks and stole like dogs! [3] How could he be said to be capable of attracting scholars to his circle?

If he had been, given the prowess of Ch'i, he could have subdued Ch'in and become its master with the aid of a single scholar. Would it have been necessary to rely on the effort of men who crowed like cocks and stole like dogs?

The fact that those who crowed like cocks and stole like dogs came to his door explains why scholars failed to join him.

孔子世家議

太史公叙帝王則曰「本紀」，公侯傳國則曰「世家」，公卿特起則曰「列傳」，此其例也。其列孔子爲世家，奚其進退無所據邪？

孔子，旅人也。棲棲衰季之世，無尺土之柄。此列之以傳，宜矣。曷爲世家哉？豈以仲尼躬將聖之資，其敎化之盛，鳥奕萬世？故爲之世家以抗之，又非極摯之論也。

夫仲尼之才，帝王可也。何特公侯哉？仲尼之道，世天下可也。何特世其家哉？處之世家，仲尼之道不從而大，置之列傳，仲尼之道不從而小。而遷也自亂其例，所謂多所牴牾者也。

[1] See p. 27, note 15, above.

Criticism of the Form of Confucius' Biography

The Grand Historian[1] adopted different forms for the biographies of emperors and kings, dukes and marquises, and prominent officials, using respectively the designations of *Pen-chi, Shih-chia* and *Lieh-chuan*. When he classified the biography of Confucius as a *Shih-chia,* his approach was utterly unjustified.

Confucius was an itinerant and traveled in a decadent age. He did not possess an inch of territory. It would have been appropriate to give his biography the form of *Lieh-chuan*. What was the need of using that of *Shih-chia*? Was it because of his sage character and the greatness of his teachings, which held the promise of being handed down to innumerable generations? If so, the decision could not be exactly considered a legitimate one.

The ability of Confucius could indeed have qualified him for the position of emperor or king, and not merely for that of duke or marquis. His teachings were fit to be transmitted through the ages for the empire, and not merely for the family. The adoption of the form of *Shih-chia* in no way elevated the Way of Confucius, and the use of that of *Lieh-chuan* would in no way have diminished it. In acting as he did, Ssu-ma Ch'ien caused confusion in his own classifications. He was indeed what might be called a man who was in many ways self-contradictory.

遊褒禪山記

褒禪山，亦謂之華山。唐浮圖慧褒，始舍於其址而卒葬之，以故其後名之曰褒禪。今所謂慧空禪院者，褒之廬冢也。距其院東五里，所謂華陽洞者，以其乃華山之陽名之也。距洞百餘步，有碑仆道。其文漫滅，獨其為文猶可識，曰花山。今言「華」，如「華實」之「華」者，蓋音謬也。

其下平曠，有泉側出，而記游者甚衆，所謂前洞也。由山以上五六里，有穴窈然，入之甚寒。問其深，則雖好遊者不能窮也。謂之後洞。余與四人擁火以入。入之愈深，其進愈難，而其見愈奇。有怠而欲出者，曰：「不出，火且盡。」遂與之俱出。蓋予所至，比好遊者尚不能十一，然視其左右，來而記之者已少。蓋其又深，則其至又加少矣。

方是時，予之力尚足以入，火尚足以明也。既其出，則或咎其欲出者，而予亦悔其隨之，而不得極夫遊之樂也。

於是余有歎焉。古人之觀於天地山川草木蟲魚鳥獸，往往有得，以其求思之深，而無不在也。夫夷以近，

---

[1] A mountain sixty *li* north of Chüyung *Hsien* 句容縣 , Kiangsu Province.

A Visit to the Pao-ch'an Mountain[1]

The Pao-ch'an Mountain is also known as the Hua Mountain. Hui-pao, a monk of the T'ang dynasty, was buried there after having dwelt on the site. Hence the name Pao-ch'an. What is today called the Hui-k'ung Abbey used to include the monk's home and grave. Five *li* east of the abbey is the Hua Yang Cave, so named because of its location south of the Hua Mountain. Something more than one hundred paces from the cave is a tablet, which had fallen to the ground. The writing thereon is blurred, but the name "Hua (花) Mountain" is still recognizable. The character "Hua" is different from the one used today, "hua 華 ," the mistake having arisen from the identical pronunciation of the two characters.

Down below, the ground is flat and spacious. A spring issues from one side of the mountain. This is the Front Cave, which is the subject of many travelogues. Five or six *li* further on is another cave, called the Rear Cave, which is dark and cold inside. Its depth is not fully known even to those who are fond of visiting it. I entered with a torch in the company of four other men, and, the more deeply we penetrated, the more difficult our progress became and the more spectacular was the sight. Those who were unenterprising wanted to get out. "If we do not get out," they said, "our light will soon fail." At this, we all made our exit, when we had not even seen one-tenth of the area covered by those who are fond of this excursion. But I could see on the side walls only few recordings left by visitors. The reason is that the deeper down the cave, the less likely it is for the visitors to stay on.

At the time I still had enough strength to go further and the torch enough light to lead us on. When we emerged, some of us complained of those who had suggested turning back, and I for one regretted that I had followed them without deriving the maximum pleasure from the visit.

This sets my mind to thinking. The ancients frequently benefited greatly from their observation of heaven and earth, mountains and rivers, grasses and trees, insects and fishes, fowls and animals, because they sought to deepen their thinking on everything under the sun. Generally speaking, many people visit places that are safe and near

353

則遊者衆；險以遠，則至者少。而世之奇偉瑰怪非常之
觀，常在於險遠，而人之所罕至焉。故非有志者，不能
至也。有志矣，不隨以止也。然力不足者，亦不能至也。
有志與力，而又不隨以怠，至於幽暗昏惑，而無物以相
之，亦不能至也。然力足以至焉而不至，於人爲可譏，而
在己爲有悔。盡吾志也，而不能至者，可以無悔矣，其孰
能譏之乎？此予之所得也。

　余於仆碑，又以悲夫古書之不存，後世之謬其傳，而
莫能名者，何可勝道也哉？此所以學者不可以不深思而愼
取之也。

　四人者，廬陵蕭君圭君玉，長樂王回深父，余弟安國
平父，安上純父。

---

[2] Chi-an *Hsien* 吉安縣, Kiangsi Province.
[3] A district in Fukien Province.

while few frequent those that are dangerous and distant. But the strange, magnificent and extraordinary sights of the world are often in the latter category. Hence, few have access to them, except those who have the will power. With this will power, they do not follow the example of others and cut short their visit. But those who lack adequate strength still cannot reach their destinations. With will power and strength and without following the example of others in giving up easily, when they reach a dark and bewildering place, they still cannot complete their visit with nothing to assist them. However, if they have the strength and do not try, they are ridiculed by others and cannot be free from regret on their own part. On the other hand, if they execute their plan fully and fail, not only do they have no regret, but who can point a finger at them? This is what I have learned from this visit.

As to the fallen tablet, I deplore the fact that the relevant ancient books are no longer in existence to explain it. How can I in consequence enumerate all those who have been responsible for giving in later generations the wrong name? It is for this reason that scholars cannot dispense with deep meditation and careful selection when a choice has to be made.

The other four men mentioned above are Hsiao Chün-kuei, with the courtesy name Chün-yü, of Luling,[2] Wang Hui, with the courtesy name Shen-fu, of Ch'anglo,[3] and my younger brothers An-kuo, with the courtesy name P'ing-fu, and An-shang, with the courtesy name Shun-fu.

泰州海陵縣主簿許君墓誌銘

君諱平，字秉之，姓許氏。余嘗譜其世家。所謂今泰州海陵縣主簿者也。

君既與兄元相友愛稱天下，而自少卓犖不羈，善辨說，與其兄俱以智略爲當世大人所器。寶元時，朝廷開方略之選，以招天下異能之士，而陝西大帥范文正公，鄭文肅公，爭以君所爲書以薦。於是得召試，爲太廟齋郎。已而選泰州海陵縣主簿。

貴人多薦君有大才，可試以事，不宜棄之州縣。君亦常慨然自許，欲有所爲，然終不得一用其智能以卒。噫，其可哀也已。

士固有離世異俗，獨行其意，罵譏,笑侮,困辱而不悔。彼皆無衆人之求，而有所待於後世者也。且齟齬固宜。

若夫智謀功名之士，窺時俯仰，以赴勢物之會，而輒不遇者，乃亦不可勝數。辯足以移萬物，而窮於用說之時。謀足以奪三軍，而辱於右武之國。此又何說哉？嗟乎，彼

[1] Title of a local subordinate official.
[2] T'ai *Hsien* 泰縣 , Kiangsu Province.
[3] Prefecture in modern Kiangsu Province.
[4] Reign of Emperor Jen-tsung.
[5] Respectively 范仲淹 and 鄭戩 .
[6] Title of an official in charge of sacrificial affairs.

Inscription on the Tomb Tablet of Mr. Hsü, Chu-pu[1] of Hailing *Hsien*,[2] T'aichow[3]

Mr. Hsü was named P'ing; his courtesy name was Ping-chih. He served as Chu-pu of what is today Hailing *Hsien*, T'aichow. I have tabulated his family history before.

He was widely noted for his fraternal love for his elder brother, Yüan. From his youth, he had been outstanding and unconventional and had great forensic ability. He and his brother were equally respected by the great men of the time for their wisdom and tact. During the reign of Pao-yüan,[4] the imperial court opened a campaign for the selection of men of extraordinary ability who could formulate strategic plans. Fan Chung-yen and Cheng Chien,[5] Commanders-in-Chief in Shensi, both recommended books written by Hsü. As a result, he was summoned to the court to be examined, after which he was appointed Chai-lang[6] of the Imperial Ancestral Shrine. Later, he was transferred to Hailing *Hsien*, T'aichow, as its Chu-pu.

Most men of distinction commended him for his great ability, which qualified him for other probationary positions. They were of the opinion that he should not have been relegated to prefectures and districts. For his own part, he had also entertained the wish to perform important tasks; but, before he died, he had never had the opportunity to apply his wisdom and capabilities. Alas, how deplorable!

True, there are scholars who forsake the world, conduct themselves differently from the vulgar and seek to do what they think best. They may be berated, derided, ridiculed, insulted and distressed, but they have no regrets. They are free from the demands of the multitude, and they wait for [the judgment of] subsequent generations. No wonder they cannot get along with their times.

As to the accomplished and crafty scholars who take every opportunity to engage in power politics, there are countless numbers of them, but they are usually unable to attain their objective. Though their forensic ability can present everything in a distorted light, they are frequently at their wit's end when they need their persuasive power. Though their strategy can succeed in capturing the foe's three armies, they are often humiliated in a country exalting militarism. What can we say of all this? Alas, those who have something to wait for and who

有所待而不悔者，其知之矣。

　君年五十九，以嘉祐某年某月某甲子，葬眞州之揚子縣甘露鄉某所之原。夫人李氏。子男瓌，不仕，璋，眞州司戶參軍。琦，太廟齋郎，琳，進士。女子五人，已嫁二人，進士周奉先，泰州泰興縣令陶舜元。

　銘曰：「有拔而起之，莫擠而止之。嗚呼，許君而已於斯，誰或使之？」

---

[7] Reign of Emperor Jen-tsung, 1056-1063.

[8] Icheng *Hsien* 儀徵縣, Kiangsu Province.

[9] Prefecture in modern Kiangsu Province.

[10] Title of a local subordinate official.

[11] T'aihsing *Hsien* 泰興縣, Kiangsu Province.

have no regrets realize it.

Hsü died at the age of fifty-nine, and was buried on the . . . day of the . . . month of the . . . year of Chia-yu,[7] on the plains of Kanlu Hsiang of Yangtzu *Hsien*,[8] Chenchow.[9] His wife was née Li. They had four sons: Kuei, who never had any official position; Chang, who became Ssu-hu-ts'an-chün[10] of Chenchow; Ch'i, the Chai-lang of the Imperial Ancestral Shrine; and Lin, a *chin-shih*. Two of the five daughters married, respectively, Chou Feng-hsien, *chin-shih*, and T'ao Shun-yüan, Magistrate of T'aihsing.[11]

Here is his epigraph:

> He who was selected for promotion
> Should not be refused it. Deeply moved,
> I sigh: "Alas, Hsü was stopped in mid-career!
> Who was responsible for this setback?"

Bibliography

I. BOOKS IN CHINESE

Ch'en Chao-lun (ed.), *Ch'en T'ai-p'u p'i-hsüan pa-chia wen-ch'ao*, 6 vols. Tzu-chu Shan-fang, 1880.

陳太僕批選八家文鈔，清陳兆綸選評，六册。清光緒六年紫竹山房影印手批本。

Chiang Jui-tsao (ed.), *Hsin Ku-wen tz'u-lei-tsuan*, 6 vols. Taipei: Taiwan Chung Hua Book Company, 1967.

新古文辭類篹，六十卷六册，蔣瑞藻輯。民國五十六年台北台灣中華書局印行。

Emperor Ch'ien-lung (ed.), *Yü-hsüan T'ang-Sung wen-shun*, 20 vols. Palace edition, 1738.

御選唐宋文醇，五十八卷二十册，清高宗選。乾隆三年內府刊本。

Ch'üan T'ang wen (Imperial ed.), 200 vols. Kuang-ya Book Company, 1901.

欽定全唐文，一千卷二百册。清光緒二十七年廣雅書局。

Han Yü, *Ch'ang-li hsien-sheng chi*, 8 vols. Shanghai: Chung-hua Book Company, undated.

昌黎先生集，四十卷，外集十卷，附錄二種八册，唐韓愈撰。上海中華書局。

————, *Ch'ang-li hsien-sheng shih chi-chu*, 4 vols. Hsiu-yeh Ts'ao-t'ang edition, 1699.

昌黎先生詩集註，十一卷四册，唐韓愈撰。清康熙三十八年秀野草堂本。

————, *Chu-wen-kung chiao Ch'ang-li hsien-sheng chi*, 12 vols. Early Ming dynasty (*circa* 14th century).

朱文公校昌黎先生集，五十二卷十二册，唐韓愈撰，宋朱熹考異。明初建刊十三行本。

————, *T'ang Han-wen-kung wen*, 8 vols. K'un-hsüeh An edition, K'ang-hsi period (*circa* 17th century).

唐韓文公文，八册，唐韓愈撰。清康熙間困學閣刊本。

Emperor K'ang-hsi (ed.), *Ku-wen yüan-chien*, 24 vols. Early Ch'ing dynasty (*circa* 17th century).

古文淵鑑，六十四卷二十四冊，清聖祖選。清初刊本。

Liu Tsung-yüan, *Ho-tung hsien-sheng chi*, 20 vols. Yin-yin Lu edition, 1923.

河東先生集，四十五卷，外集二卷，外集補遺一卷，龍城錄二卷，附錄二卷，集傳一卷，二十冊。蟫隱廬影印宋世綵堂本。

————, *Liu wen*, 8 vols. Edited by Liu Yü-hsi. Hsinhui: Mo Ju-shih's edition, 1556.

柳文，四十三卷，別集二卷，外集二卷，附錄一卷，八冊，唐柳宗元撰，劉禹錫編。明嘉靖三十五年新會莫如石刊本。

Lu Hsin-yüan (ed.), *T'ang-wen shih-i*, 2 vols. Yungho Chen, Taipei Hsien: Wen-hai Publishing Agency, 1962.

唐文拾遺，七十二卷二冊，清陸心源輯。民國五十一年台北縣永和鎮文海出版社印行。

Mu Hsiu, *Honan Mu-kung chi*. Shanghai: Commercial Press, 1929.

河南穆公集，三卷，宋穆修撰。民國十八年上海商務印書館（四部叢刊本）。

Ou-yang Hsiu, *Liu-i t'i pa*, 2 vols. Shanghai: Commercial Press, 1939.

六一題跋，十一卷二冊，宋歐陽修撰。民國二十八年上海商務印書館（叢書集成本）。

————, *Ou-yang Wen-chung-kung ch'üan-chi*, 64 vols. Edition of Ch'eng Tsung, Prefect of Chi-an, 1461.

歐陽文忠公全集，一五三卷，附錄五卷，六十四冊，宋歐陽修撰。明天順五年吉安知府程宗刊後代修補本。

————, *Ou-yang hsien-sheng wen-ts'ui*, 5 vols. Edited by Ch'en Liang. Wuhui: Pao-shan T'ang, 1547.

歐陽先生文粹，二十卷五冊，宋歐陽修撰，陳亮編。明嘉靖二十六年吳會郭雲鵬寶善堂刊本。

Shen Ping-chen (ed.), *T'ang shu ho-ch'ao*, 40 vols. Haich'ang: Cha Shih-t'an's edition, 1803.

唐書合抄，二百六十卷四十冊，沈炳震輯。清嘉慶八年海昌查世倓刊本。

Su Ch'e, *Luan-ch'eng chi*, 16 vols. Governor of Szechwan's edition, 1541.

欒城集，五十卷，後集二十四卷，三集十卷，十六冊，宋蘇轍撰。明嘉靖二十年蜀藩刊本。

Su Hsün, *Chia-yu chi*, 4 vols. Undated old hand-copied edition.

嘉祐集，十五卷四册，宋蘇洵撰。舊鈔本。

——, *Su Lao-ch'üan hsien-sheng ch'üan-chi*, 4 vols. Soochow: An-lo Chü edition, 1698.
蘇老泉先生全集，二十卷，附錄二卷，四册，宋蘇洵撰。清康熙三十七年吳郡邵氏安樂居藏版。

Su Shih, *Su Wen-chung-kung ch'üan-chi*, 30 vols. Governor of Kiangsi's edition, 1534.
蘇文忠公全集，一百十卷，附年譜一卷，三十册，宋蘇軾撰。明嘉靖十三年江西布政司重刊本。

——, *Tung-p'o chi*, 48 vols. Pao-hua An edition, 1909.
東坡集，一百十卷四十八册，宋蘇軾撰。清宣統元年寶華盦本。

T'ang-Sung shih-ta-chia ch'üan-chi-lu, 32 vols. Kiangsu Book Company, 1882.
唐宋十大家全集錄，五十二卷三十二册。清光緒八年江蘇書局刊本。

Tseng Kung, *Yüan-feng lei-kao*, 12 vols. Yang Ts'an's edition, 1470.
元豐類稿，五十卷，附錄一卷，十二册，宋曾鞏撰。明成化六年楊參刊本。

——, *Nan-feng Tseng hsien-sheng wen-ts'ui*, 8 vols. Wusi: An Ju-shih's edition, 1549.
南豐曾先生文粹，十卷八册，宋曾鞏撰。明嘉靖二十八年無錫安如石刊本。

Tseng Kuo-fan (comp.), *Ching-shih pai-chia tsa-ch'ao*, 2 vols. Taipei: Taiwan Chung Hua Book Company, 1962.
經史百家雜鈔，二十六卷二册，清曾國藩輯。民國五十一年台北台灣中華書局印行（四部備要集部）。

Tung Tso-pin, *Chung-kuo nien-li tsung-p'u* (Chronological Tables of Chinese History), 2 vols. Hong Kong: Hong Kong University Press, 1960.
中國年曆總譜，二册，董作賓編著。一九六〇年香港大學出版社出版。

Wang An-shih, *Lin-ch'uan hsien-sheng wen-chi*, 14 vols. Edition of Yin Yün-luan, Magistrate of Linch'uan, 1546.
臨川先生文集，一百卷十四册，宋王安石撰。明嘉靖二十五年臨川知縣應雲鸞刊本。

——, *Lin-ch'uan hsien-sheng wen-chi*, 20 vols. Shanghai: Chung Hua Book Company, 1928.

臨川先生文集，一百卷，目錄二卷二十冊，宋王安石撰。民國十七年
上海中華書局印行（四部備要本）。

Wang Hsien-ch'ien (ed.), *Hsü Ku-wen kuan-chih,* 2 vols. Taipei: International Book Company, 1960.

續古文觀止，三十四卷，卷首一卷，目錄一卷，二冊，清王先謙編。
民國四十九年台北世界書局印行。

Wang Pin (ed.), *Pa-tai wen-ch'ao,* 54 vols. Early Ch'ing dynasty (*circa* 17th century).

八代文鈔，五十四冊，明王賓編。清初刊本。

Wu Ch'u-ts'ai (ed.), *Ku-wen kuan-chih p'ing-chu.* Shanghai: Tatung Book Company, 1926.

古文觀止評註，清吳楚材編。民國十五年上海大東書局印行。

Yao Hsüan (ed.), *T'ang-wen ts'ui,* 16 vols. Kiangsu Book Company, 1883.

唐文粹，一百卷十六冊，宋姚鉉編。清光緒五年江蘇書局印行。

Yao Nai, *Ku-wen tz'u-lei-tsuan,* 4 vols. 2nd edition. Taipei: International Book Company, 1956.

古文辭類纂，七十四卷，重印本四冊，清姚鼐編。民國四十五年台北
世界書局印行。

II. BOOKS IN ENGLISH AND FRENCH

Birch, Cyril (ed.), *Anthology of Chinese Literature from Early Times to the Fourteenth Century,* 2 vols. New York: Grove Press, 1965-1972.

Chai, Ch'u & Winberg (tr. & ed.), *A New Treasury of Chinese Literature, a Prose Anthology, Including Fiction and Drama.* New York: Appleton-Century, 1965.

Ch'en, Shou-i, *Chinese Literature, a Historical Introduction.* New York: Ronald Press, 1961.

Clark, C. D. Le Gros, *The Prose-Poetry of Su Tung-p'o.* Shanghai: Kelly & Walsh, 1935.

————, *Selections from the Works of Su Tung-p'o.* London: Jonathan Cape, 1931.

Edwards, E. D., *Chinese Prose Literature of the T'ang Period,* 2 vols. London: Probsthain, 1937-1938.

Giles H. A., *Gems of Chinese Literature*. Shanghai: Kelly & Walsh, 1922. First published in 1884.

Hightower, J. R., *Topics in Chinese Literature*. Rev. ed. Cambridge: Harvard University Press, 1962.

Li, Tien-yi, *The History of Chinese Literature, a Selected Bibliography*. New Haven: Far Eastern Publications, Yale University, 1968 (Sinological Series No. 15).

Lin, Yutang, *The Gay Genius*. New York: John Day, 1947.

————, *The Importance of Understanding*. Cleveland: World Publishing Company, 1960.

Liu, James T. C., *Reform in Sung China: Wang An-shih and His New Policies*. Cambridge: Harvard University Press, 1959.

————, *Ou-yang Hsiu: An Eleventh-Century Neo-Confucianist*. Stanford, Calif.: Stanford University Press, 1967.

Liu, Wu-chi, *An Introduction to Chinese Literature*. Bloomington, Ind.: Indiana University Press, 1969.

Margouliès, G., *Le Kou-wen Chinois*. Paris: Orientaliste Librairie, Paul Guenthner, 1926.

Meskill, John (ed.), *Wang An-shih—Practical Reformer*. Boston: D. C. Heath & Co., 1963.

Watson, Burton, *Early Chinese Literature*. New York: Columbia University Press, 1962.

————, *Su Tung-p'o: Selections from a Sung Dynasty Poet*. New York: Columbia University Press, 1965.

Williamson, H. R., *Wang An-shih, a Chinese Statesman and Educationist of the Sung Dynasty*. London: Probsthain, 1937.

3